The
# Houseplant
## Handbook

BNK - bow

THC —Tenet Health Corp.

CRY - Cryolife.

FVRL

AHO- foodservice

TLM

CFP- Canfor - Lumber.

# The
# Houseplant
## Handbook

### Elaine Smallwood

## STRATHEARN BOOKS LIMITED
### Toronto, Canada

For Jem Smallwood, with thanks for all of his help.

© 2004 D&S Books Ltd

D&S Books Ltd
Kerswell
Parkham Ash,
Bideford
Devon, England
EX39 5PR

e-mail us at:-
enquiries@dsbooks.fsnet.co.uk

This edition printed 2004

ISBN 1-895464-47-1

Creative Director: Sarah King
Editor: Sally MacEachern
Project editor: Anna Southgate
Designer: Axis Design

This edition published by
STRATHEARN BOOKS LIMITED
36, Northline Road
Toronto, On, Canada
MB4 3E2

Printed in China

1 3 5 7 9 10 8 6 4 2

# Contents

Introduction 6
    Plant Names 7
    The Parts of a Plant 8
    Terms Used in the Text 10
1. Selecting and Cultivating Houseplants 12
    Buying and Conditioning Houseplants 13
    Choosing the Correct Environment for a Houseplant 15
    Some Tools of the Horticultural Trade 24
    Potting on, Repotting, Top-dressing 30
    Hydroponics 33
    Feeding Houseplants 34
    Watering Plants 35
    Resting Houseplants 39
    Cleaning Plants 39
    Grooming Plants 40
    Propagating Houseplants 41
    When Plants are Ill 52
2. Houseplant Families and Categories 59
    Bulbs 60
    Indoor Trees and Shrubs 62
    Bonsai 64
    Cacti 65
    Succulents 66
    Bromeliads 68
    Palms 69
    Ferns 70
    Orchids 71
    Carnivorous Plants 73
    Feng Shui and Houseplants 74
    Eco-friendly Houseplants 76
    Potentially Dangerous Plants 77
3. An A to Z of Houseplants 79
Index 253
Bibliography 256
Credits and Acknowledgements 256

# Introduction

More and more people are enjoying looking after houseplants, and are doing so with increasing understanding. Often used as an integral part of the decor of both the home and workplace, plants can be victims of fashion swings, but offer little pools of calm in a busy world in return for some care and attention. So love them! And if a plant has served you well, but has now become straggly and withered, take a cutting before consigning it to the trash. It will then live on, a true immortal.

Not only can indoor gardening be as rewarding as outdoor gardening, but it is also an occupation that is accessible to everyone throughout the seasons, regardless of the climate or location in which you live, or of your own physical limitations.

As long as they receive sufficient light, plants can be placed in any room in the home or workplace, perhaps as a focal point or merely as background decoration. Most houseplants are impulse buys, but when choosing one, remember that time spent on reconnaissance is never wasted, and try to think about where it would be best positioned before parting with your money.

Start your career as an indoor gardener with plants that are reputedly easy to look after, and when you have proved yourself successful, move on to those that are more difficult to foster. Always try to take pleasure in the experience because if you enjoy your plants, they seem to have an uncanny knack of being nice in return! It's a phenomenon called having a green thumb.

# Plant nNames

In 1753, Carl Linnaeus, a Swedish botanist, founded the binomial (two-name) system of naming plants that is now used by gardeners all over the world. This means that although we often call a plant by its common name, it is also universally recognized by its botanical, Latin name. Only one type of plant in the whole world can have this name.

A plant's botanical name is made up of at least two parts. The first is the name of the plant's genus, which starts with an upper-case (capital) letter and is written in italics; the genus name represents a group of plants with similar characteristics. The second is the name of the plant's species, which starts with a lower-case letter and is written in italics; the species name represents a subgroup of plants within the genus. The botanical name of the plant commonly called mother-in-law's tongue in England, for example, is

| Genus | *Sansevieria* |
| Species | *trifasciata* |
| Common name | mother-in-law's tongue |

*Sanseviera* (the genus name) *trifasciata* (the species name).

If there are variations within a species, these are identified separately. When the variation is naturally occurring, it is called a variety, and its name is written in italics, starting with a lower-case letter (*Sanseviera trifasciata laurentii*, for instance). A bred variety is called a cultivar (which is an abbreviation of "cultivated variety"), and its name is enclosed in single quotation marks and written in the roman typeface, starting with an upper-case letter (for example, *Sansevieria trifurcate* 'Golden Hahnii').

Note that once a plant's full Latin name has appeared in a text for the first time, the genus name is subsequently abbreviated to its initial letter, followed by a full point (*S. trifasciata*, for instance).

# The Parts of a Plant

Each part of a plant serves a particular purpose.

The roots hold the plant firmly in the soil. They take up water and nutrients from the soil and store nutrient reserves (sometimes in the form of bulbs and tubers).

The main root (the tap root) has lateral roots branching out from it.

Some plants have aerial roots, which grow above the compost from the stem.

The stem provides above-ground support for the plant. A stem can be single or branched, soft or woody, thick or thin. The stem carries water and nutrients from the roots to the leaves and flowers that are attached to it.

Stems can twist themselves to turn toward the light.

A runner, sometimes called a stolon, is a stem that grows horizontally and puts down roots from its nodes (*Chlorophytum comosum* 'Vittatum', or the spider plant, has these).

A node is a point on a stem from which a leaf grows.

An internode is the space on the stem between two nodes.

Leaves contain the cells within which photosynthesis and respiration take place. Photosynthesis is the process by which a plant uses the energy from light to produce food for itself. Respiration is the process by which cells release energy to fuel the growth of the plant. Leaves release excess water from the plant by the process of transpiration.

A leaf is made up of a network of veins and the leaf stalk. Leaves grow in a variety of shapes, sizes, and colors; a variegated leaf consists of more than one color.

A frond is the leaf of a fern.

A simple leaf is not divided into leaflets, but a compound leaf is. A bract is a modified leaf that is sometimes mistaken for a flower (as often occurs with the poinsettia, *Poinsettia pulcherrima* or *Euphorbia pulcherrima*).

Flowers are a plant's organs of sexual reproduction and contain the female egg cell (the ovary) and the male pollen (the stamen). Flowers attract insects, which then carry pollen from flower to flower in a process called pollination. Pollination is often confused with fertilization, which is the fusion of male pollen with a female ovule to produce a seed.

Flowering is the final stage of a mature plant's cycle, leading to seed formation and fruit growth. Plants generally produce enough flowers to be fertilized, then stop blooming. By removing wilted flowers, we force the plant to continue growing more blooms, during which time it will need extra feeding.

Flowers are sometimes produced in clusters, called inflorescences. There is a variety of cluster patterns. A single flower has petals arranged in a single row, while a double flower has petals arranged in more than one row. A spathe flower is really a large bract surrounding a fleshy flower spike (as displayed by the *Spathipyllum wallisii*, or peace lily).

A pedicel is the stalk that supports the flower.

A bud is an undeveloped stem or flower. Apical buds, which grow at the end of stems, are where new cells are formed to produce longer stems. Removing these buds encourages a plant to become bushier. Auxiliary buds are formed in the angle (axil) between the stem and leaf.

# Terms Used in the Text

The meanings of certain terms used in the text are explained below.

**Acid compost:** a growing medium that contains no lime.

**Aerial root:** a root that grows from the stem of a plant that is used for climbing and absorbing moisture.

**Air-layering:** a method of propagation (see page 47).

**Alternate:** a word used to describe leaves that are arranged at different heights on a stem.

**Annual:** a plant that completes its life cycle in one year.

**Axil:** the upper angle between the stem and leaf, from which a new leaf or side shoots grow. (Buds growing here are called auxiliary buds.)

**Biennial:** a plant that completes its life cycle in two years.

**Bottom heat:** heat provided at the base of a plant.

**Bract:** a modified, often colorful, leaf that may be mistaken for a flower.

**Bulb:** a plant's underground storage organ.

**Bulbil:** an immature small bulb.

**Calyx:** a ring of green sepals.

**Compost:** a mix of decomposed organic matter in which plants live and grow.

**Corm:** a plant's swollen underground organ.

**Crock:** a piece of broken earthenware that can be placed in the bottom of a plant pot to aid drainage.

**Crown:** the growing point of a plant.

**Cultivar:** a plant that has been developed and named by plant breeders.

**Cutting:** a piece of a plant (usually a stem) that is used to produce a new plant.

**Deadheading:** removing dead or faded flower heads.

**Deciduous:** a plant or tree that sheds its leaves at the end of its growing season.

**Double flower:** a flower that has more than one layer of petals.

**Epiphyte:** a plant that grows on another plant, but does not live off it.

**Evergreen:** a plant or tree that retains its leaves all year round.

**Frond:** the leaf of a fern, usually deeply dissected (narrowly lobed or segmented).

**Fruit:** the ripe seeds of a flower.

**Germination:** the first stage of a seed's development.

**Growing point:** the tip of a shoot from which new growth appears.

**Hydroponics (or hydroculture):** a method of growing plants in water.

**Insecticide:** a chemical used to destroy insects.

**Leggy:** the spindly growth of a plant.

**Margin:** the border of a leaf or petal.

**Misting:** the spraying of a plant with a thin film of water.

**Node:** a joint on a stem from which a leaf or bud grows.

**Offset:** a new plant produced by a parent plant.

**Peat:** a growing medium consisting of decomposed sphagnum moss.

**Pebble tray:** an arrangement of stones or pebbles sitting in water in a shallow tray.

**Photosynthesis:** the process by which plants use energy from light to produce food for themselves.

**Pinching out:** the nipping-out of the growing point of a stem to induce bushiness.

**Plunging:** placing a pot in soil up to its rim.

**Pot-bound:** a plant that has become too big for its pot.

**Potting on:** transferring a plant to a pot that is one size larger than its previous pot.

**Pricking out:** transferring seedlings from the pot in which they have been growing to a larger one.

**Resting period:** the period when a plant stops growing.

**Rhizome:** a creeping stem growing below the surface of the compost.

**Root ball:** a plant's roots and the compost around which they remain entwined when removed from a pot.

**Rooting hormone:** a liquid or powdered chemical that encourages a cutting to form roots.

**Rosette:** an arrangement of leaves radiating from the center of a stem.

**Seed:** the fertilized part of a flower.

**Seedling:** a young plant that has been raised from seed.

**Sepal:** the outer part of a flower before it blooms.

**Short-day plants:** plants that are covered over for at least twelve hours every day in order to induce flowering.

**Shrub:** a woody stemmed, bushy plant.

**Spadix:** a small spike bearing minute flowers.

**Spathe:** a prominent bract, often highly colored.

**Spore:** a reproductive cell.

**Stamen:** a flower's male sex organ.

**Standard:** a plant that is trained to grow like a tree, with no lower stems.

**Succulent:** a plant that has fleshy leaves.

**Tendril:** a thin stem that twines itself around a support, enabling it to climb.

**Top-dressing:** replacing the top few inches of the potting compost in which a plant is growing with fresh compost.

**Tuber:** a thick, fleshy root that acts as a plant's storage organ.

**Variegated:** a term applied to green leaves that display areas of a different color, usually cream or white.

**Wintering:** the resting of plants in cold conditions.

# Chapter 1
# Selecting and Cultivating Houseplants

This chapter advises you on choosing and cultivating your houseplants.

# Buying and Conditioning Houseplants

Look for healthy flowers, fruits, or leaves.

Houseplants are now accepted as being integral to the interior-design strategies of homes, public buildings, and workplaces. So it is important to consider the best balance between plant and environment and effect. Most workplaces have high indoor temperatures for most of the day and are much cooler at night, which affects plants. Plants may also suffer from a lack of sunlight in such environments, and may be watered irregularly, too.

With so many plants to choose from, care is needed to ensure that you choose the best species for the location. When making your choice of plants, consider the following points carefully.

• What is your budget?
• Is foliage or flowers the priority, or are both important?
• Are you buying the plant for the short term, or should it last for a long time?
• Where will it be positioned: in a warm or cool area; in sunlight or shade?
• What size should it be?
• Will it fit in with the design of the room or area for which it is destined?
• Will it need a lot of looking after?
• Are there any specific, or general, advantages inherent in your choice? (Does the plant remove polluting gases, for example?)

Provide plenty of light, but not direct sunlight.

## Buying Houseplants

It is not always easy to ascertain the quality of the plants on sale in stores or markets, and it is generally better to buy from a reputable supplier, who should be able to offer advice on the conditions and care that a plant needs. (There should also be a label in the pot giving similar advice.)

When buying houseplants, look out for the following points.

• Is the pot clean and labeled?

• Do the leaves show any signs of damage, discoloration, or pests?

• If it is a flowering plant, is it mainly in bud? (If not, it won't last long.)

• If it is a foliage plant, does it show signs of new growth, and are the leaves firm? (Droopy or withered leaves are a sign of disease.)

• Is the compost moist, rather than dried up or very wet?

• Is the plant being displayed outside? (If so, it could be damaged by cold conditions).

### Tip
Remember that the biggest plant is not always the best.

Be wary of bargain offers.

## Conditioning Houseplants

Houseplants are usually grown in glasshouses, in ideal conditions. They are then moved to a wholesaler and on to a retail outlet, where they are displayed before being bought and taken to someone's home. No wonder they sometimes sulk.

After buying a houseplant, make sure (especially in winter) that it has been correctly wrapped before taking it out of the store because this will protect the foliage from being damaged and, more importantly, will shield the plant from the cold and drafts. Take the plant home as soon as possible; don't leave it in the trunk of an automobile for hours and then expect it to look fresh.

Once you have returned home, gently condition the plant to become accustomed to its new environment. To start with, expose it to as much bright light as possible (but not direct sunlight), don't keep it too warm and position it away from drafts. Do not overwater it or add fertilizer to the compost during this time. At the end of about four weeks, the plant will usually be ready to be moved to its final position. Now is the time to use horticultural skills in order to maintain its health and happiness.

# Choosing
# the Correct Environment for
# a Houseplant

Most houseplants are raised in glasshouses whose microclimate is totally different to that of the home or office, but in order to care for a houseplant successfully, it is important that its environment suits it. If a houseplant is to thrive, it will need to be positioned in a location that resembles its natural habitat as closely as possible. This section discusses the effect that temperature, light, and humidity have on plants, as well as the pros and cons of positioning houseplants in specific rooms.

## Temperature

Most plants grow in temperatures ranging from 55 to 77°F (13 to 25°C), and a fluctuation of a few degrees on either side during the day is acceptable, while plants generally prefer a lower temperature at night. It is important not to expose houseplants to sudden changes in temperature, however, because no plant likes being on the receiving end of a sudden blast of hot or cold air, and no houseplant will tolerate frost either, with the exception of desert cacti and some succulents.

Modern heating systems tend to boost the temperature in a house during the day, but when they are switched off at night, the temperature can drop dramatically, especially in winter. And when the curtains are drawn, windowsill plants can be trapped in a chilly microclimate between the curtains and the cold glass (although the drop in temperature is less drastic if the windows are double-glazed). So if your house is likely to cool considerably in this way at night, move your houseplants

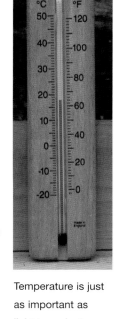

Temperature is just as important as light to a plant.

> ## Tip
> Keeping a thermometer in a room that houses plants will save you from having to guess the temperature.

into the center of the room. Note that African violets (*Saintpaulia*), crotons (or Joseph's coat, *Codiaeum*), and prayer plants (*Maranta leuconeura*), in particular, prefer even temperatures. It may also be advisable to move plants from windowsills on sunny days, when the temperature on a windowsill may reach 104°C (40°C), scorching a plant's leaves.

Remember, too, that sudden drafts can enter a room through windows and doors, and that such drafts are extremely harmful to houseplants, particularly during the winter, when a sudden lowering of the air temperature will cause leaf and flower buds to drop.

Plants that are positioned in areas that are warmer than they prefer will exhibit rather weak and spindly growth, while too low a temperature may lead to a plant's leaves yellowing or dropping prematurely.

## Light

All plants need light, which is one reason why they grow better in a greenhouse or conservatory than in a conventional room. In addition, a plant will need to be housed in conditions that are similar to those of its native habitat, which means that the amount of light that prevails in its place of origin will dictate the lighting conditions that it requires if it is to flourish in your home.

All-round light is most suitable for houseplants.

Plants that grow naturally in shady areas are more tolerant of poor lighting conditions than others, but often become leggy. By contrast, plants with variegated or brightly colored leaves require more light, and if they don't receive it, their leaves may lose their attractive variegation or striking coloring. Good light doesn't always mean sunlight, however, and succulents, cacti, and some plants with brightly colored leaves enjoy this type of bright light. The brightest indoor location is usually near a south-facing window, and the darkest near a north-facing one.

As a general rule, flowering plants need more light than nonflowering plants because they require good light in order to produce the hormone responsible for initiating flowers. So if such a plant fails to flower, it may just need to be repositioned so that it receives better light. The length of time flowering plants are exposed to light is also critical to their flowering: to encourage a Christmas cactus (*Schlumbergera truncata* or *Zygocactus truncatus*) to flower at Christmas, for example, you will need to keep it in darkness for a long period until it begins to bud (darkness helps flower buds to form, while artificial light delays flowering).

Plants on a windowsill will benefit from their pots being given a quarter-turn every day to prevent their growth from becoming imbalanced. And when moving a plant from a shady area to a bright windowsill, do so gradually to enable the plant to acclimatize to its new conditions.

## Artificial Light

The artificial light provided by conventional light bulbs is not really suitable for growing plants. Halogen lamps are more suitable, as long as they are placed at least 5 ft (1.5 m) above plants (if the leaves have a scorched appearance, the light is too close). Plants that can be grown under artificial light include African violets (*Saintpaulia*), orchids, and bromeliads.

## Full Sun

If a plant is described as needing full sun, it should be placed close to a south-facing window that receives at least five hours of direct sunlight a day. The plant should not touch the window, and will require some shade in summer.

## Bright Semisunlight

Most flowering plants will bloom if they are either set about 3 to 5 ft (1 to 1.5 m) back from a south-facing window or receive a couple of hours of direct sunlight every day.

## Semishade

If semishade is specified for a plant, this means bright, indirect light, such as the light that filters through sheer curtains. Most foliage plants like this sort of light, but few flowering plants thrive under it.

## Shade

A shady position receives no direct sunlight and may be over 6½ ft (2 m) away from a window. Only a few foliage plants can survive in the shade, and no flowering plants are suitable for shady locations.

### Tip
Always check a plant's light requirements.

Always cover plants at midday if the sun is too hot.

## Humidity

Humidity levels reflect air temperatures, and the warmer the air, the more rapidly moisture is lost from it. Because plants constantly lose water through their leaves in the form of water vapor, they are sensitive to a lack of humidity, and if the atmosphere is dry, the rate of water loss will increase, causing plants to become stressed. While some plants (cacti, for instance) have adapted to dry conditions, others, such as philodendrons and bromeliads, need constant high humidity. The ideal humidity level for most plants ranges between 40 and 65 percent.

Dry air is a problem for most indoor plants, and one that has become more common in recent years as a result of the increase in central-heating and air-conditioning systems. There are various steps that you can take to increase the humidity level around your plants.

• Hang humidifiers over radiators to add moisture to the air, but try to ensure that disease-causing micro-organisms don't develop within them by changing their water regularly.

• Create a pebble tray by placing a ¾ in (2 cm) layer of pebbles, gravel, or colored glass chippings in the bottom of a shallow tray or pot. Add water, ensuring that it does not reach the top of the pebbles, and put the plant pot on top. Then place the tray or pot on either a shelf above a radiator or windowsill, and remember to change the water frequently.

• Pack moss, tree bark, or clay granules between the plant pot and a decorative container and keep this material moist. Ensure that no excess water is allowed to stand in the bottom of the pot.

Place the plant pot on top of moist pebbles to increase humidity.

• Misting (spraying a plant's leaves with a fine mist of water) is a vey effective humidifying method, especially for ferns. It also helps to keep leaves clean and to prevent red spider mite. Fill a spray container with tepid water and spray the plant in the mornings (but not when it is in direct sunlight because this can cause its leaves to be scorched). Take care not to soak furniture or furnishings when misting (a time-consuming alternative is to move a plant to a basin or bath before misting it).

When plants are misted, water is absorbed through the leaves.

• Grouping plants together is a natural way of growing them and also increases the local humidity by trapping moist air between them. Check plants regularly when using this method, however, because gray mold (or botrytis, see page 57) and other diseases may develop.

## Where to Place a Plant

When deciding where to position a houseplant, remember that each room has its advantages and disadvantages.

## Living Rooms

Living rooms are rooms in which people spend a lot of their time and where houseplants are most often displayed. Before positioning a plant in this room, however, check the light level and remember that plants are used to receiving

light from all sides, so even if there is a large window, they may still need to be turned around regularly.

The temperature will probably vary the most in this room, especially in winter, when the central heating is turned up high, causing the room to become very dry and lacking the humidity that plants need. Placing pebble trays on a windowsill or grouping plants together in a larger container, with moist compost or clay granules between their pots, will increase the humidity, as will regularly misting the plants.

## Conservatories and Garden Rooms

Conservatories and garden rooms can be ideal locations for plants because they provide them with more light than almost anywhere else in the home. Because conservatories are often an extension of a living area, your first consideration should be for your comfort when selecting plants to display in it. Alternatively, if your children use your conservatory as a playroom, safety considerations should be uppermost in your mind, and you should therefore steer clear of any poisonous or sharp-leaved plants (see pages 77 to 78); however, an inspired selection may fire a lifelong interest in plants in your children.

Try to ascertain your conservatory's suitability for housing plants by asking yourself the following questions.

• Is there adequate ventilation?
• Is there some way of shading plants from the hot, midday sun?
• Is there convenient access to a faucet?
• Will the floor surface and furniture rot if the atmosphere is too humid? (Tiles, bricks, and stone are suitable flooring materials, while cane or plastic furniture withstands humidity best.)
• Is there any form of heating? Note that if you are intending to overwinter plants in your conservatory, a minimum temperature of 44.6°F (7°C) must be maintained for ordinary plants, and 53.6°F (12°C) for exotic plants.

If you are satisfied that your conservatory fulfills these requirements, consider growing such impressive plants as *Bougainvillea* (paper plant), *Hoya* (wax plant), and *Rhoicissus* (grape ivy). Also think about how best to display them, for instance, in deep troughs or individual pots, in hanging baskets or on shelving or climbing structures. Finally, aim to position plants so that there is interest at every level of the conservatory.

## Kitchens and Bathrooms

Kitchens and bathrooms offer their own, special environments, within which the humidity and temperature are both usually higher than in other rooms. Remember that there are certain hot spots in a kitchen, such as near an oven door or close to a kettle or toaster, that may cause plants to become scorched, although a container of herbs may thrive on a kitchen windowsill.

Well-lit bathrooms are ideal for ferns, bamboos, Swiss cheese plants (*Monstera deliciosa*), and hanging baskets. Note that although these plants do not require misting, their leaves will need frequent cleaning (especially if family members use generous amounts of talcum powder).

Bathrooms are ideal for plants that like conditions of high humidity.

## Bedrooms

A light, cool bedroom that is heated for part of the night is ideal for plants that dislike too much heat during the winter, such as the grape ivy (*Rhoicissus*), ivy tree (x *Fatshedera lizel*), and false caster-oil plant (*Fatsia japonica*).

## Halls and Stairwells

As long as they are draft-free, halls and stairwells may be good places in which to position large plants. Many halls are often both poorly lit and cold, however, so if a plant starts to look sickly here, you may have to remove it to a well-lit area to recover before returning it. That having been said, halls and stairwells can be suitable locations for plants that require a winter rest period at a low temperature.

A well-placed plant can add a touch of color to an otherwise dull hallway or stairwell.

Plants can add a calming feel to a bedroom.

## Office Environments

The furniture, fittings, and electronic devices in offices can all emit unpleasant chemicals into the working atmosphere. Choosing plants that assist in the removal of these pollutants can be beneficial to the workforce (see page 76 for eco-friendly plants). In addition, displays of plants in office buildings can have a calming effect.

Plants that can survive lack of care are also useful for the office environment. *Chlorophytum comosum* 'Vittatum' (spider plant), for example, can tolerate neglect for quite long periods, and revives after a good watering. Note that because office environments often lack natural light, plants need to be rotated more frequently.

## Putting Plants Outside in Summer

Putting houseplants outside in summer will often revitalize them, as long as they have been acclimatized beforehand by being moved to a sunny position gradually, and not suddenly placed in full sun and then left there. Before positioning any plants outside, make sure that the danger of frosts has passed and that the temperature is above 53.6°F (12°C).

Certain houseplants in particular enjoy spending time outside in the summer, notably citrus plants, genista brooms (*Cytisus*), euonymus plants, forest cacti, busy Lizzies (*Impatiens*), bay trees (*Laurus*), pelargoniums, and yuccas. Others need plenty of fresh air during the summer months to build them up for the winter, and chrysanthemums, palms, most cacti and succulents, plumbagos, and euphorbias will all benefit from this treatment.

A sheltered area in a yard or on a patio is the ideal position for plants that are spending the summer outside, but if only a balcony is available, try to protect the plants from drafts. Remember, too, that although fresh air and sunlight are beneficial, scorching midday sun can damage plants, so either move the pots or position them so that they are always in the shade at this time.

When they are outside, plants need more frequent watering and should be fed (see page 34) about once a fortnight. Feeding should be tailed off before the plants are brought back inside at the end of the summer however, otherwise, with the subsequent lack of intense light, it will result in soft, leggy shoots. Before taking them back inside, carefully check the plants for such pests as aphids (see page 55) to avoid introducing them to the house and infecting other plants.

# Some Tools
## of the Horticultural Trade

You will need a few tools to help you to care for your houseplants, and at least the following.

• A book that identifies houseplants and advises on their cultivation.

• Appropriate compost for potting on.

• Plant pots (which you will need to keep clean in order to avoid introducing pests and diseases).

• A watering can with a long, thin spout with which to get under leaves. (1.)

• A pump-action spray for misting. (2.)

• A good-quality houseplant fertilizer, preferably in liquid form (a liquid is easier to administer than a powder).

• A pair of sharp scissors or pruning shears, which you should always clean after use,

and especially after cutting away any part of a diseased plant. (3.)

• Plastic-coated wire, or else string or raffia, with which to tie up plants. (4.)

• Supports, hoops, and canes in a variety of sizes. (5.)

• An indoor thermometer. (6.)

### Tip
Keep a small piece of cloth soaked in oil in a plastic bag to rub over scissors or pruning shears after use. This will keep them sharp and prevent them from rusting.

## Compost

Compost holds the moisture and air that enable roots to develop, also providing nutrients that feed a plant, as well as offering it stability.

Houseplants are best planted in the specially commercially prepared composts that are readily obtainable from garden centers. Never use garden soil because this

Choose a reliable compost suitable for your plant.

may contain pests and diseases, which will flourish in the warmer household environment.

You will usually need to choose between soil- or loam-based composts and soil-less- or peat-based composts.

Soil- or loam-based composts are made to the John Innes formula, their main ingredient being sterilized loam, which provides substance and weight, making them useful for larger plants. Their other constituents include peat, sand, or grit, and sometimes added fertilizer. Such composts are less prone to drying out and therefore hold nutrients better than soil-less- or peat-based composts.

Soil-less- or peat-based composts are light and easy to handle and make the best growing medium for certain plants, such as African violets (*Saintpaulia*). These composts dry out much more quickly than soil- or loam-based composts, however, and are even harder to remoisten (when it will be necessary to use the immersion method, see pages 36 to 37). It is consequently harder to tell if a plant needs rewatering, while large plants with lots of top growth may fall over through lack of support. Soil-less- or peat-based composts are nevertheless useful, especially in the early stages of a houseplant's growth. Note, however, that peat is a natural resource that is rapidly becoming depleted, as a result of which sensitive gardening suppliers have produced environmentally friendly alternatives, such as cocoa shell.

Certain groups of plants need specialist composts (which are available from good garden centers).

• Lime-hating plants, such as azaleas, require ericaceous compost.
• Cacti (see page 65) and palms (see page 69) need compost that contains a high percentage of sharp sand.

• Orchids (see pages 71 to 72) require free-draining, open compost (compost whose components do not stick together and that usually contains bark chips and moss).

## Pots and Containers
There is a wide variety of pots and containers to choose from.

### Pots
Pots are made of either clay (earthenware) or plastic, and there are devotees of both.

Being heavier, clay pots are less likely to fall over than plastic ones, making them a stable home for larger plants. Waterlogging is also less likely to occur because moisture evaporates faster from clay pots, but this means that the pots need to be soaked thoroughly before use and that you have to water plants more often. In addition, clay pots are less likely to break than plastic pots, which become brittle when constantly exposed to sunlight. Finally,

terracotta's natural color suits most plants.

Plastic pots are lightweight and are manufactured in a variety of colors, often with decorative designs. They retain moisture better than clay pots, as a result of which plants require watering less often and the compost is less likely to dry out. Plastic pots are also better insulators than clay pots and provide plants with better protection from temperature changes. New plants are almost always sold in plastic pots because they are clean, easy to handle, and an inexpensive option for growers.

Whichever type of pot you choose for a houseplant, make sure that it is the correct

Select a clean pot a size larger than the one in use.

Pots must have drainage holes or the plants will become waterlogged.

## Tip
Make sure that a pot has at least one good-sized drainage hole in its base.

size to enable the plant to root properly: too small, and the plant may become pot-bound; too large, and waterlogging may then occur.

Bulbs (see pages 60 to 61) are the exception to the general rule that plants should be planted in pots that have drainage holes in the bottom. For this reason, it is important to plant dormant bulbs in bulb fiber, which is made up of peat, charcoal, and oyster shell and quickly absorbs water, making you less likely to overwater the bulbs. After the bulbs have flowered, the bulb fiber remains dry, allowing them to dry out.

## Containers

Containers, or planters, are the outer pots that house clay or plastic pots. When choosing containers, remember that they should show off plants to their best advantage and should not compete with the display for the viewer's attention.

Containers come in many shapes, sizes, and materials; you could either buy a new one or use a household item like a watering can or basket. In fact, the only requirement for a container is that it should be waterproof.

A container for a single pot should be large enough to enable you to insert a finger between the two pots, indicating that air will be able to circulate between

Containers should always complement plants.

them. The rim of the pot should be just hidden by the container (and note that you can raise a pot by placing a lid or some pebbles in the bottom of the container).

A number of plants in individual pots can be arranged within a planter, perhaps surrounded by compost, bark, decorative glass chippings, or crushed shells or sitting on a bed of pebbles. The plants can then be rearranged at any time without disturbing them unduly.

Choose a container that is larger than the pot to allow air to circulate.

> ## Tip
> After watering, make sure that the container does not remain full of water, otherwise the plant may become waterlogged.

Add pebbles to the bottom of the pot for drainage.

Leave sufficient space to insert a finger between the pot and the container.

# Potting on,
# Re-potting, Top-dressing

When you buy a houseplant from a store or garden center, it will already be growing in suitable compost. When the plant becomes pot-bound, however, it will be necessary to pot it on into a pot that is slightly larger than the previous one. There are also times when it may be necessary to repot or top-dress a plant.

## Potting on

When trying to ascertain whether a plant is pot-bound, don't be misled by the sight of a few roots growing through the drainage holes. Instead, make the following checks.

• Is the plant growing more slowly than normal, and have the leaves remained small and the blooms poor?

• Does it need more frequent watering?

• Is there any green algae or moss on the surface of the compost? If so, this is a sign of waterlogging.

• Check the root ball by holding the plant by the base of its stem, inverting it, and gently tapping the rim of the pot on a hard edge or table, whereupon the plant should fall out of the pot. If you can then see a mass of roots growing in a circle and very little compost, you should pot the plant on. (If the plant is not pot-bound, however, gently return it to the pot.)

Tap the pot on a table to help loosen the plant from the pot.

Gently ease out the plant and the root ball.

### Tip
When handling cacti, always wear thick gloves and wrap a piece of strong paper around the thorns when lifting these plants.

Potting on should be done in the spring, and never during a plant's resting period (usually the winter) or while it is in bloom.

Never pot plants on as a matter of course, however, because some, such as kaffir lilies (*Clivia*) and orchids, prefer being pot-bound and grow better in this state. Palms (see page 69) only need potting on every three to four years, when they have totally outgrown their pots. And rubber plants (*Ficus elastica* 'Decora') only require the top 1½ to 2 in (4 to 5 cm) of soil removing and replacing with fresh compost (see below). Bromeliads (see page 68) never need repotting because their roots are used for anchorage only.

Note that plants don't appreciate being disturbed in this way because it upsets their roots. It takes about six weeks before the roots have settled down and begun growing again, so don't expect instant results after potting on. The appearance of new shoots, leaves, or flower buds indicate that a plant is happy in its new home.

**1.** With the plant still in its original pot, plunge the pot up to its rim in water and leave it until the plant's root ball has become saturated.

**2.** Select suitable compost (see pages 26 to 27) and a new pot. Choose a pot that is slightly larger than the previous one because too large a pot can cause waterlogging (this occurs when the compost contains too much water for the roots to absorb). Make sure that the pot is clean because a dirty pot can introduce pests and disease to the plant. If you are using a clay pot, soak it in water. Now dampen the compost, but do not allow it to become too wet because this can cause the plant's roots to rot.

**3.** Cover the drainage holes with crocks and then place a layer of compost over the crocks.

**4.** Remove the plant from its existing pot as described above for checking the root ball, take the old crocks from the base, and strip away any rotten roots, which are usually dark brown, soft, and smell foul. Although you should try to avoid damaging the smaller roots as much as you can, gently tease out some of the outer roots.

**5.** Position the root ball in the center of the new pot and then add fresh, damp compost, gently firming it in around the edges of the pot with your fingertips until it is level with the base of the plant's stem.

**6.** Do not pack the compost too tightly, or you may damage the roots. Leave a space of about ½ in (1 cm) between the surface of the compost and the top of the pot to facilitate watering.

**7.** If the plant requires a support, provide it now, so that you don't damage the roots at a later date.

**8.** Water the compost carefully before placing the plant in a warm, sheltered position, out of full sun, for about a week. Note that misting the plant daily will help to prevent the leaves from wilting. Finally, return the plant to its normal position.

## Repotting

Plants that you don't want to grow any bigger should be repotted rather than potted on. To do this, take the plant out of its pot, remove any compost attached to its roots and then, using scissors, trim the roots by a quarter of their length. Next, clean the pot and repot the plant in fresh compost, following steps 5 to 7 for potting on.

> ## Tip
> Do not repot a plant any deeper than it was planted previously because this can cause stem rot. Add extra compost to the bottom of the pot if necessary.

## Top-dressing

When plants, such as trees or palms, become too large to repot, or when they have been trained up a structure--perhaps a room divider or window--they will need to be top-dressed. Do this by carefully removing the top 1 to 2 in (4 to 5 cm) of compost and then replacing it with fresh potting compost and watering it in. Note that top-dressing is best done in the spring.

# Hydroponics

Hydroponics, or hydroculture, a growing method in which compost is replaced with a water solution containing all of the nutrients that plants require, is useful if you have little time to care for your houseplants. Foliage plants respond better to hydroponics than flowering plants, as, perhaps surprisingly, do cacti.

Two pots are required: an inner pot and a larger outer pot. The inner pot holds the plant's root ball, from which any compost has been gently washed away, surrounded by material that supports and anchors the plant, which may be porous clay granules, washed pebbles, or gravel. This pot should have lots of slits or holes in its sides to enable the nutrient solution to be easily absorbed. The inner pot is placed in a larger outer container, perhaps a decorative one. If a collection of plants is to be displayed, a trough or tank could be used as the outer container, the individual inner pots being grouped together within it.

The inner pot is placed in a larger outer pot containing the nutrient solution.

The gap between the two containers is filled with the nutrient solution, namely water mixed with the appropriate amount of hydroponic solution (available from garden centers and florists). The nutrient solution will need to be replaced about every eight weeks. Leave the two pots to dry out for a few days before refilling with new nutrient solution.

Before watering, allow the solution in the container to dry out first and do not add any more nutrients. A water gauge placed in the inner pot will show when the water needs topping up. Note that plants that receive nutrients in this way need to be kept warm as the combination of water and coldness may cause the roots to rot.

Slits in the inner pot allow the nutrient solution to be absorbed.

# Feeding Houseplants

All plants need feeding, and the correct manner of feeding can make the difference between a plant that merely survives or one that thrives. Plants need:

- nitrogen for leaf formation;
- phosphates for root formation;
- and potash for flower and fruit formation (it also helps to ward off diseases).

It is preferable to use a fertilizer that has been specially formulated for houseplants. It is best applied as a liquid, which is both the easiest to administer and the best absorbed. Follow the maker's instructions carefully, and do not overfeed a plant or make up a stronger solution than is recommended because too much feed can be as bad as too little. (A sign that you have been giving a plant too much feed is when the tips of the leaves turn brown.)

## When to Feed Houseplants

Most plants should be regularly fed from late spring until fall, the natural growing season for foliage and flowering plants, and not at all during their resting period, which is usually winter (note that winter-flowering plants should be fed more in winter, however, because this is their growing season).

- During their growing season, feed plants about every ten to fourteen days.
- A plant that grows rapidly needs feeding more than a slow-growing one.
- At the end of the growing period, slowly decrease feeding to none at all.
- After the resting period, gradually increase feeding.
- Never add fertilizer directly to dry compost, but make sure that it is moist first.
- Feeding a plant a weak dose regularly is better than giving it a stronger dose at less frequent intervals.
- For a quick pick-me-up, spray a foliar feed onto a plant's leaves, but try to prevent it from coming into contact with any flowers.

# Watering Plants

Water both transports nutrients around a plant and, through promoting cell turgidity by osmosis, essentially supports it.

Plants need the most water during their growing period and when they are in full bloom, but less water during their resting period. Along with the time of year, several factors determine how much, and how often, a plant needs watering:

- the size and type of pot;
- the type of plant;
- the environment;
- a plant's location in a room;
- if a plant is root-bound;
- a plant's individual watering needs (some plants need to be kept moist, and others relatively dry).

Although some houseplants need watering more frequently than others, more houseplants die from being overwatered than from receiving too little water. (Waterlogging kills plants by blocking the air spaces within the compost and preventing the roots from breathing, which then encourages root rot.)

Giving plants the correct amount of water is a combination of experience and, more importantly, observation. Although you could buy a water meter that measures the compost's water content through the insertion of a probe, be warned that this can damage a plant's roots, and a water meter that is permanently positioned in a pot may detract from a plant's attractiveness.

The compost is the best guide to whether a plant needs watering, but never judge by its appearance alone because although the surface may appear dry, the roots may still be damp. Check the compost regularly during the growing season by pressing a finger down the inside of the pot--if the compost here is dry, then water the plant. Never let a plant get to the wilting stage because it may have reached the point of no return by then.

## Danger Signs

The following signs indicate that a plant is being underwatered:

- the leaves have become limp, have wilted, and no new growth is visible;
- the leaves are curling up at the edges;
- the leaves are falling off;
- the flowers are fading and dropping quickly.

These signs indicate that a plant is being overwatered:

- the leaves have become limp, soft, and rotten;
- rather than blooming, the flowers are rotting;
- the stem is rotting;
- the roots smell of rot;
- the roots are rotting.

## How to Water Houseplants

Water from the faucet is usually suitable for plants (and plants that are being cultivated using the hydroponic method, see page 33, must be watered with it), unless you live in a hard-water area, in which case boil the water and let it cool before using it. Remember that it's always advisable to use room-temperature water to prevent plants from receiving a thermal shock. Rainwater can be used as long as it is clean and fresh, but note that suspect rainwater (water that contains insects or is stagnant) may introduce disease to a plant. Rainwater is best used for lime-hating plants like camellias, azaleas, and ericas.

Remove the pot from its container and place it in an area where the water can

Water slowly from the top of the pot.

drain from the pot, such as a basin, bath, or outside. If you cannot remove the plant from its position, or do not wish to, then water it carefully and slowly, making sure that the pot does not end up sitting in any excess water in the bottom of its container by pouring it away (failure to do so causes root rot, which in turn can kill the plant).

It's best to water plants using a watering can specially designed for indoor watering, with a long, narrow spout. Fill the watering can with water, insert the spout under the plant's leaves, pour the water steadily until it reaches the rim of the pot and then wait until the water has drained through the pot. If the plant absorbs the water, add more until it runs out of the bottom of the pot. Allow any excess water to drain away before returning the pot to its usual position. Water most plants generously in this way, but make sure that you do not leave a plant standing in excess water.

If the compost has dried out and shrunk away from the sides of the pot, it will be necessary to water the plant using the immersion method. This method should also be used for plants that don't like getting their leaves wet, such as African violets (*Saintpaulia*), gloxinias (*Sinningia speciosa*), cyclamens, and corms. Fill a basin or large container with tepid water, immerse the pot in the water to just below its rim (you may have to hold the pot

Fill the container to just below the rim of the pot and allow the compost to soak up the water.

down for the first few minutes), and leave the compost to soak up the water until the surface is damp. It is important to allow any excess water to drain away before returning the plant to its container or growing area.

> ## Tip
> Always check whether a plant needs watering before doing so, and remember that it's better to underwater than overwater a plant.

## Vacation Watering

The best way of ensuring that your plants survive your vacation is to ask a friend to water them regularly (and be sure to explain to him or her the consequences of overwatering).

If you are going to be away for less than about five days, water your plants well and place them a shady area (the middle of a room, for example) before leaving. Most cacti and succulents will happily survive for ten to fourteen days without water if

they are moved to a shady position. Note that if you are using a hydroponic unit, you can leave the plants for two to four weeks, as long as there is sufficient water in the reservoir and the plants are not standing in direct sunlight.

Don't stand your plants in a bowl of water before leaving them, however, because this will probably cause the roots to rot before the water has dried up.

If no one is available to look after your plants, use one of the following watering methods, having first removed any flower heads and watered the plants generously (but don't add any feed).

• Select a plastic bag big enough to enclose one plant. Place the plant in the bag, tie some twine around the bag, and then loosely do the same at the top of the bag, leaving a small air space. (If the plant has fleshy leaves, you may need to arrange some wooden sticks--perhaps food skewers--inside the bag to prevent it from touching the leaves.) Finally, place the shrouded plant in a shady, cool position.

• Fill a waterproof box with a thick bed of wet sand and place the pots in the sand (capillary action will draw up moisture). The sand will need to be kept damp, and you can dispense more water by inserting an animal's water-feeder bottle into the sand.

• Group the plants together in a light, shady area and set a reservoir, such as a large bowl full of water, nearby, at a higher level than the plants. Now place a wick

(cotton or glass-fiber wicks are available from garden centers, but you could alternatively use strands of thick wool or even old stockings) in the water and then, using a stone or hairpin, firmly anchor the other end of the wick into each plant's compost (use one wick per pot).

• The wick watering system can similarly be used to water a plant by inserting one end of the wick through a pot's drainage hole and placing the other into a tub of water.
• You could alternatively use any of a variety of automatic-watering systems available from garden centers, but note that these are more expensive options.

## Tip
Check that any watering system works before setting off on vacation.

# Resting Houseplants

Most plants require a resting period, which generally coincides with winter, the only exception being such winter-flowering plants as cyclamen and Christmas cacti (*Schlumbergera truncata* or *Zygocactus truncatus*).

When they are resting, plants need no feeding and reduced watering (but don't allow the root ball to dry out) and some will benefit from being placed in a cool environment, for example, an unheated bedroom. Regularly check plants during their resting time because if their foliage withers, drops off, and is not removed, it may cause fungal diseases.

The sign that a plant's resting period is over is when new growth appears, usually in the spring.

# Cleaning Plants

In common with all items in a home, houseplants become dusty over a period of time, spoiling their appearance, blocking the leaf pores through which they breathe, and reducing some of the daylight that they receive. In the workplace, dust may even contain plant-damaging chemicals.

An easy way of removing the dust from a lot of plants is to put them in a bath and gently spray them with tepid water from the showerhead, then leaving them to dry before returning them to their original positions. Some plants, such as big rubber plants (*Ficus elastica* 'Decora'), are too large to be moved, however, and therefore have to be cleaned *in situ*. Do this by wiping their leaves with a soft cloth or sponge moistened with clean water,

supporting each leaf with your hand as you work. Note that plants with hairy leaves--velvet plants (*Gynura*) or cacti, for instance--should not be wiped, and that the dust should instead be removed with a soft brush.

If a glossy shine is required, use a proprietary leaf-shine product that can be sprayed or wiped on, but remember that this will only make the plant's leaves look shiny, and will not promote growth.

### Tip
Leaves should be washed in the morning so that the foliage has time to dry before the evening, when the temperature may drop.

# Grooming Plants

Just as we check our own appearance each day, so we should cast a quick eye over our houseplants, especially flowering ones, to ensure that they are looking their best.

## Removing Dead Flowers

Removing dead flowers always makes a plant look better, as well as prolonging its flowering season and reducing the risk of fungal infections striking.

## Removing the Growing Tip

Carefully pinching out (removing) the growing tip immediately above the top leaves can produce a much bushier plant.

## Pruning Houseplants

Although houseplants don't need to be pruned regularly, they may become a bit unsightly. If so, prune them in spring using a sharp knife or pruning shears, cutting just above an outward-pointing bud wherever possible. Weak shoots will need to be cut off at their bases, and always remove dead and diseased stems as soon as you see them. And if the leaves on a variegated-leaf plant are reverting to green, cut their stems back to a variegated leaf.

## Staking Houseplants

A houseplant may need staking either to support the stem or to train the plant to grow in an attractive manner. Staking should always be as inconspicuous as possible, so avoid using a single cane, which can be more eye-catching than the plant that it is supporting. Instead, use a framework of canes, wire loops, or pot spirals. Tie the stems to the support with twine (not wire) at frequent intervals to spread the plant's weight, leaving enough room between the twine and stems to enable stem growth and minimize the danger of the plant being strangled.

When potting a plant that you think will require staking in the future, place the support in the pot while you are potting the plant because adding a stake––especially a moss stick––at a later stage can damage its roots.

## Making a Moss Stick

Vines, philodendrons, and Swiss cheese plants (*Monstera deliciosa*) can be grown very effectively up moss sticks. You can buy them from most garden centers, or make one yourself. First make sure the pot is large enough to hold both the pole and the plant and still provide enough room for the roots to grow. Then select a thick stick or cane measuring about 1½ in (4 cm) in diameter and wrap a thick layer of sphagnum moss around it, securing it with twine or plastic netting. The moss stick should always be kept moist by spraying it with water every day.

# Propagating Houseplants

It is possible to buy a wide variety of houseplants, of course, but there is great satisfaction to be had in propagating them yourself, either directly from seed or from cuttings.

No special equipment is needed, although a propagator (a propagating tray with a transparent lid) will ensure that the surrounding temperature encourages seeds and cuttings to grow. The basic requirements for propagation are air, moisture, the correct temperature, a seed tray, and compost that contains a small amount of minerals. The best sowing medium is loam-based compost, but there are also many commercially prepared seed composts available (but note that there is little real difference between them). Under no circumstances use garden soil, however, and always make sure that the equipment that you are using is clean because it is all too easy to introduce disease.

Another point to note is that you should not overwater because seedlings and cuttings cannot tolerate standing in root-rotting water.

## Propagating From Seed

Many pot plants are easy to propagate from seed.

**1.** Fill a seed tray, pot, or module to the top with compost.

### Tip

Modules are individual containers that take a variety of forms, such as trays, blocks of polystyrene, or compost. Their advantage is that the plant suffers less disturbance when it is transplanted, and grows more rapidly.

**2.** Firm the compost, but do not compress it because there must be space within it for air and water.

**3.** Wet the compost by watering it using a fine rose attached to a watering can or placing the tray in water up to its rim. Leave it to drain before sowing the seeds.

**4.**

4. Scatter the seeds thinly over the surface of the compost so that they do not touch each other. (It is easier to distribute very fine seeds if they have first been mixed with sand.)

5. Cover the seeds with finely sieved compost or vermiculite to a depth of about twice the seeds' diameter.

6. Gently firm down the compost.

**7.**

7. Either place the seed tray, pot, or module in a propagator or cover it with a plastic bag or sheet of glass and ensure that the temperature remains between 60 and 70°F (16 and 21°C).

8. When the first leaves (seed leaves) start to show, remove the cover.

9. As soon as the second leaves (which are the true leaves) have appeared, the seedlings are ready to be pricked out or planted separately.

10. To transplant an individual seedling, first fill a suitable pot with a good-quality, multipurpose compost (the seedling will now need feeding) and poke your finger into it to make a hole.

11. Handling the seedling by its leaves, not its stem, ease it out of its existing compost with a pencil, trying not to damage the roots, and then place it in the hole in the compost.

12. Gently firm the compost around the seedling with a pencil. (Do not use your fingers because they may damage the stem and compact the compost.)

13. Place the pot in a tray of water until the surface of the compost is damp, then leave it to drain.

14. Position the pot in a shady spot for a couple of days to allow the seedling to revive.

15. Finally, place the pot in a lighter position (but not in direct sunlight, which may scorch the young plant).

## Propagating From Stem Cuttings

Sometimes called softwood or tip cuttings, stem cuttings are generally taken from the end of a shoot, together with two or three leaves. Most houseplants can be propagated by this method.

**1.** Select a young side shoot without flower buds and then, using pruning shears, cut it away from its parent plant just below a leaf bud or joint, about 2 to 4 in (5 to 10 cm) from the tip.

**2.** Remove any lower leaves, but leave the top two or three in place.

**3.** Moisten the base of the cutting by dipping it in water and then dip it into some rooting powder.

**4.** Fill a suitable pot with a specially formulated cutting compost or a mixture of 50:50 peat and sand. Insert one-third to one-half of the stem's length into the compost. (Note that you could plant several cuttings around the edge of the pot.)

**5.** Water the compost gently and leave it to drain.

**6.**

**6.** Either insert four canes into the pot (to make sure that the bag's sides do not come into contact with the cutting) before covering it with a plastic bag or place the pot in a propagator. Keep the cutting at a constant temperature of 64 to 68°F (18 to 20°C).

**7.** Do not allow the compost to dry out.

**8.** Rooting can take ten to thirty days, and sometimes longer. As soon as you can see new growth at the tips of the cutting, you can be fairly certain that it has rooted.

**9.** You can now remove the cutting and pot it up into a larger pot, using multipurpose compost.

> ### Tip
> The best time to take cuttings is in the spring or summer.

## Propagating From Leaf Cuttings

New plantlets can be propagated from the leaves of certain plants, and there are four methods of doing this.

Whichever method you use, first prepare a pot or tray with moist cutting compost (as described in step 3 for propagating from seed, see above) and finally either place the container in a propagator or cover it with a plastic bag before leaving it in a warm and shady position.

## Propagating From a Whole Leaf and its Stem

The following method is suitable for African violets (*Saintpaulia*), begonias, and peperomias. It can also be used for rubber plants (*Ficus elastica* 'Decora'), but roll up the leaf vertically and secure it with an elastic band before planting it to encourage the stem to root.

Using a pair of sharp scissors, detach a leaf and its stem from the parent plant and then push one-half of the stem into the compost. As soon as you can see new plantlets growing where you buried the stem, carefully lift the plantlets and pot them on.

## Propagating From a Whole Leaf

Propagating from a whole leaf is a suitable method for succulents.

Remove a whole leaf from the parent plant with a pair of sharp scissors and then leave it to dry for a couple of days before planting the cut end in compost. You could cover the surface of the compost with a thin layer of sharp sand to aid drainage.

## Propagating From Part of a Leaf

Cape primroses (*Streptocarpus*) and mother-in-law's tongue (*Sansevieria*) are best propagated from part of a leaf.

1. Detach a whole leaf from the parent plant with a sharp pair of scissors, lay it flat on a hard surface, and then cut across the leaves, dividing them into sections 2 in (5 cm) wide.

2. Dip the bottom end of each section in rooting powder.

3. Insert the bottom end of each section vertically into the cutting compost, to one-half of its length.

New plantlets will form at the base, which should be potted on when they are large enough to handle.

## Propagating From a Leaf Blade

The following propagation method is suitable for *Begonia rex* and *B. masoniana*.

1. Using a pair of sharp scissors, detach a leaf (without its stem) from the parent plant and then, using the point of the scissors or a sharp knife, nick the main veins on the leaf's reverse side.

2. Place the leaf on the surface of the compost so that it is lying flat, with the cut side facing downward.

3. Gently place some pebbles, small stones, or hairpins on the surface of the leaf to keep it in contact with the compost.

4. New plantlets will form from the cuts.

## Propagating From Plantlets

Many plants throw out shoots that are easily detached from the mother plant's leaves or stems to grow into plantlets, notably spider plants (*Chlorophytum comosum* 'Vittatum'), piggyback, or pick-a-back, plants *(Tolmiea),* and hen and chicken ferns *(Asplenium bulbiferum).*

Let the plantlet produce three or four leaves before detaching it from the mother plant, and then follow the propagation method used for stem cuttings (see pages 43 to 44). Alternatively, leave it in a glass of water until it has produced roots and then pot it on.

**1.** Using a sharp knife, cut the offset from the parent plant as close to the stem as possible, protecting any roots.

**2.**

## Propagating From Offsets

Some plants, such as begonias, rosary vines *(Ceropegia woodi),* hot-water plants *(Achimenes hybrida),* and cacti, produce small versions of themselves from their sides, called offsets. And offsets can be propagated into new plants, as follows.

**2.** Then pot it up using ordinary compost.

## Propagating From Bulblets

Bulblets are small bulbs that grow at the base of plants like amaryllises and lilies.

To propagate, remove the largest bulblets from the parent bulb, using a sharp knife or just pull them away with your fingers. Pot them on in their normal compost mix, leaving just the tip of the bulb showing. Surround the tip with grit and put the pot in a sheltered place. (It may take two or three years before the plants flower.)

## Propagating by Air-layering

The air-layering method of propagation is suitable for rubber plants (*Ficus elastica* 'Decora'), Swiss cheese plants (*Monstera deliciosa*), and philodendrons.

**1.** Select a healthy young stem, and while it is still attached to its parent plant, remove all of the leaves growing about 6 to 10 in (15 to 25 cm) from the tip.

**2.** With a sharp knife, cut a diagonal slit upward, through the stem.

**3.** Place some rooting power in the slit.

**4.** Tie some transparent plastic film, such as Saran wrap, polythene, or a plastic bag that is open at both ends under the lower part of the cut section so that it forms a bag and then fill it with some damp sphagnum moss. Now close up the top, securing it with tape, such as electrical tape, to make it waterproof.

**5.** As soon as the moss ball is filled with roots (which can take up to two to four months), carefully cut below the bottom tie, remove the plastic film. and pot the plant on.

## Propagating by Division

Some houseplants' roots form thick clumps in the compost that can be divided into two or more sections. The division method of propagation is suitable for ferns, certain cacti and succulents, umbrella plants (*Cyperus*), and pelargoniums.

**1.** Extract the parent plant from its pot, which is easily done when the compost is slightly dry. Now remove some of the compost to expose the roots.

**2.** When you can see where the roots of the main plant and the new growth are connected, cut through this joint with a sharp knife.

**3.** You may need to separate additional compacted growing areas with two hand forks, positioned back to back.

**4.** Transplant the plants into normal compost at once and water them well.

### Tip

Always try to leave the roots as intact as possible when using the division method, and never simply cut a plant in half because this may kill both sections. Check that all sections have roots.

## Growing Plants From Fruits and Vegetables

Producing houseplants from the seeds, pips, stones, or tops of fruits and vegetables can be rewarding. Children especially enjoy this activity, which can be a pleasing introduction to gardening. But do note that although these plants need little attention, some demand patience on the part of the grower because they can take a long time to mature (and even then, often don't produce any edible fruits).

### Ananas Comosus (Pineapple Plant)

Remove the top of the pineapple with about 1½ in (4 cm) of the flesh. Remove the "shoulders," or sections of flesh on each side, leaving the hard, fibrous center. Now let it dry out for two to three days to prevent it from rotting. Remove the lower leaves and pot up the pineapple part in sandy compost. Place the pot in a warm, sunny position and keep the compost moist, but not wet, which would rot the base.

A miniature pineapple may grow from the center, but this will not ripen.

### Persea Americana (Avocado Tree)

It is easy to grow an avocado tree from an avocado stone. Insert three toothpicks into

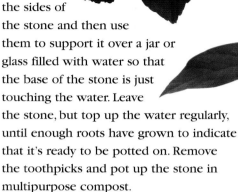

the sides of
the stone and then use
them to support it over a jar or
glass filled with water so that
the base of the stone is just
touching the water. Leave
the stone, but top up the water regularly,
until enough roots have grown to indicate
that it's ready to be potted on. Remove
the toothpicks and pot up the stone in
multipurpose compost.

The tree may grow to around 3 to 5 ft (1
to 1.5 m) in height, and if you want a
bushy plant, pinch out the growing tips
when it reaches the required height.

*Citrus sinensis* is easily grown from seed.

## Citrus and Other Fruit-bearing Plants

The pips of lemons (*Citrus limon*), oranges
(*C. sinensis*), grapefruits (*C. paradisi*), and
tangerines (*C. deliciosa*) germinate very
easily. Soak the pips in water overnight to
soften the outer shell and then insert them
individually in a small pot of multipurpose
compost to a depth of ½ in (about 1 cm).
Keep the pot in a warm, dark place until
shoots appear, watering the compost when
necessary, then move it to a sunny position.
Pot on the seedlings when they are large
enough to handle.

Once they have become established, all
citrus plants prefer to spend the summer
months outside (see page 120). If you
move them inside for the winter, avoid
positioning them in an overly warm place.

Other plants that can be grown from
pips and stones include apples (*Malus
domestica*), almonds (*Prunus amygdalus*),
lychees (*Litchi chinensis*), peaches
(*Prunus persica*), plums (*Prunus
domestica*), and pomegranates (*Punica
granatum*).

## Coffea Arabica (Coffee Tree)

To propagate a coffee tree, sow an unroasted coffee bean in a small pot filled with multipurpose compost and keep it warm and moist. Once a shoot has appeared, move the pot to a warm position that receives light, but not direct sunlight.

The leaves will be copper colored at first, before turning dark green with wavy edges. You can prune the bush to encourage it to branch out. Note that although small, white, sweet-smelling flowers may appear, they will rarely develop into beans.

## Phoenix Dactylifera (Date Palm)

If you'd like to propagate a date palm, remove the stone from a preserved date and plant it vertically in a pot filled with multipurpose compost, to a depth of ½ in (about 1 cm). Keep it very warm--at a temperature of 68°F (20°C)--and moist until a shoot appears, which can take three to four months. Then pot it on.

Alternatively, germinate the stone in warm water, and as soon as a seedling appears, plant it in very damp, multipurpose compost.

The seedling will grow into a date palm with long, stiff leaves measuring up to 6 ft 6 in (2 m) in height.

## Zingiber Officinale (Ginger Plant)

You can grow a ginger plant from a ginger root (rhizome). Put the rhizome in water until it forms roots, then pot it up in multipurpose compost and leave the pot in a warm, well-lit position, making sure that you keep it moist.

The result will eventually be a wide plant, with erect, dark-green leaves.

### Daucus Carota (Carrot)

To grow a carrot plant, cut the top ¾ in (2 cm) from a healthy carrot and trim away the outer leaves. Place the cut endin a pot filled with moist, multipurpose compost, leaving the crown exposed. Put the pot in a light position, but not in direct sunlight, and in a few weeks the carrot part will have developed into a feathery, bushy plant.

### Arachis Hypogaea (Peanut)

Propagate a peanut plant by planting an unshelled peanut in a pot filled with multipurpose compost. Keep the compost moist and ensure that a temperature of 68°F (20°C) is maintained around it.

The plant will display yellow flowers before the stems bend into the compost to produce peanuts.

### Sinapis Alba (Mustard) and Lepidium Sativum (Cress)

Mustard (*Sinapis alba*) and cress (*Lepidium sativum*) are particularly interesting for children to grow because they are both edible and sprout rapidly.

Although their seeds are usually sown on a damp paper towel, they can be grown on any moist surface, such as cones or balls of florist's sponge soaked with water. Roll or press the seeds into the wet sponge and then hang it up and spray it with water every day to keep it damp.

Sow the cress first by sprinkling its seeds evenly over a damp paper towel and then exposing them to a temperature of 64°F (18°C), keeping the paper towel damp by spraying it daily. After three days, sow the mustard seeds among the cress and then place the paper towel in a plastic bag until the seeds have germinated, at which point remove the paper towel from the bag and place it in a light position. When the leaves have opened, harvest the crop with a pair of scissors and perhaps enjoy your mustard and cress with fish paste and pepper in a sandwich.

# When Plants

Remember that the most common ways of killing plants are over- or underwatering them, and that most of the pests and diseases that afflict plants are brought into the home on a new plant. It is therefore important to check a plant thoroughly before buying it, and if you receive a plant as a gift, do not put it with others until you have checked its leaves. Examine plants regularly (don't forget plants that are resting or wintering) because a problem that is caught early is easier to control than one that has really taken hold.

Hygiene is most important when caring for plants, so always make sure that your equipment and hands are as clean as possible. Also ensure that there are never any dead or diseased leaves lying on the surface of the compost or in any plants' trays and containers.

Regularly check over your plants for damage or disease.

Finally, when treating a plant, it is best to isolate it. And if the plant is really sick, throw it away.

> ### Tip
> A healthy plant is less prone to pests and diseases.

## Cultivation Problems
A number of cultivation problems can cause plants to suffer, and this section outlines their symptoms and remedies.

## Cold
Cold slows down a plant's growth, also causing its leaves to curl and their tips to turn yellow and brown. Some plants may even collapse.
REMEDY: remove dead or dying flowers or foliage and move it to a warm spot.

## Heat
If a plant is too hot, the tips of its leaves may turn brown, it may loose its lower leaves, and any flowers may quickly die.
REMEDY: remove any damaged leaves, gradually move the plant to a cooler position over a period of days, and mist the leaves to increase the humidity level.

## Too Much Sun
Scorched or brown leaves may be the result if a plant is receiving too much sun.

# Are Ill

REMEDY: remove damaged leaves; either move the plant out of the sun or provide it with shade at the hottest time of the day.

## Too Little Light

If a plant receives too little light, it will become thin and straggly and the lower leaves will drop off. The leaves of variegated plants will revert to green.
REMEDY: move the plant to a lighter spot, but not in direct sunlight. Cut off all of the spindly growth to encourage bushiness.

## Low Humidity

If a plant is suffering from low humidity, the leaves will wilt and have brown edges, and any flowers will fade very quickly.
REMEDY: mist the plant daily with warm water, and once a week mist it with water in which fertilizer has been diluted.

## Underfeeding

Underfeeding results in poor growth, with flowers and leaves being smaller than usual.
REMEDY: make sure that the compost is wet before introducing a fertilizer diluted to half-strength; thereafter, gradually bring it to full strength over a period of weeks. (Adding full-strength fertilizer straightaway would shock the plant, making it sicker.)

## Overfeeding

Overfeeding causes the tips of a plant's leaves to turn brown, plant tissue to become soft, stems to droop, and a flowering plant to fail to flower. Another sign of overfeeding can be a white deposit on the outside of clay pots.
REMEDY: soak the pot in plenty of water, let it drain, and repeat the process a few times. Repot the plant in new compost, do not feed it for six weeks, and follow the instructions on the fertilizer package.

## Overwatering

Overwatering causes a plant to droop, its leaves to turn yellow, and its roots to rot. If the plant is in a clay pot, a sure sign of overwatering is green slime on the sides.
REMEDY: remove the dead roots and yellow leaves; repot the plant in fresh compost and then place it in a warm spot.

## Underwatering and Infrequent Watering

The symptoms of underwatering are flaky, brown patches on a plant's leaves and dry compost shrinking away from the sides of the pot. Infrequent watering can cause buds or flowers to drop off.
REMEDY: submerge the pot in water and keep it there until all of the air bubbles have come to the surface. Then leave the pot to drain. The next day, water it with diluted fertilizer.

## Pests

Pests are insects that have a damaging effect on a plant. And although they are less common inside than they are in the garden, they can still infest houseplants. Inspecting your plants once a week should enable you to spot any pests before they get out of hand.

A list of common pests and the measures that can be used against them appears below. When dealing with them, always try the easiest remedy first--a few are outlined here--and avoid using houseplant insecticides unless absolutely necessary.

• Some pests, such as scale insects, can be scratched off leaves, but before doing so, place an aluminum-foil collar around the neck of the plant to catch the scale insects and prevent reinfection.

• Certain pests, such as aphids, can be washed off a plant with warm or soapy water. Place the pot in a plastic bag, tie some string around the bag at the stem, invert the pot in a bowl of warm or soapy water for thirty seconds, and then place it upright on a sheet of newspaper, which will collect the aphids as they fall off.

• To protect a plant from aphids, regularly spray it with liquid manure made from stinging nettles (see the box above).

• Insert small, yellow, plastic traps (from garden centers) into a plant's pot to trap flying insects like whiteflies.

> ### Tip:
> ### A Recipe for Stinging-nettle Manure
> Roughly chop 1 lb (about 500 g) of fresh, young stinging nettles and place them in a very large plastic bowl. Add 9 pt (5 l) of water to the bowl and leave it for twenty-four hours. Sieve the nettle mixture over a bowl and retain the liquid. Transfer the liquid to a bottle and label it. This manure will keep indefinitely, as long as you seal the bottle after using it.

• Regularly spraying a plant with water will deter red spider mites. If the plant is already infested, spray the leaves with water, place a plastic bag over the top of the plant and tie it with string at the base of the stem; leave the plant like this for a week before removing the bag. Note that this method works best when the shrouded plant is placed in an area of high humidity.

• Remove mealy bugs from a plant by brushing them with cooking oil.

• If you have an infestation in your conservatory or garden room, you could buy a biological-control product from a company that suppliies natural predators for pests. Aphids, for example, are controlled by *Aphidoletes*, a predatory midge; red spider mites, by *Phytoseiulus persimilis*, another midge; vine weevils are eaten by nematodes (worms); and whiteflies are feasted on by *Encarsia formosa*, a parasitic wasp.

## Aphids
Aphids are sap-sucking insects that inject a poison into the plant and excrete a sticky, sweet liquid (honeydew) that attracts sooty mold. Aphids can be green, black, or orange. They attack green, sappy growth and new tips of flowering plants.
TREATMENTS
PRACTICAL: wash with soapy water.
BIOLOGICAL: introduce *Aphidoletes*, a predatory midge, or spray with stinging-nettle manure.
CHEMICAL: spray with a general-purpose houseplant insecticide.

## Caterpillars
Caterpillars are not often found on pot plants, but may be seen in a garden room or conservatory. A symptom of a caterpillar infestation is holes in a plant's leaves.
TREATMENTS
PRACTICAL: pick off the caterpillar and destroy it.
BIOLOGICAL: introduce *Bacillus thuringiensis* bacteria, which kills caterpillars without harming other insects.
CHEMICAL: spray with Fenitrothion or a general-purpose houseplant insecticide.

## Earwigs
Earwigs have dark-brown bodies with pincerlike tails. They hide under leaves during the day, come out to eat vegetation after dark, and can strip a leaf to its skeleton overnight.
TREATMENTS
PRACTICAL: pick off the earwig and destroy it.
BIOLOGICAL: none.
CHEMICAL: spray with a general-purpose houseplant insecticide (this step is rarely required, however).

## Mealy Bugs
Mealy bugs leave secretions on the undersides or crowns of plants and hide under a whitish substance that looks like fluffy cotton. They multiply very quickly and are very fond of cacti, palms, and ferns.
TREATMENTS
PRACTICAL: pick off the mealy bugs and destroy them, or else dab the fluffy evidence of their presence with a brush soaked in cooking oil.
BIOLOGICAL: introduce the predatory beetle *Cryptolaemus*.
CHEMICAL: spray weekly with a general-purpose houseplant systemic insecticide.

## Red Spider Mites
Red spider mites are tiny pests that multiply rapidly in hot and dry conditions

and move from one plant to the next. The mites and their larvae are greedy feeders that sit on the underside of leaves, pierce holes in them, and then suck out the sap.

TREATMENTS

PRACTICAL: spray the plant regularly with water and pick off, and destroy, any red spider mites that you can see.

BIOLOGICAL: introduce the predatory midge *Phytoseiulus persimilis*, which eats the mites faster than they can reproduce.

CHEMICAL: use a general-purpose houseplant systemic insecticide.

## Scale Insects

Scale insects inject a toxic substance into plants, which causes them to turn yellow or brown. The protective scales that they secrete around themselves are circular, waxy, and brown.

TREATMENTS

PRACTICAL: scrape, or wipe off, the scales with a damp cloth or cotton bud.

BIOLOGICAL: introduce *Chilocorus nigritus*, a black ladybird that will bite a hole in the waxy secretions and kill the scale insects.

CHEMICAL: spray with a general-purpose houseplant insecticide.

## Vine Weevils

Vine weevils have become the new scourge of the gardening world. The adult beetle eats plants' leaves at night, while the grub attacks their roots, thereby causing the most damage, which is often done before you notice that the plant is wilting.

TREATMENTS

PRACTICAL: use a potting compost containing perimiphos-methyl, a vine-weevil insecticide. Pick off the adult insects whenever you see them.

BIOLOGICAL: introduce the nematode *Heterorhabditis* when watering plants.

CHEMICAL: water the plant with Provado Pest Free, according to the manufacturer's directions.

## Whiteflies

Whiteflies are usually noticed as tiny, white, mothlike insects on the undersides of leaves. They spread rapidly from plant to plant as the pupae suck out the leaves' sap, causing them to turn yellow and drop off.

TREATMENTS

PRACTICAL: wash the affected plant with soapy water (this treatment is not very effective, however).

BIOLOGICAL: introduce the parasitic wasp *Encarsia formosa*, which will kill the pupae. (Note that this wasp is harmless to other insects.)

CHEMICAL: spray with a general-purpose houseplant insecticide.

# Diseases

A plant often succumbs to disease when it has been cared for incorrectly. The easiest remedy is to make sure that it is exposed to the correct conditions and that plenty of air is circulating around it.

## Tip

When treating a diseased plant, quarantine it from other plants to prevent them from becoming infected and remove all diseased parts. Before returning it, thoroughly clean the area in which it will be displayed.

## Blackleg

Blackleg attacks the stems of plants and cuttings, causing the stem closest to the compost to turn black and rot. Pelargonium cuttings, African violets (*Saintpaulia*), and begonias are especially prone to blackleg.

There is no cure for this disease, so destroy infected plants and cuttings to prevent it from spreading.

TREATMENTS
PREVENTATIVE: make sure that the compost isn't too wet. When potting on a plant, place plenty of drainage material in the base of the pot and ensure that the plant is not positioned any lower in the compost than it was in its previous pot

## Corky Scab

As its name suggests, corky scab (edema) causes corky growths to appear on the undersides of a plant's leaves, and can often be seen on Christmas cacti (*Schlumbergera truncata* or *Zygocactus truncatus*). It is caused by the plant being waterlogged and positioned in an area that receives poor light and is too high in humidity.

TREATMENTS
PRACTICAL: remove the affected leaves, place the plant in a brighter position, and reduce your watering regime.

## Gray Mold

Gray mold (botrytis) manifests itself on leaves, buds, and stems as soft, furry, rotting patches covered with gray mold, which cause a plant to rot. Soft-leaved plants like African violets (*Saintpaulia*), begonias, and fuchsias are particularly prone to gray mold.

TREATMENTS
PRACTICAL: cut off and destroy all of the affected parts and replace the top ½ in (1 cm) of compost with fresh compost. Don't overcrowd plants, and reduce your misting and watering regimes.
CHEMICAL: spray with a general-purpose systemic fungicide for houseplants.

## Powdery Mildew

Powdery mildew causes a white, floury film to develop on the tops of leaves. Although it is unsightly, it is not fatal.

TREATMENTS

PRACTICAL: cut off and destroy the damaged parts and then dust the plant with sulfur powder (which is available from garden centers).

CHEMICAL: spray with a general-purpose systemic fungicide for houseplants.

## Rust

When a plant is infected with rust, circular, reddish patches appear on the leaves. Pelargoniums, fuchsias, and palms are particularly susceptible to rust.

TREATMENTS

PRACTICAL: remove and destroy the infected leaves and improve the circulation of air around the plant.

CHEMICAL: spray at regular intervals with a preventative fungicide containing mancozeb.

## Sooty Mold

Sooty mold, which appears on leaves as a black coating, results from the honeydew droppings that have been deposited on the leaves by scale insects, mealy bugs, and aphids. Although sooty mold does not directly harm a plant, it blocks the pores of its leaves and shades them from the light, thereby preventing photosynthesis (see page 11).

TREATMENTS

PRACTICAL: using a damp cloth, wash the affected leaves with warm water.

CHEMICAL: spray with a general-purpose houseplant fungicide to target the honeydew-producing pests.

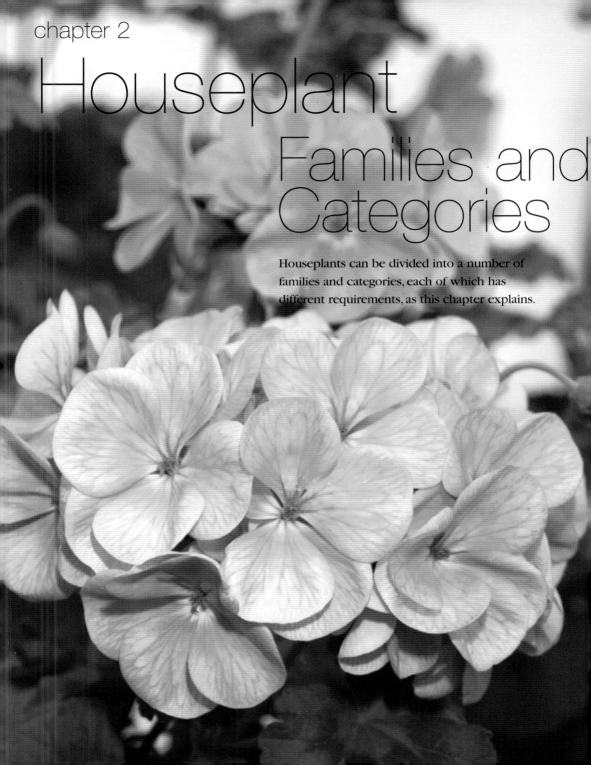

# chapter 2

# Houseplant
## Families and
## Categories

Houseplants can be divided into a number of
families and categories, each of which has
different requirements, as this chapter explains.

# Bulbs

A variety of bulbs can be grown and displayed in the home, including hyacinths (*Hyacinthus*), narcissi (*Narcissus*), crocuses, snowdrops (*Galanthus*), colchiums, scillas, lilies (*Lilium*), hippeastrums, and lilies of the valley (*Convallaria majalis*). Bulbs do not like warm conditions, so it's important to keep them in a cool, but light, area when you bring them into your home.

## Planting and Cultivating Winter- and Spring-flowering Bulbs

It is always good to see a container full of bulbs in bloom at Christmas, reminding us of the spring flowers to come. If Christmas flowering is to be guaranteed, however, you must buy specially prepared bulbs (which are relatively expensive) and plant them by September (in the northern hemisphere).

Bulbs are easy to grow. Winter- and spring-flowering bulbs are planted in bulb fiber (which consists of peat, charcoal, and oyster shell), in bowls without drainage holes. Another suitable compost is John Innes No. 2, which provides a firmer basis and includes some initial feed.

**1.** Select a suitable pot. Bulbs can be planted in any type of pot, as long as there is good drainage material at the bottom.

**2.** If your chosen pot has drainage holes, cover them with crocks.

**3.** Half-fill the pot with bulb fiber, which should be moist, but not wet.

**4.** Arrange the bulbs closely together, but ensure that they are not touching one another or the sides of the pot. Now add more bulb fiber until just the tips of the bulbs are visible in the case of large bulbs like hyacinths, but cover the tips of smaller ones, such as *Iris danfordiae*.

**5.** Place the pot in either a cool, dark place or cover it and plunge it (that is, place it in a hole in the earth) in a shady spot in the garden. It is important to keep the bulbs cool to enable roots to develop.

**6.** Constantly check the pot to ensure that the bulb fiber is moist, but not wet, and water it carefully if necessary.

**7.** When you can see shoots measuring 1 to 2 in (2.5 to 5 cm) in height, move the pot to a light position, but shield it from direct sunlight and keep it cool until the flower buds have developed.

**8.** Continue to keep the bulb fiber moist, but do not overwater because most bulbs fail when their conditions are too wet.

**9.** Turn the container each day to ensure even growth (the shoots will lean toward the light).

**10.** When the bulbs have stopped flowering, move their pot to a cool, dry position and let the leaves die back. Because the quality of their blooms will lessen each year, it's then best to plant the bulbs in the garden.

Hyacinth bulbs can be grown over water. To do this, use a specially designed hyacinth glass and select a large, healthy bulb that fits snugly into the neck of the glass. Fill the glass with water, but ensure that the water level is below the bottom of the bulb (the bulb will rot if it is in constant contact with water). Keep the hyacinth glass in a cool place, topping up the water when necessary (and note that adding a few pieces of charcoal will keep the water fresh), until shoots begin to develop.

Some narcissi and crocuses can be grown on pebbles or moist sand in a trough. Select a variety that has lots of small flowers, such as *Narcissus* 'Cragford' or *N.* 'Paper White', rather than one big bloom. Follow the same rules of cultivation as described above for hyacinths. Smaller varieties, such as *Narcissus* 'Tête-à-Tête' and *N.* 'Peeping Tom' are also suitable.

Tulips that are traditionally grown in the garden can be unruly and difficult to manage as houseplants, although single and double early flowering varieties are worth a try. The dwarf tulips make good pot plants, and thrive best in sandy soil.

Small flowering bulbs have a beauty all of their own. Winter aconites (*Eranthis*), snowdrops, chionodoxas, scillas, and irises can all be raised in pots, but should not be brought inside until their flower buds have appeared.

## Summer- and Fall-flowering Bulbs

Some of the most spectacular bulbs flower during the summer, notably amaryllises, lilies, cannas (*Canna hybrida*), nerines, and forest lilies (*Veltheimia*). After they have flowered, these bulbs should remain in their pots until the foliage has died. They should then be stored in almost dry conditions until new growth appears, when they should be repotted. Summer- and fall-flowering bulbs cannot tolerate frost or very cold or wet conditions.

Members of the *Colchicum* genus of flowering bulbs, including *Colchicum autumnale* (which is commonly, and incorrectly, called autumn crocus), will bloom if they are positioned in a bright, sunny spot, such as a windowsill, even without being planted in compost.

# Indoor Trees and Shrubs

Eucalytus makes a good indoor tree.

Many trees and shrubs that are usually grown in the garden can be cultivated as houseplants, including hollies (*Ilex aquifolium*), Japanese maples (*Acer palmatum* 'Dissectum Atropurpureum'), and cedar gums (*Eucalyptus gunnii*). And some houseplants assume treelike proportions over a period of years in any case.

Certain trees, such as Norfolk Island pines (*Araucaria heterophylla*), can add a different dimension to a room by providing an unusual focal point, particularly if they are tall or have unusual foliage. Their positioning needs thought, however, not least because trees and shrubs are generally housed in large, and very heavy, pots, and

should therefore be placed on a secure base. As long as this is done and their natural growing conditions are roughly met, they should thrive.

When planting a tree or shrub, always remember that the pot needs to be large enough to hold the root ball and also to be in proportion with the height of the mature plant. It's best to use a soil-based compost like John Innes No. 2 or 3, which contains plant food and is also firm enough to anchor a tree that may become top-heavy with foliage. Rhododendrons, azaleas, ericas, and other acid-loving plants must be planted in ericaceous compost and the surface of the compost weighed down with grit or gravel to prevent the plant from overbalancing should the compost dry out (ericaceous compost is very light).

As the tree or shrub grows larger, potting it on will be impractical, which means that it will need top-dressing (see page 32).

The plant should be watered regularly (the compost should be moist, but not wet), and it should also be fed once a month from spring through to fall. Evergreen trees and shrubs should be watered throughout the year, but still require a resting period during the winter, while deciduous types, such as fuchsias, can be overwintered in cool conditions and watered sparingly.

Because the tree or shrub will lean toward the light, remember to turn it regularly, that is, unless it has a "face side," or definite front, like Swiss cheese plants (*Monstera deliciosa*) and weeping figs (*Ficus benjamina*).

Once the tree or shrub has reached the required height, consider pruning out the central stem in the spring to encourage the development of side shoots, but be warned that pruning it like this may cause it to develop an unnatural shape over time.

Shrubs that are grown for their flowers should be pruned after the flowers have faded, while foliage shrubs are best pruned in the spring.

*Acer palmatum* can provide an unusual focal point in a room.

## Tip

Once a tree or shrub becomes large and heavy, it is difficult to turn, so think ahead and place its container on an easily moveable base.

# Bonsai

The leading principle underpinning the art of bonsai (a Japanese word that means "to plant in a container") is restricting the root growth of trees or shrubs severely, thus stunting their overall growth, but without causing them to lose their natural shape or attractiveness. The aim is to cultivate a perfect tree, but in miniature.

Unless you are an experienced bonsai-grower, it is best to buy a bonsai that has already been trained (but you could have fun trying to create one yourself from scratch!) You will also need to choose any bonsai that you intend to keep inside carefully because although the plants are miniature, they still require the same growing conditions that they would if they were full size. Traditionally, bonsai are outdoor plants that cannot survive for long indoors, and perhaps four to five days at the most. If a bonsai is to be kept inside for longer, the best choices are woody plants from Mediterranean regions, such as *Bougainvillea glabra*, species of *Ficus,* and *Hibiscus rosa-sinensis*. Remember that a bonsai will need plenty of natural light (but not direct sunlight) and a cool, draft-free position.

## Cultivating Bonsai

Although growing bonsai can be very rewarding, it can cost a lot of money and take a great deal of time. It is certainly not for the faint-hearted. If you are interested in cultivating bonsai, however, it's best to research the subject by reading specialist publications. The following general tips may nevertheless prove helpful.

• Never let a bonsai dry out (this is the quickest way of killing it).

• Feed a bonsai with weak fertilizer every ten to fourteen days during the growing season, but never apply it to dry compost. After repotting it, do not feed a tree for six weeks.

• Constant attention and skill are required for training and pruning bonsai. New growth is slow, but when shoots do appear, they should either be pinched back or trained with soft, plastic-covered wire. The branches of evergreen bonsai should be pruned regularly, with shoots being pinched back to two or three buds. If the bonsai is deciduous, remove the first flush of leaves to encourage the growth of a second set of smaller ones.

### Tip
When watering a bonsai tree, use a watering can to which a fine rose has been attached to discourage the compost from running out of the container.

# Cacti

There are over two thousand species of cacti and stem succulents, whose swollen stems act as water reservoirs and that have stemless flowers in all colors, apart from blue. Most flower annually in early summer, but although a plant may have many blooms, they do not last for long. There are two types of cacti: forest cacti and desert cacti.

Forest cacti--Christmas cacti (*Schlumbergera truncata* or *Zygocactus truncatus*), for example, are the easiest to grow and to persuade to flower. These cacti need watering throughout the year, but note that the compost must always be allowed to dry out beforehand. They should initially spend three months (from June to August in the northern hemisphere) in the yard to harden their stems before being transferred to a cool, indoor environment to encourage bud development, after which they should not be moved again.

Desert cacti include some of the smallest-growing plants, such as *Echinopsis*, and also some of the largest, in the form of prickly pears (*Opuntia*). Desert cacti do not thrive on neglect.

They need plenty of natural light, and are ideal plants for a conservatory (see page 20) or south-facing windowsill. They can tolerate high daytime temperatures of 90°F (32°C) and higher, and night temperatures as low as 41°F (5°C). A winter resting period in cool, light conditions is essential if desert cacti are to reflower in the spring.

## Cultivating Cacti

Cacti are often sold in tiny pots with very little growth medium, so it is advisable to pot them on as soon as you buy them. You can buy many types of commercial cactus compost, but try a mixture of 2 parts peat-based potting compost, or John Innes No. 2, to 1 part grit or coarse, washed sand, which provides a quick-draining element.

It's best to repot cacti in the spring, gently firming the compost and then watering it thoroughly before allowing the surface to dry out. The compost should be moist, but not wet, throughout the growing season, and dry during the resting period. Water sparingly during the fall, and not at all during the winter, unless a cactus starts to shrivel. It is, however, vital to mist cacti occasionally. Feed cacti at intervals of two to three weeks during the spring using a high-potassium feed (such as that used for tomatoes), and revert to a normal fertilizer in summer.

# Succulents

There is a vast range of succulents with amazing shapes and sizes; the most popular are *Mesembryanthemum,* or living stones.

Succulents originate in the dry regions of Africa and America, and in order to withstand these dry, hot climates, they have developed thick, fleshy leaves that store large quantities of water and often have a waterproof, waxy coating to prevent water loss. To reduce evaporation further, the leaves are packed closely together and are covered either with hairs or a web of thin fibers.

## Cultivating Succulents

Because their root system lies just below the soil, succulents can be planted in shallow containers or half-pots to enable the flat, branched roots to soak up every available drop of water. Ensure that a pot has good drainage holes, however, and repot succulents only when absolutely necessary. Use a free-draining compost, at least one-third of which should be sand, and never allow it to become waterlogged because this makes the base of the plant susceptible to rotting.

Succulents need full sun, fresh air (especially during the summer), warm temperatures, and plenty of water during their growing period. The best way to water them is to stand their pots in water until the compost is moist and then leave the pots to drain. If you are watering succulents from above, however, do not allow any water to come into contact with the leaves because it may become trapped between them, causing them to rot.

Feed succulents little and often, with a fertilizer that has been diluted to half of its normal strength.

Succulents enjoy spending the summer in the garden, and if you are hoping that they will flower in spring, overwinter them in a cool, but light, position.

These plants are best propagated in spring or summer, either by division or by taking stem or leaf cuttings (see pages 43 to 45). Remember to let the cut ends of the cuttings dry out before planting them in compost, and then not to cover them.

## Creating a Dish Garden

Make a dish garden as follows.

**1.** Select a large, shallow dish with drainage holes.

**2.** Add a thin layer of grit to the bottom of the dish and then fill it with free-draining compost.

**3.** Arrange the succulents in the dish without overcrowding them, perhaps so that some trail over the sides.

**4.** Cover the compost with pebbles or colored glass chippings.

**5.** Water the plants, leave the compost to drain, and then place the dish on a sunny windowsill.

## Living Stones

Living stones (*Lithops*)--pebblelike succulents--are members of the *Mesembryanthemum* family, each plant being made up of a pair of extremely thick leaves. They are very slow-growing plants and reach a height of only 2 in (5 cm).

Living stones need little attention. Plant them in free-draining compost (compost containing sand or grit) in a shallow pot with drainage holes, cover the surface of the compost with sand or grit, then place the pot in a light position. Living stones produce new leaves every year (the old ones die off), so keep them dry from the end of their flowering period (usually early winter) until the new leaves are visible in the summer. Water them sparingly during their flowering season and don't allow any water to come into contact with the leaves. Although they can survive without being fed, note that giving living stones a little weak fertilizer once a month will encourage them to flower.

# Bromeliads

Some of the most exotic houseplants are bromeliads, the best-known being the pineapple plant (*Ananas comosus*). Bromeliads grow wild in the subtropical areas of America, where they live as epiphytes (plants that grow on other plants, but are not parasitic), clinging directly to the branches and trunks of trees. They have leathery leaves arranged in rosettes, which act as water reservoirs.

## Cultivating Bromeliads

Bromeliads (but not tillandsias, or air plants, see below) can be grown in small, shallow pots, and should be planted in a moist, all-peat compost mixed with an equal part of sphagnum moss to which some charcoal has been added (alternatively, use a commercially prepared mixture specifically formulated for bromeliads). They should be planted firmly, but not deeply, because they have poorly developed root balls.

*Aechmea fasciata.*

Bromeliads that have hard, silvery-gray leaves need plenty of light and a temperature of 50°F (10°C), but if their leaves are soft and green, they prefer shadier conditions and a temperature of 64°F (18°C).

Unless you live in a very cold region, water your bromeliads throughout the year, letting the compost dry out between waterings. If the center of the plant forms a "vase," always fill it with soft water or rainwater, unless a flower bud is forming or it is cold. Misting a bromeliad daily from spring to fall encourages growth.

During their growing period (usually spring or summer), feed bromeliads with an organic fertilizer, at the strength recommended by the manufacturer. Do not feed them during their resting period (which is generally winter, or when they are exposed to cool temperatures).

Propagate bromeliads by removing their offsets during the growing period, letting them dry out, and then potting them in free-draining compost.

Note that tillandsias, or air plants, are not suited to pot culture and should instead be attached to rough-barked branches, skeletal wood, or cork bark. Do this by placing sphagnum moss around their roots and attaching them to the wood or bark with plastic-coated garden wire. Water air plants by spraying them with soft water twice a day during the growing season, and twice a week during the winter.

# Palms

Although palms live in the world's tropical and subtropical areas, they are not difficult to grow as houseplants. But be warned: because some species can reach heights of 13 to 16 ft (4 to 5 m), they may soon outgrow a room.

Some of the palms that make good houseplants are:

- *Cocos nucifera* (coconut palm);
- *Phoenix canariensis* (Canary date palm);
- *Neathe bella* (parlor palm);
- *Chamaerops humilis* (European fan palm, or dwarf fan palm);
- *Rhapis excelsa* (little lady palm); and
- *Cycas revoluta* (sago palm).

## Cultivating Palms

Palms prefer temperatures ranging from between 60 and 72°F (16 and 22°C) and require good light (but avoid positioning them in direct sunlight because their leaves are easily scorched). They tend to die back if placed in a dark corner.

Palm leaves grow from a single point on the stem, and will usually thrive in a variety of composts that provide good drainage, although a mixture of peat, leaf mold, and loam-based compost in equal parts will generally produce the best results, while some more exotic species prefer a loam-less mixture. As a plant grows larger, compost containing more loam and some sand will be necessary.

Palms produce lots of roots, which often push the root ball upward, out of the pot, and when a palm's roots start growing through a pot's drainage holes, it is time to repot it. Alternatively, rather than repotting such palms as *Caryota* and *Cocos nucifera* into a larger container, you could prune their roots.

When potting them, note that palms need to be anchored into their pots much more firmly than most plants, and that the compost should be watered thoroughly and then left for a couple of weeks to become slightly dry before being watered again. The watering requirements of different species of palm vary, but none should be allowed to become waterlogged. All benefit from regular misting, too, which also helps to keep red spider mites at bay.

Feed palms little and often during the spring and fall. After potting them on, don't feed them for six months, however.

*Cocos nucifera.*

# Ferns

Ferns are some of the oldest plants on the planet. Although they do not flower, they make up for it by displaying a variety of beautiful fronds or leaves, ranging from the fine leaves of the maidenhair fern (*Adiantum raddianum*) to the broad, coarse leaves of the stag's-horn fern (*Platycerium bifurcatum*). When buying a fern, ensure that its leaves are fresh-looking and bright green in color, and that there is no dry or shriveled foliage.

Most ferns grow well in the home, and aren't difficult to look after. They need more shade and humidity than the average houseplant, however, and make good specimens for bottle and tank gardens.

Some suitable ferns to cultivate as houseplants are:
- *Cyrtomium falcatum rochfordianum* (holly fern);
- *Asplenium nidus* (bird's-nest fern);
- *Dicksonia antarctica* (soft tree fern);
- *Nephrolepis exaltata* (sword fern).

## Cultivating Ferns

Although most ferns tolerate being planted in ordinary potting compost, they prefer peat-based compost and, being acid-lovers, dislike lime.

Water ferns regularly--if possible, with rainwater--keeping them moist throughout the year. You should also ideally either fill the space between the pot of an

The delicate grace of a maidenhair fern.

individual fern and its container with damp moss or peat or stand the pots of a number of ferns on a moist, pebble-filled tray. (Indeed, ferns benefit from being grouped together.)

No fern likes direct summer sunlight, preferring to stand in a shady window area, although they can tolerate weak winter sunlight. Keep them away from drafts, too.

Once a fern has established itself in its pot (usually when it is about one year old), feed it little and often from spring through to fall. Note that ferns respond well to foliar feeding, which means misting them with a fine spray of diluted fertilizer.

## Propagating Ferns

Dividing them in the spring is the usual way of propagating most ferns. You could alternatively raise them from their spores, although be warned that this process requires a great deal of patience.

# orchids

Orchids are exotic plants whose flowers' lifespan ranges from only a week to several months, depending on the species. The orchid family is a huge one, comprising as it does over seventeen thousand species, most of which are found in the tropics. Orchids are divided into two main groups: epiphytic orchids (which grow on trees) and terrestrial orchids (which root in the soil). All orchids have swollen, bulblike stems known as "pseudobulbs," which store water and food and also support the plant's roots, leaves, and flowers.

*Cymbidium* orchids have masses of long-lasting flowers.

Orchids are tolerant plants that can survive when given only the minimum of attention. The epiphytic group is the one most closely associated with houseplants, and with such a large number of species to choose from, it is possible to have a flowering orchid in your home every month of the year. *Cymbidium* and *Phalaenopsis* are the two most popular genuses of orchidaceous plants that can be grown as houseplants, but note that cultivating orchids is an arcane art, and that it's best to research the subject by reading specialized publications before trying your hand at it.

## Cultivating Orchids

Orchids require a special compost, and although you could mix it yourself, it is much easier to buy a commercially prepared pack, which should be open (that is, it should contain some grit) and free-draining and should be made up of 2 parts sphagnum moss, 2 parts plastic or bark chips, 1 part rough moss peat, and a small amount of charcoal.

Because orchids prefer to be pot-bound and flower better in this state, they only need potting on when their roots start to grow through the sides of the pot. Another signal that a plant should be potted on is when it has pushed its roots over the rim of the pot. Do not repot an orchid when it is actively growing, however.

Pot an orchid on into a pot that is only one size larger than the old one. Too large a pot can cause the roots to rot. Although you could use a clay pot, a slatted basket or perforated pot made especially for orchid culture is far better. Note that if you are using a clay pot, you should fill one-third of it with crocks to improve the drainage. When potting an orchid on, place a layer of compost in the bottom of the pot and arrange the orchid's roots on top, even if this means curling them around the plant. Pour more compost around the roots and tap the pot to firm it in. Water the plant after two or three days.

Although orchids require regular watering, the compost must never be wet, and you should allow it to dry out before immediately watering it. And because the recommended compost is very free-draining, you can water an orchid by submerging its pot in water for thirty seconds before leaving it to drain. Preferring as they do a humid atmosphere, orchids enjoy being misted and having their leaves sponged with water.

Most orchids are best screened from the sun, except in winter. They need as much light as possible (but not direct sunlight) and a cool nighttime temperature of about 50°F (10°C).

Orchids will grow and flower without being fed, but may benefit from being given a half-strength fertilizer during their growing season.

Note that these plants require a resting period, during which time you do not need to water them, that is, as long as their bulbs remain plump (start watering them again as soon as you see new growth). During this period they should, however, receive plenty of light to encourage the

bulbs to ripen, ready for flowering.

Propagate orchids by division (see page 48), ensuring that each section comprises several pseudobulbs, leaves, and roots. After planting these sections, water them sparingly until new shoots appear.

Large varieties will need careful staking.

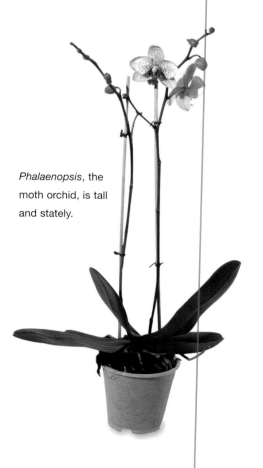

Phalaenopsis, the moth orchid, is tall and stately.

# Carnivorous Plants

Carnivorous, or insectivorous, plants live in boggy areas whose soil contains few nutrients. They therefore rely on flies, which they trap and digest, to provide them with nitrates. Carnivorous plants snare their prey using one of two primary methods: either by snapping together two hinged leaves and trapping the fly inside, the method used by Venus flytraps (*Dionaea muscipula*); or by drowning any insects that are attracted by their sweet smell or bright color to venture inside them in digestive fluid, the method employed by pitcher plants (*Nepenthes coccinea* and *Darlingtonia californica*, for instance). Another method entices the unfortunate insect to become stuck to the hairs that cover parts of such carnivorous plants as sundews (*Drosera binata*).

## Cultivating Carnivorous Plants

Carnivorous plants must be kept constantly wet, so plant them in pots containing equal parts peat and spaghnum moss and then place them in deep containers and keep one-third filled with rainwater. They can also be secured with peat within a waterproof container--perhaps a bog garden--which should be topped up with water to a depth of around ¾ in (2 cm).

You can give carnivorous plants an occasional extra feed of tiny pieces of raw meat or fly maggots (available from fishing-tackle stores) during the summer. Don't feed them in winter, but ensure that they are kept moist in a cool position. (At this time of the year, such plants are less than attractive, and are probably in any case best regarded as short-lived entertainment.)

# Feng Shui
## and Houseplants

According to the Chinese theory of feng shui, everything about us, wherever we are, possesses a vital energy that circulates around us, constantly affecting our lives.

It is thought that surrounding ourselves with healthy plants, which are reputed to be powerful carriers of the more positive effects of feng shui, will cause us to feel generally better, but that the proximity of any dead or dying plants will offset this effect. If you, like many people, have kept a sick plant out of affection for your old friend and it cannot be saved, feng shui would therefore advocate disposing of it, or at least moving it outside so that it doesn't negatively affect the energy of the room.

Not only do plants connect us with the natural world, but, according to the principles of feng shui, if they are well-placed, they can also help to promote positive energy (chi) by adding oxygen to the air and increasing the natural energy that all materials possess. This is why installing houseplants in a room is one of the most effective life-enhancing measures recommended by feng-shui practitioners.

## Selecting Plants
From the feng-shui perspective, the best plants with which to surround yourself are those that have round or soft leaves, while plants that have spiky leaves are usually best avoided. (The one exception to the rule banning spiky plants is to place them near windows to discourage unwanted intruders.)

The most popular plant in feng shui is the luck-bringing bamboo (*Bambusa*), which, because it requires very little natural light, can be positioned anywhere in a building. Other plants are also believed to exude positive influences, including:
• the jade plant (or money tree, *Crassula argentea*), said to enhance prosperity and supply energy;
• the African violet (*Saintpaulia*), said to have the power to increase your wealth;
• the Chinese evergreen (*Aglaonema*), which bestows security;
• the silver crown (*Cotyledon undulata*), which radiates good fortune;
• any dark-green climbing plant is said to impart the desire for growth.

It is also important to give careful thought to a plant's container when practicing the art of feng shui. Big terracotta planters represent stability, and may therefore prove helpful in areas where people tend to feel insecure, for example. The sight of lots of little, fussily decorated pots can be irritating, on the other hand, and may make people feel on edge. Remember that simplicity is fundamental when feng shui meets plants.

## Where to Position Plants

First impressions are important, and can, if intelligently manipulated, promote positive feelings. And what people notice first on entering a room can set the tone for the rest of the day. The color or scent of a stylish flowering plant can make an immediate impression if it provides an unexpected treat for the eye in contrast to an otherwise dull area.

Western architecture tends to prefer sharp angles, but corners are considered offensive in the East, with feng shui holding that the sharp corners of tables and counters emit and lose energy, while the corners of rooms are areas of stagnant energy. Positioning a tall plant in an empty corner will even out this pooling effect by keeping the energy flowing smoothly. Placing plants that have soft, arching stems (such as *Adiantum raddianum*, the maidenhair fern) or trailing foliage (such as *Hedera*, ivies) on tables and counters will counteract their corners' negative effect.

Electrical paraphernalia gives off a great deal of energy, but surrounding electrical equipment like televisions and computers with plants can balance such energy loss and counteract the negative effect on you.

To reap further benefits from plants' positive energies, position them:
• inside an unused fireplace to keep positive energy in the room rather than letting it escape up the chimney;
• under sloping ceilings to prevent negative energy from pressing down on you;
• in long hallways to encourage the flow of positive energy and to calm nervous energy.

Finally, if you are skeptical about the effectiveness of feng shui, try placing a potted cactus in your bedroom, but don't be surprised if you sleep fitfully because prickly cacti release negative energy and attract bad luck, according to feng shui. Replace the cactus with a feathery fern, however, and you will enjoy sweet dreams. (Try doing this in the bedroom of an unsuspecting family member or friend; in my experience, it really does work!)

# Eco-friendly
# Houseplants

Over the years, we have been encouraged to make our homes and offices more energy-efficient, consequently creating an atmosphere in which the pollutants given off by modern materials are threatening our health. Sick-building syndrome has caused a big increase in allergies, asthma, headaches, sneezing attacks, and lethargy, which is, perhaps, hardly surprising given that we are estimated to spend 90 percent of our time inside.

It has long been known that plants have a positive effect on people by providing a calming atmosphere and relieving stress. Research carried out by Dr. Bill Wolverton over the past twenty-five years, primarily at N.A.S.A. (the U.S.A.'s National Aeronautics and Space Adminstration), has furthermore found that certain plants act as air filters that suck pollutants out of the atmosphere, thereby improving a room's air quality. Such plants have a high transpiration rate, which means that they absorb carbon dioxide from the atmosphere through their leaves, in return adding healthy moisture to the air. And in a recent survey of British schoolchildren carried out by researchers at Reading University, it was discovered that they performed much better when plants were displayed in their classrooms.

The following plants, all of which have high transpiration rates, are recommended for their ability to remove polluting chemical vapors from the air:
- *Chysalidocarpus lutescens* (areca palm);
- *Rhapis excelsa* (little lady palm);
- *Ficus robusta* (rubber plant);
- *Dracaena deremensis* 'Janet Craig' (dracaena 'Janet Craig');
- *Hedera helix* (ivy);
- *Chlorophytum comosum* 'Vittatum' (spider plant);
- *Spathiphyllum sp.* (peace lily);
- *Nephrolepis exaltata* 'Bostoniensis' (Boston fern);
- *Gerbera jamesonii* (gerbera daisy); and
- *Epipremnum aureum* (golden Pothos).

Spider plants remove indoor pollutants.

# Potentially
# Dangerous Plants

Some very attractive plants are poisonous, making them extremely dangerous if ingested, while others can irritate or wound the skin.

Amaryllises contain sap that can cause vomiting.

## Poisonous Plants

The following plants are poisonous:
• the *Solanaceae* group of plants, including the winter cherry, *Solanum capsicastrum,* and the nightshade *Solanum jasminoides*;
• *Browallia* (bush violet) and *Brunfelsia* (yesterday, today, and tomorrow), which have attractive colored berries that children may be tempted to eat;
• *Nerium oleander* (oleander), *Allamanda cathartica* (dogbane), *Dipladenia sanderi* (Chilean jasmine), *Cycas revoluta* (sago palm), and *Datura candida* (angel's trumpet), which are very bitter and cause nausea if eaten in sufficient quantities;
• the tubers of *Gloriosa superba* (glory lily) and *Colchicum autumnale* (autumn crocus);
• the bulbs of *Lilaceae*, such as *Amaryllis* (belladonna lily), *Tulipa* (tulip), narcissus, *Hyacinthus* (hyacinth), and *Clivia* (kaffir lily), which can cause vomiting and sickness if swallowed.

## Emergency Treatment

If a child has swallowed part of a poisonous plant, do not give him or her anything to drink and take the child and a cutting from the plant responsible to hospital immediately. If you know it, tell the medical team the plant's botanical name.

## Skin-irritating Plants

Plants that can irritate the skin include:

Primula leaves can cause irritation.

• all *Euphorbiaceae* (poinsettia), *Codiaeum* (croton or Joseph's coat), and *Acalypha*, which contain a skin-irritating white sap;

• some *Araceae*, which contain a poisonous sap that can cause swelling of the mouth and throat and inflammation of the eye. These plants include *Dieffenbachia* (leopard lily or dumb cane), *Aglaonema*, (Chinese evergreen), *Anthurium* (pig-tail plant), *Monstera deliciosa* (Swiss cheese plant), *Philodendron*, and *Zantedeschia* (arum or calla lily);

• *Primula* (primroses) and *Lycopersicon* (tomatoes), whose fine hairs can trigger an allergic reaction, resulting in a raised rash.

Before touching these plants, always put on gloves, and after handling or coming into contact with them, wash your hands or skin thoroughly. Never rub your eyes while working with them either.

Note: allergies are often person-specific, so while one person may react badly to touching a skin-irritating plant, someone else may suffer no ill effects.

## Spiky Plants

Try to discourage children from playing near plants that have sharp points, prickles, or leaves with lethal edges, such as cacti, *Ananas* (pineapples), yuccas, agaves, certain succulents, palms, *Euphorbia milii* (crown of thorns), and aloes.

The sharp points and prickles of a yucca can cause damage to the skin.

# Chapter 3
# An A to Z
## of Houseplants

The houseplants in this chapter are listed by their genus names (which are often also their common names, although these are not italicized) and appear in alphabetical order.

Dictionaries usually define houseplants as being any plant that is grown inside. There is therefore no reason why herbs and vegetables shouldn't be included in this chapter, particularly in view of their usefulness to the household's cook.

## Key to Symbols

The following symbols are used in the directory for quick reference.

Location of plant

Watering advice

Feeding advice

Potting and pruning

Advice for propagation

Pests and diseases

# Abutilon

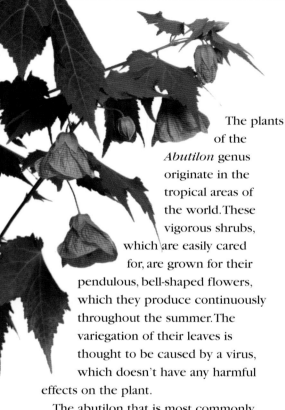

The plants of the *Abutilon* genus originate in the tropical areas of the world. These vigorous shrubs, which are easily cared for, are grown for their pendulous, bell-shaped flowers, which they produce continuously throughout the summer. The variegation of their leaves is thought to be caused by a virus, which doesn't have any harmful effects on the plant.

The abutilon that is most commonly seen in stores is *A. hybridum* 'Canary Bird', which has bright-yellow flowers. The variegated *A. striatum* 'Thompsonii' will grow to 6 ft 6 in (2 m) and has attractive, orange-red-flowers, while *A. megapotamicum* is a trailing variety.

## Cultivating *Abutilon*

*Abutilon* thrives best in bright, indirect sunlight. In summer, it prefers temperatures ranging from 60 to 77°F (16 to 25°C), but will tolerate temperatures as low as 50°F (10°C) in winter. It makes a good plant for a conservatory.

Keep the compost moist from spring through to fall, and only water sparingly during the winter.

Feed every two weeks, except in winter, when it should not be fed at all.

This plant is easy to look after. It should be repotted each spring unless it is being grown in a large pot, when it should be top-dressed instead. (Note that *Abutilon* flowers better if it is slightly pot-bound.) Stand it outside during the summer, but protect it from any winds. Prune it back to half its size in fall to produce a more bushy plant.

Propagate either by taking stem cuttings or by sowing seeds in a well-draining compost in the spring. It is best to take stem cuttings from variegated species, however, because any plants grown from their seeds may not truly reflect the parent plants' characteristics.

Prone to red spider mites, mealy bugs, and scale insects. If it is too cold in winter, it will often shed some leaves.

# Acer

As its common name, Japanese maple, suggests, *Acer palmatum* 'Dissectum Atropurpureum' originates in Japan. It is a very attractive, slow-growing, deciduous tree or shrub, whose foliage forms a mound of palmate (deeply divided or lobed), bronze-red or deep-purple leaves that change to a spectacular russet in fall. Usually grown for its foliage, this maple can reach nearly 5 ft (1.5 m) in height.

A. *japonicum* 'Aureum' has yellow leaves, while A. *palmatum* 'Dissectum' has green leaves.

## Cultivating *Acer*

*Acer* tolerates temperatures of 41 to 50°F (5 to 10°C), but is best kept away from drafts, which can cause the leaves to shrivel and drop off. It likes some shade, dislikes direct sun, and benefits from spending time outside during the summer. It is best grown as a conservatory or specimen plant.

Water *Acer* frequently, don't let the compost dry out once the leaves have formed, and keep it moist during the winter, after it has shed its leaves. It needs regular misting when grown inside.

Feed only during the growing season.

Prefers a free-draining, acid soil. Pot it on in ericaceous compost roughly every two years. Once installed in a large pot, top-dress it every year.

Very hard to propagate, *Acer* is best bought from a garden center.

Be warned that aphids can plague this plant.

# Achimenes

*Achimenes* grows from small rhizomes, which should be stored dry over the winter and will then grow in spring. The foliage is heart-shaped, dark-green in color, and hairy. It is thought that *Achimenes'* common name--hot-water plant--refers to its need to be watered with warm water, but today's centrally heated buildings have made this requirement redundant.

*A. hybrida* is the most popular species, and comes in a variety of colors. *A. erecta* is a trailing plant with red stems and bright-red flowers. *A. grandiflora* has large blooms and grows up to 12 in (30 cm) in height.

## Cultivating *Achimenes*

Shade *Achimenes* from direct sunlight, but place it in a bright position. It prefers temperatures between 50 and 59°F (10 and 15°C), making it suitable for a light, warm position. If it is a spreading species, you could plant it in a hanging basket.

Keep the compost moist and don't allow it to dry out. Stop watering once *Achimenes* has finished flowering.

Feed *Achimenes* fortnightly during the growing season.

During the winter, store the rhizomes in dry peat at a constant temperature of 64°F (18°C). In spring, water them with warm water to encourage growth. Once shoots have appeared, pot the rhizomes on into multipurpose potting compost, which should just cover them. Note that most species of *Achimenes* will need supporting when they are growing, and that pinching out young shoots will result in a bushy plant. After *Achimenes* has flowered, cut back straggly branches and remove dead blooms to encourage it to flower again.

Propagate by either dividing the rhizomes in spring or sowing seeds in early spring.

Aphids can afflict *Achimenes*.

# Adiantum

*Adiantum* (maidenhair fern) originates in tropical America. These plants have delicate, deeply dissected, tufted leaves, the blades of the fronds being roughly triangular and the stems looking like pieces of thin, black wire. Quite delicate plants, they require warmth, moist air, and shade.

A. *raddianum* is the most popular species, and probably the easiest to grow. It reaches a height of only around 12 in (about 30 cm). A. *tenerum* 'Farleyenseis' is, by contrast, an arching variety.

## Cultivating *Adiantum*

*Adiantum* requires partial or complete shade and should be protected from the sun throughout the year. It does not respond well to any change in its conditions and must be kept out of drafts. It enjoys a humid position and temperatures between 64 and 68°F (18 and 20°C), making it a suitable plant for a terrarium or bathroom.

Always keep the compost moist (preferably with rainwater), but don't allow the plant to become waterlogged. Mist regularly, and, if necessary, position it on a pebble tray to increase the humidity levels around it.

When it is producing new foliage, it likes to be fed once a week with a weak solution of liquid fertilizer. Stop feeding it in winter, however.

*Adiantum* prefers a peat-based, well-draining compost, and should be potted on each year. Remove accumulations of dead leaves from the center of the plant to prevent them from causing rotting.

Propagate in the spring, either by division or by propagating its spores (providing some heat from below will encourage them to grow).

*Adiantum* may be attacked by aphids.

# Aechmea

The plants of the *Aechmea* genus are tough, epiphytic bromeliads that originate in Brazil. The common name of the best-known species, *A. fasciata*--urn plant--reflects how the hard, spiky-edged leaves appear to form a waterproof funnel or urn. In its natural, jungle habitat this central "cup" is always full of rainwater, helping to keep the plant moist.

The rosette-forming leaves of the popular *A. fasciata* 'Silver King' are marbled and banded in white, although colors can vary from light gray to dark red. The leaves can grow up to nearly 20 in (50 cm). The purple-blue flowers are held in spikelike panicles (clusters) on long stems, each bearing pink-colored bracts. These plants may take up to five years to produce flowers, which appear between spring and fall, and after flowering only once (albeit often for six months), the rosette dies, offsets then forming at its base.

## Cultivating *Aechmea*

*Aechmea* requires a light position, although not one in full sun. It will flower the most readily at temperatures between 68 and 86°F (20 and 30°C), but can tolerate temperatures as low as 53.6°F (12°C). This attractive flowering plant is ideal for a light, warm place or a bromeliad tree. It is also an eco-friendly plant that effectively removes the formaldehyde fumes commonly found in busy offices.

Allow the compost to dry out between waterings, but make sure that the rosette is always filled with about 1 in (2.5 cm) of rainwater.

Feed *Aechmea* every two weeks with a liquid feed.

This plant rarely needs repotting. Remove the dead rosette as soon as possible after flowering.

Propagate in late spring by planting offsets into their own pots.

*Aechmea* may be troubled by scale insects or mealy bugs.

# Aeonium

*Aeonium* (stonecrop crassula) originates in Arabia. A sparsely branched succulent that thrives in the home, it has rosettes of dark-green, glossy leaves on bare, long or short stems, depending on the species or variety. *Aeonium* blooms attractively in spring and summer, its starlike, yellow flowers forming a rounded pyramid above a thinly branched shrub base that can reach around 3 ft (1 m) in height.

A. *arboreum* 'Atropurpureum' is notable for its dark-purple, glossy leaves, while A. *tabulaeforme* is commonly known as saucer plant because its tightly packed leaves form a shape that resembles a saucer.

## Cultivating *Aeonium*

*Aeonium* requires a sunny, warm position during the daytime, but prefers a lower temperature at night. It should be kept at temperatures above 50°F (10°C) during the winter. It makes an ideal plant for a succulent collection or dish garden, and is especially suited to bright windowsills. It enjoys plenty of fresh air, too. Note that if A. *arboreum* 'Atropurpureum' is kept in too dark a position, its rosettes will turn green.

Water it generously in summer, but give it little or no water during the winter.

Feed *Aeonium* every two weeks during its growth period.

Repot in the spring, in a shallow pot filled with free-draining compost (perhaps John Innes No. 2, to which coarse sand has been added). The stems die after flowering, and should then be cut off.

Propagate in spring or summer by planting rosettes, leaf or stem cuttings (remember to let the cut edges dry out before planting them) in sandy compost. It can also be raised from seed, with the help of some heat from below.

*Aeonium* often attacts mealy bugs and red spider mites in winter.

# Agave

A genus of evergreen perennials originating in southern North America, whose long, thick, fleshy, sword-shaped leaves (which are usually tipped with spines) form rosettes, *Agave* are grown as foliage plants. In order to flower, all *Agave* species need to be grown in large tubs, the plentiful, blooms, which are carried as very tall, candelabralike clusters, taking twenty to twenty-five years to appear. Although agaves make good houseplants in their early stages of growth, they can grow too large for the average home. Once they have flowered, the rosettes die, and are replaced by offsets from which new plants grow.

  *A. americana*, commonly called century plant, has gray-green leaves measuring up to 3 ft (1 m) in length. *A. americana marginata* has green leaves edged with yellow. *A. filifera* is smaller and more delicate, with dark-green leaves that have threads of white along their top edges.

## Cultivating *Agave*

*Agave* likes full sun all year round, and can be placed outside during the summer. Although it enjoys warm days, it prefers to spend its nights in temperatures ranging from 41 to 50°F (5 to 10°C). It should be kept cool, but should not be allowed to become too cold during the winter. Note that a large specimen or display plant requires plenty of space, and that smaller species are often best displayed in cactus gardens.

Do not water during the winter.

Feed once a month.

Plant in a free-draining compost, which should be kept moderately moist during the spring and summer.

Propagate by planting any offsets or bulbils in separate pots. *Agave* seeds (which are rarely available, however) can be sown in spring.

It is rarely attacked by pests, but overly cold winter conditions may cause it to rot.

## Caution
*Agave's* spines present a danger to young children.

# Aglaonema

*Aglaonema* is a genus of slow-growing, bushy plants that originate in tropical Southeast Asia. Most species have attractive, oblong, spear-shaped leaves that are mottled grayish-green, and short stems about around 20 in (50 cm) long.

Variegated strains require bright light if their leaves are to retain their variegation, but the all-green variety *A. modestum* (Chinese evergreen) thrives in poor light. The foliage of the popular *A.* x 'Silver Queen' is almost silvery in color, while the small flowers lack petals.

## Cultivating *Aglaonema*

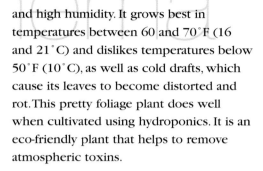 *Aglaonema* relishes warmth, shade,

### Caution
Although *A. modestum* rarely fruits when in cultivation, its red fruits are poisonous.

and high humidity. It grows best in temperatures between 60 and 70˚F (16 and 21˚C) and dislikes temperatures below 50˚F (10˚C), as well as cold drafts, which cause its leaves to become distorted and rot. This pretty foliage plant does well when cultivated using hydroponics. It is an eco-friendly plant that helps to remove atmospheric toxins.

Keep its compost moist from spring to fall, but water it sparingly during the winter. Mist *Aglaonema* regularly, too, ensuring that it receives a fine spray of water because any droplets that remain on the leaves may result in leaf spot (a disease caused when the leaves rot).

Feed with half-strength liquid fertilizer every two weeks during the growing season.

Repot every two or three years in a peat-based compost and, if necessary, place its pot on a pebble tray to increase the humidity around it.

Propagate in spring by division or by taking suckers or rooted basal shoots.

Red spider mites, mealy bugs, and aphids can all target this plant.

# Allium

allium

*Allium schoenoprasum* plants, or chives, are easily grown from seed sown in multipurpose potting compost.

## Cultivating *Allium Schoenoprasum*

*A. schoenoprasum* requires a sunny position (a warm windowsill is ideal), regular watering, and feeding about every two months.

Don't thin the seedlings, but when the foliage is about 2 ¾ in (7 cm) high, cut it back by about ¾ to 1 in (2 to 3 cm), after which the plants will grow again, so that it should be possible to "cut and come again" for as long as is required. After a year, the seedlings will have become thicker and more mature and will fill the pot.

Propagate by division in spring.

# Alocasia

*Alocasia* (or kris plant) is an increasingly popular genus of plants that originates in tropical Asia. The plants' fleshy rhizomes produce tall evergreens that can grow to a height of over 3 ft (1 m). They display striking, deeply lobed, arrow-shaped leaves that are dark green in color, with white veining, and measure 12 to 16 in (30 to 40 cm) in length. The flowers, which lack petals and resemble those of arums, are not so attractive, however.

*A.* x *amazonica* (Amazon lily) has glossy, white-veined, dark-green leaves, with wavy white edges.

## Caution
*Alocasia* can irritate some people's skin.

## Cultivating *Alocasia*

 If it is to thrive, *Alocasia* requires a warm and humid atmosphere and plenty of light. It needs a minimum temperature of 59°F (15°C) in winter (the leaves will turn brown if conditions are too cold) and can tolerate temperatures of up to 86°F (30°C) in summer. This plant prefers bright, indirect sunlight, but can be grown in a semi-shaded position for a short time. It does best in a warm, sunny, enclosed space, making it ideal for a conservatory that is heated in winter.

Keep its compost moist during spring and summer, but let it dry out a little in winter. It likes high humidity, so mist it regularly and stand its pot on a pebble tray.

Give a weak feed every two weeks.

Wipe the leaves frequently throughout the year. Repot the plant every spring.

Propagate in spring by taking either suckers or cuttings from the rhizomes; encourage them to grow by exposing them to gentle heat from below.

Red spider mites and scale insects can infest this plant.

# Aloe

Originally from South Africa, the plants that belong to the *Aloe* genus are succulents whose juices apparently benefit the skin. Tubular in shape, *Aloe's* flowers usually appear at the end of long stalks. Their triangular-shaped leaves, which measure 1 in (3 cm) in length, are arranged in rosettes and exude a thick juice when cut.

The best-known plant of this genus is *A. variegata* (the partridge-breasted aloe), which has white bands around its leaves and salmon-red flowers. *A. aristata* is a smaller species, with white-spotted leaves and orange-red flowers. The skin-nurturing juice of *A. vera* (sometimes called *A. barbadensis*, or burn plant) is frequently used for cosmetic purposes.

## Cultivating *Aloe*

*Aloe* tolerates temperatures between 41 and 50°F (5 and 10°C) and enjoys fresh air. Suitable for a bright, warm windowsill, it can be placed outdoors in full sun during the summer. In winter, position it in a light place.

Water *Aloe's* compost moderately, but allow it nearly to dry out between waterings and do not let the plant become waterlogged. Keep the compost almost totally dry during the winter. Don't let the rosette become wet or it will rot off.

Feed with a very diluted cactus feed every six weeks during the summer.

*Aloe* prefers a shallow container and free-draining compost and should only be potted on when it becomes pot-bound.

Propagate using stem cuttings, offsets, or leaf cuttings, allowing the cut edges to dry before planting them in compost. The cuttings will root easily, that is, as long as they are dry and are not covered with compost.

*Aloe is* rarely attacked by pests or diseases, but note that the stem may rot if the compost is too wet.

# Amaryllis

*Amaryllis belladonna* (belladonna lily) is of South African origin. Its flowers grow in clusters of up to four, straight from the bulb on bare, solid stalks that reach heights of between 20 and 27 in (50 and 70 cm). These trumpet-shaped flowers, which measure 3 to 4¾ in (8 to 12 cm) in width, bloom from spring until late summer. After it has flowered, the bulb produces deciduous, strap-shaped, deep-green leaves that appear in late winter and last until spring.

A. *belladonna* is best grown in a conservatory and should only be brought into the house when it is ready to flower. Although its bulbs are usually on sale in the fall, note that you will need to buy a specially prepared one if you require it to flower at Christmas.

## Caution
Parts of *A. belladonna* are toxic to pets.

## Cultivating *Amaryllis Belladonna*

A. *belladonna* prefers a sunny, warm position, possibly outside during summer and before its flowering period. In winter, don't let the temperature around it drop below 50˚F (10˚C), and keep it in a well-lit position. Ideally suited to any conservatory that can accommodate its height, cultivate a single bulb for the best display.

Keep its compost moist in summer and almost dry in winter.

To ensure that it will flower the following year, feed it with a high-potash fertilizer every two weeks from the end of the flowering period until fall.

Unless you have bought a ready prepared bulb, plant only half of it in good-quality, free-draining compost. After the plant has flowered and the foliage has died back, allow it to rest for three to four months before repotting or watering it.

Propagate by planting its offsets in the spring.

This plant is rarely bothered by pests, apart from the occasional red spider mite.

# Anthurium

*Anthurium* originates in the humid rainforests of tropical America. An evergreen, upright plant, it has leathery, dark-green leaves and exotic spathes, which are usually brightly colored or spotted and contain a twisted flower spike (hence its common name, pig-tail plant).

A. *scherzerianum* (flamingo flower) has elongated, waxy, bright-scarlet spathes, each containing a long, yellow, spiral-twisted flower spike. Cultivars are available with white, pink, dark-red, and spotted spathes.

*Anthurium* is vulnerable to cold conditions, so buy it only from a reputable retail outlet.

## Cultivating *Anthurium*

Place *Anthurium* in a light or partially shaded position and protect it from direct sunlight. *Anthurium* dislikes sudden changes of temperature, so maintain a minimum temperature of 50°F (10°C) around it. If it is to flower, temperatures of between 60 and 75°F (16 and 24°C) are preferable, and plenty of light is required. This humidity-loving plant is suitable for hydroponics and is also eco-friendly, helping in the removal of harmful chemical vapors from the immediate atmosphere.

Keep compost moist throughout the year, but ensure that it does not become waterlogged, especially during the winter. Mist it regularly, too.

Feed with diluted liquid fertilizer once a week, but stop this feeding regime in winter.

Repot every two or three years, placing plenty of crocks in the pot. Provide it with an atmosphere of high humidity by standing its pot in a pebble tray. Because its roots should always be kept damp, push any roots that appear at the base of the stem back into the compost. Clean the leaves with a damp cloth.

Propagate in spring, by division or by planting offsets in free-draining compost, soaked with warm rainwater or soft water.

Targeted by red spider mites, mealy bugs, scale insects, and aphids.

## Caution
*Anthurium* is poisonous, making good hygiene essential after handling it.

# Aphelandra

Originating in tropical America, *Aphelandra squarrosa* (zebra plant) is a striking plant, having glossy green foliage with contrasting pale-cream or silver-white veining. It produces angular, spiked, bold-looking flowers with overlapping yellow bracts in the fall, which can last for six to eight weeks. It grows to a height of 24 in (60 cm) in favorable conditions.

*A. squarrosa* 'Louisae' is the most suitable variety for a houseplant.

Before purchasing a zebra plant--which is attractive as both a flowering and foliage plant--make sure that the leaves don't have a yellow tinge and that the flowers are not too advanced in growth.

## Cultivating *Aphelandra Squarrosa*

*A. squarrosa* needs a light, warm position, but should be protected from direct sunlight. Although it is capable of withstanding cool conditions, it prefers temperatures ranging from between 60 and 68°F (16 and 20°C) and should not be kept at a temperature of less than 50°F (10°C) during the winter. *A. squarrosa* is suitable for hydroponics.

Water the compost freely in summer, but keep it merely moist in winter. Mist frequently with warm water.

If it is to flower, it is vital that you feed this plant every two weeks from spring to early fall.

Pot on in the spring. After the flowers have finished blooming, cut the stems back to a single pair of leaves.

Propagate by taking stem cuttings in spring or summer. These must be exposed to a constant temperature of 75°F (24°C) in order to take root.

Prone to receiving the attention of aphids. Its leaves will fall off if the air is too dry or if the plant is standing in a draft.

# Aporocactus

*Aporocactus* is a genus of epiphytic cacti. Trailing or pendent plants that grow on trees or rocks, their cylindrical stems--which are usually ¾ in (2 cm) thick, grow several inches in length a year, and can be as long as 5 ft (1.5 m)--have aerial roots and are covered with prickly spines. The fiery red, or pink to purple, trumpet-shaped flowers, which measure 3 in (7 cm) in length, last for several days.

A. *flagelliformis* (rat's-tail cactus) displays pink or bright-red flowers in spring.

> ## Caution
> Approach *Aporocactus*'s prickly spines with caution, not least because they are difficult to remove from the skin.

## Cultivating *Aporocactus*

To encourage flowering, *Aporocactus* needs a warm, bright position and cool conditions during the winter. Although it does well in full sun and can be positioned outside during the summer, it must be protected from rain. Being a trailing plant, it is suitable for hanging baskets, while the smaller species are ideal for cactus gardens.

Water generously when the plant is flowering, letting the compost dry out between waterings. Keep the compost almost dry in winter, however.

Feed with a high-potash fertilizer once a month from February to June (in the northern hemisphere) until it has finished flowering.

Do not move this plant once the buds have set lest they fall off. Repot only when it becomes essential, and then after flowering, placing plenty of gravel in the base of the pot before adding free-draining compost.

Propagate in summer by taking stem-tip cuttings and allowing the cut surfaces to dry out before planting them in compost.

Red spider mites and mealy bugs can be a problem. Note that overwatering can cause the stems to rot.

# Araucaria

Northwestern New Zealand is the place of origin of *Araucaria heterophylla*, commonly called Norfolk Island pine and sometimes Christmas-tree plant. A tall, evergreen conifer with graceful, horizontal branches that are arranged in spirals on the main stem, the crown produces bright-green leaves that resemble pine needles.

Another popular species of *Araucaria*, *A. glauca*, is noted for its blue-gray needles. Before buying, check that the needles look fresh and there are lots of lower branches.

## Cultivating *Araucaria*

*Araucaria* prefers a light position, with no direct sun, and should be placed in a shady spot outside during the summer. It should be kept cool, but shielded from drafts, at a temperature ranging between 50 and 64°F (10 and 18°C) in summer and 41 and 50°F (5 and 10°C) in winter. As long as it receives enough light, it can suit a large space, such as a hall or stairwell. Turn it regularly if it is placed in a corner. Because it helps with the removal of chemical vapors from the atmosphere, *Araucaria* is eco-friendly and can also be cultivated as a bonsai tree or grown in a hydroponic system.

Water regularly with soft water. Allow the compost to dry out between waterings, but don't let it become waterlogged. Mist the leaves regularly, especially in winter.

Feed a weak fertilizer every two weeks, but stop in winter.

It grows slowly, and disturbing its roots harms it, so top-dress, rather than repot, it.

This plant is hard to propagate.

*Araucaria* often attracts scale insects. If needle growth is weak, it is probably too warm. Needle drop is usually due to the air being too dry, while limp branches are a sign that it is suffering from too much water or heat.

# Arbutus

*Arbutus unedo* is an evergreen shrub originating in Western Europe. It grows to a height of 6 ft (2 m) and has shiny, dark-green, oval leaves and pale-pink-to-cream, bell-shaped flowers that hang in panicles (clusters) and develop into round, orange fruits that resemble strawberries, which is why the plant's common name is strawberry tree. The flowers and the fruits (which, although edible, are tasteless) often appear on the tree simultaneously.

A. *unedo* is not often sold as a houseplant, so look for it in garden centers.

## Cultivating *Arbutus Unedo*

An attractive plant for an unheated conservatory, A. *unedo* tolerates temperatures of between 37 and 59°F (3 and 15°C). It requires a very light position and benefits from spending time outside during the summer (as long as it is protected from strong winds).

Water regularly during the summer (with rainwater if possible), but keep the compost merely damp in winter.

Feed with a weak fertilizer every two weeks during the spring and summer.

Because frequent disturbances can cause the plant to drop its flowers and fruits, repot it in good-quality, multipurpose compost only when it is pot-bound, and then in late winter, before the flowers have appeared.

Propagate in spring by taking stem-tip cuttings. Note that although you could sow its seeds, the resulting plants will take a long time to produce flowers.

A. *unedo* is rarely attacked by either pests or diseases.

# Asparagus

*densi-*
*rus*
*eyeri'.*

The shrublike, South African plant *Asparagus densiflorus* 'Meyeri' has a short trunk and thickly leaved, arching stems measuring up to 12 in (30 cm) in length that resemble both the fronds of ferns and foxes' tails, which is why the plant is commonly called foxtail fern. The dark-green, needlelike leaves that form the stems' bottle-brush shape are actually modified side shoots (phylloclades or cladodes).

*A. densiflorus* 'Sprengeri', commonly called emerald fern, also originates in South Africa. Its arching, multibranched stems, which reach 35 in (90 cm) in length, hold numerous, quite dainty, bright-emerald-green, needle-type leaves (really modified branchlets) that give the plant a fernlike appearance. It occasionally produces bright-red berries. This plant is favored by florists when making up bouquets.

## Cultivating *Asparagus Densiflorus*

*A. densiflorus* likes bright, indirect sunlight, but can cope with semishaded conditions. It prefers average temperatures of 50 to 59°F (10 to 15°C). Too hot a room temperature can cause its leaves to drop. The plant can be placed outside in summer. It makes an ideal plant for a hanging basket situated in a cool room.

Water regularly from spring to fall, but keep its compost barely moist during the winter. Although it should be misted occasionally, it does not require a humid atmosphere.

Feed weekly during the summer, and occasionally in winter.

Propagate in the spring, by division.

*A. densiflorus* may fall prey to red spider mites and aphids.

A. densiflorus 'Sprengeri'.

# Aspidistra

*Aspidistra elatior* (cast-iron plant), which originates in China, was a popular houseplant during Victorian times that is still often used to add interest to dark corners. Its dark-green leaves are reminiscent of spears. It flowers rarely, but when it does, individual, dark-purple blooms appear at compost level.

A. *elatior* 'Variegata' has attractive white banding on its leaves. It will not withstand neglect, however.

Don't buy any A. *elatior* that has split or speckled leaves or shows signs that the leaves have been cut back to their base.

## Cultivating *Aspidistra Elatior*

A. *elatior* is an undemanding plant that will thrive in most places. It tolerates both dark and light positions. If it is to maintain its variegation, the variegated variety requires more light, however. But it enjoys diffused sunlight and can be stationed outside during the summer. It grows best in temperatures ranging from 50 to 70˚F (10 to 21˚C). An eco-friendly plant, A. *elatior* effectively removes formaldehyde and benzene vapors from the atmosphere.

Keep the plant's compost consistently moist in summer, but barely moist during the winter.

Feed monthly with a weak fertilizer solution, but stop feeding it in the winter or if its leaves begin to split.

Trim back any old leaves and sponge the remaining leaves regularly with a damp cloth. Either repot every two or three years or, if it has reached the required size, top-dress it (older plants do not like their roots to be disturbed) in the spring.

Propagate in the spring by division (note that each part should have at least two leaves), and do not feed the new plantlets until the following spring.

Apart from the occasional attack from red spider mites triggered by dry conditions, this plant is rarely bothered by pests. Indeed, it is very hard to kill, unless it is overwatered.

# Asplenium

AThe *Asplenium* genus of plants. commonly called spleenworts, which originate in tropical Asia and Australia, have a tufted appearance, with fronds measuring up to 35 in (90 cm) long growing from either one or several crowns.

In the wild, *A. nidus* (bird's-nest fern) is an epiphyte. It has a rosette of undivided, fresh-looking, glossy green leaves, each with a distinct black midrib. As each leaf develops, it uncurls to reveal the plant's central well or "nest."

## Cultivating *Asplenium*

*Asplenium* requires a fairly shady location without any sunlight and a year-round temperature of between 59 and 64°F (15 and 18°C). It is a useful plant for a bathroom or terrarium.

Water it frequently, and maintain its preferred atmosphere of high humidity by placing its pot on a pebble tray and misting it often.

Give the plant a weak solution of fertilizer every two weeks during its growing season, but don't feed it at all during the winter.

Repot young plants in a peat-rich compost every year, ensuring that their crowns are level with the compost. Although young leaves should not be handled because they are easily damaged, older leaves will benefit from being sponged with water.

Propagate in the spring or summer, either by division or by encouraging the spores to germinate.

Scale insects can attack this plant. Cold and dry conditions can cause the edges of the leaves to turn brown, while waterlogging will result in the crown rotting.

# Aucuba

*Aucuba japonica* 'Variegata' (spotted laurel) is an evergreen shrub, originally from eastern Asia, that can grow to a height of 6 ft (2 m). It has glossy, cream-spotted, oval- to oblong-shaped, leathery leaves and insignificant flowers made up of four petals. The female plants produce glossy red fruits, but only if a male plant is growing alongside them.

> ## Caution
> **The fruits of *A. japonica* 'Variegata' are poisonous.**

## Cultivating *Aucuba Japonica* 'Variegata'

This plant likes partial shade and indirect sunlight. It can be located outside during the summer as long as it is sheltered from both wind and direct sunlight. During the winter, it can tolerate temperatures as low as 43°F (6°C) for quite long periods of time. It makes an impressive container shrub for an atrium, balcony, or cool conservatory.

Water *A. japonica* 'Variegata' regularly during the spring and summer, but hardly ever during the winter. Mist it occasionally, too.

Feed every two weeks during the spring and summer, but not at all during the winter.

This plant resents having its roots disturbed, so repot it in spring only if necessary. If it has grown too large, prune it and top-dress it in spring. Keep the leaves shiny by sponging them with water.

Propagate the plant in spring by taking stem cuttings.

Red spider mites can afflict this plant during the winter. If the edges of the leaves turn brown during the summer, this is a signal that you need to water the plant more.

# Azalea

Its common name is misleading, for the Indian azalea, *Azalea indica* (or *Rhododendron simsii*, its alternative botanical name), originates in China. One of the most attractive of the winter-flowering houseplants, it is a low-growing, evergreen shrub with small, oval-shaped leaves and funnel-shaped flowers.

Note that commercial growers often force this slow-growing plant to flower in time for Christmas, so always buy a specimen with plenty of buds because this will flower for some time.

## Cultivating *Azalea Indica*

If it is to thrive, the Indian azalea needs a light position out of direct sunlight and should spend some time outside during the summer. It requires temperatures of between 50 and 59°F (10 and 15°C) in order to produce flowers, and is therefore best housed in a cool conservatory.

When it is flowering, give it either soft water or rainwater every two days, and never let its compost dry out completely. It is best to water it using the immersion method and then to leave it to drain because being waterlogged will prove fatal. Mist the leaves daily during the growing season, but stop when the flower buds appear.

The Indian azalea should be fed with a weak fertilizer every two weeks during its flowering period.

Neglect is the main reason for the failure of this plant, so ensure that you keep the roots permanently moist. Pot on into ericaceous compost in spring. Indian azaleas are often discarded after they have flowered because it is difficult to encourage them to bloom again. Don't prune this plant because doing so will reduce the number of flowers that it produces. Remove dead flowers immediately.

Be warned that this plant can be propagated by taking stem cuttings, but these are difficult to encourage to root.

Whiteflies often target this plant. If the buds drop, the plant has probably been positioned in too warm a spot.

# Beaucarnea

In its natural conditions in Mexico, *Beaucarnea recurvata* (pony-tail or elephant's-foot plant) is a shrublike plant that grows up to 6 ft (2 m) in height, but when it is grown in a pot, its final height is much smaller, only about 3ft (1 m). The base of this agave is swollen like a huge bulb, and a large plume of straplike, gray-green leaves of lengths ranging from 22½ to 37½ in (65 to 95 cm) arches downward from the top. A plant that rarely flowers in containers, it is usually grown for its attractive foliage and unusual shape.

## Cultivating *Beaucarnea Recurvata*

This tall specimen plant enjoys a light, warm location and is suitable for hydroponic cultivation. It particularly likes a brightly lit position, with some sunshine and temperatures of between 59 and 70°F (15 and 21°C) in summer, but requires a lower temperature of around 50°F (10°C)--yet still sufficient light--in winter.

Water thoroughly during summer, but allow the compost to dry out completely between waterings and keep it almost dry throughout winter (the distended, bulblike base stores water). Be warned that this plant can easily be killed by overwatering.

Feed monthly from spring until the end of summer.

Prefers, and looks better in, a small pot, so repot it in spring only when necessary.

Propagate by taking offsets, but note that they are not easy to grow on.

Aphids and spider mites are the only pests that target this plant.

# Begonia

B. rex.

Plants of the *Begonia* genus often have very different characteristics, but most have ear-shaped leaves with attractive markings, and the flowers are usually held in clusters.

Tuberous begonias, whose large flowers bloom from summer to fall, make good pot plants. Some have tassel-like flowers, making them ideal for hanging baskets. *B. multiflora* has small flowers on branched stems and a compact growing habit.

*B. rex* has broad, arrow-shaped leaves with metalliclike markings. *B. masoniana* has a dark-brown cross on its leaves, hence its name, iron-cross begonia. Before buying a begonia, check that there's no root or stem rot and the leaves are firm and undamaged.

## Cultivating *Begonia*

Begonias need a bright place out of direct sunlight and a temperature range of 59 to 64°F (15 to 18°C). Suited to a light, warm location, they are useful, eco-friendly plants that remove vapor chemicals from their environment.

B. multiflora.

Water freely when flowering, but don't allow it to become waterlogged. Because it likes a very humid atmosphere, either place its pot on a wet pebble tray or surround it with moist peat. Don't not allow water to come into direct contact with the leaves.

Feed every two weeks.

Store the begonia tuber in a cool, dry place before repotting in spring. Most flowering begonias need some support; if the plant is becoming too straggly, it should be trimmed back to stem-node joints.

Propagate in spring by taking leaf or root cuttings; it can also be divided in the spring. Prepare bought tubers in February, place them in a container of moist peat, and leave it on a warm windowsill. When shoots appear, pot each tuber into its own pot, using good-quality potting compost.

Mealy bugs and powdery mildew are common problems, as is root rot if conditions are either too wet or too cold.

# Beloperone

An easy-to-grow, shrublike, evergreen plant that originates in Mexico, *Beloperone guttata*'s common name of shrimp plant refers to its unusual bracts, which resemble unpeeled shrimps. This plant has pale, nondescript leaves growing on spindly stems, and its mass of reddish-brown bracts, which fade to light green at the tip, are produced throughout the year, almost hiding the white flowers that appear in summer.

## Cultivating *Beloperone Guttata*

*B. guttata* thrives best in a sunny position that is shaded from direct sunlight, although it will tolerate some shade. It requires temperatures ranging from between 55 to 70°C (13 and 21°C) during the summer, and a minimum temperature of 50°F (10°C) in winter. It is suited to either a warm, well-lit room or a light spot in a sheltered conservatory.

Water frequently during the summer to ensure that the compost is moist, but less in winter, although the compost should still remain slightly moist.

Feed weekly, but only when flowering.

Pot on when it has finished blooming. If the plant is becoming spindly, pinch out the growing tips and prune it lightly in late winter if it is losing its shape as it grows.

Propagate by taking stem-tip cuttings, and provide some heat from below.

Aphids, whiteflies, and red spider mites all attack this plant. If the compost is too wet, or its position too shady, the leaves will turn yellow, while if the compost is too dry, the leaves will drop off.

# Bougainvillea

In their natural surroundings (the tropical areas of South America), the flowers of the paper plant, or *Bougainvillea*, will outshine all others. But it can be frustrating to cultivate because it is reluctant to flower in poor light. Most have been trained as shrubs for domestic cultivation, and are often sold trained around a framework of wires.

*B. buttiana* has large, papery bracts in vivid colors. *B. glabra*, which has purple bracts, is commonly sold by nurseries.

Make sure that a bougainvillea is in flower before purchasing it.

## Cultivating *Bougainvillea*

All species and varieties of *Bougainvillea* need full sun, and are best positioned on a windowsill because they will not survive in poor light. From spring through to fall, the temperature should ideally remain above 55.4°F (13°C). Although it prefers a cooler temperature of 50°F (10°C) during the winter, it still requires bright conditions. It is an ideal plant for a light conservatory.

Its compost must be kept damp during the growing season, but dry in winter. Water the plant from above, and do not leave it standing in excess water.

Do not feed in winter, but give it a high-potash fertilizer once a week as soon as you can see new growth.

Repot young plants every year. Note that this plant relies on a period of winter dormancy in order to produce flowers. If you want it to retain its bushy shape, prune it lightly in the fall.

Propagate in spring by taking stem cuttings and applying a growth hormone. Heat from below until shoots appear.

Fairly resistant to diseases and pests. Yellow leaves are a sign that the plant has been overwatered, and if it loses its leaves in summer, the plant is too dry (it's natural for it to drop its leaves in winter, however).

# Buxus

*Buxus microphylla* (small-leaved box), a native of Europe, is a popular, slow-growing, evergreen shrub. Densely branched, it has a mass of small, dark-green, glossy leaves. It is easily clipped into attractive shapes and can be used to make a statement in any cool room.

Before purchasing a small-leaved box, make sure that its leaves have a healthy sheen.

## Caution
**All parts of the *B. microphylla* plant are poisonous.**

## Cultivating *B. Microphylla*

*B. microphylla* likes cool, airy conditions and a temperature of around 50°F (10°C). Although it prefers bright light, it will tolerate a semishaded position during the summer (when it benefits from being positioned outside), as long as it receives good light during the winter. It makes a good specimen plant for a cool, bright room or entrance area (it is unaffected by drafts).

Water regularly, but allow the compost to dry out between waterings. Note that it is important not to overwater this plant. Mist it frequently.

Feed monthly, but not at all during the winter.

This is an easy shrub to look after. Pot it on in spring--but only when it has become pot-bound--using a John Innes No. 3 compost. It can be easily pruned into a variety of shapes.

Propagate in spring or summer by taking stem cuttings and placing their pots in a cool, shady position, but be warned that they will take a long time to root properly.

This plant is rarely attacked by diseases or pests.

# Caladium

A colorful foliage plant, *Caladium* x *hortulanum* (commonly called angel's wings or elephant's ears) originates in tropical America. It has huge, wafer-thin, heart-shaped leaves, each of which has a crinkled surface or margin, borne on long, slender stems. The color of its foliage ranges from white through pink and red to bronze, with variable amounts of green, and the leaves' attractive veining is either in similar colors or contrasting hues like rose and scarlet. The foliage dies back in fall. Although arumlike flowers appear during summer, they are not that attractive.

## Cultivating *Caladium* x *Hortulanum*

Good light is essential to maximize the color of *C.* x *hortulanum's* leaves, but note that they are easily scorched by the sun. This plant prefers a year-round temperature of between 59 and 64°F (15 and 18°C), and should be positioned well away from any drafts. It is suited to a very warm and humid room, possibly a summer conservatory.

Water it regularly and mist it often during the growing season. To increase the humidity around it, place its pot on a pebble tray. Reduce your watering regime during the fall and keep the compost only slightly damp during the winter.

As soon as the leaves unfurl in late spring, start to feed it weekly, but stop in winter.

Remove the faded foliage in fall, keep the temperature at no lower than 55°F (13°C), and allow the compost nearly to dry out. In spring, pot the tubers in a container filled with moist peat and position them on a sunny windowsill until shoots appear.

Propagate in early spring by dividing the tubers; each should have just one "eye."

Usually only aphids target this plant.

# Calathea

*C. makoyana.*

The *Calathea* genus of plants--natives of tropical America and the West Indies--consist of well over a hundred species. These plants are usually cultivated for their great variety of patterned leaves, which look as though they have been hand-painted. They often look rather drab in the home, however, and because they require conditions of constant warmth and high humidity, they present a challenge to any grower.

*C. makoyana* is a small plant that measures 8 to 10 in (20 to 25 cm) in height, but has comparatively large, upright, oval leaves that are greenish-silver in color, with contrasting, dark-green veins. Said to resemble a peacock's tail--which is why this plant's common name is peacock plant--the leaves' undersides are pale red in color, patterned with deep red.

*C. crocata.*

*C. crocata* is grown mainly for its flowers. Its plain, dark-green leaves measure 12 in (30 cm) in length, and bright-orange bracts containing orange-red petals are borne at the top of erect, sticklike spikes.

## Cultivating *Calathea*

*Calathea* requires partial shade during summer, a bright, but sunless, position in winter, and a constant temperature of 60°F (16°C). Suitable for hydroponic cultivation, terrariums and bottle gardens provide the ideal conditions for this plant. An eco-friendly plant, *Calathea* helps to remove harmful chemical vapors from the air.

It must be kept moist all year round, so either place its pot on a pebble tray or pack the space between its container and pot with damp compost. Water frequently (but less so in winter) and mist it often, too

Feed every two weeks during spring and summer.

Pot on every two to three years in free-draining compost.

Propagate in summer by carefully dividing the crowns, which should then be kept in shade until new roots have formed.

Aphids and red spider mites may attack this plant when its conditions are dry. Note that sudden changes in temperature and humidity may cause the leaves to roll up and die.

# Calliandra

*Calliandra tweedii* is an evergreen plant that originates in Brazil and has thin, hanging stems and delicate, feathery, compound leaves. Its flowers, which bloom for eight weeks during the winter, look like powder puffs (which is why one of its common names is powder-puff plant, another being fairy duster) and are distinguished by their attractive, long, red stamens.

## Cultivating *C. Tweedii*

*C. tweedii* needs a light, sunny position that is shaded from the hot, midday sun. The temperature around it must never be allowed to drop below 59˚F (15˚C), even in winter. It is suitable for a warm conservatory, where it can be trained as a standard plant.

Water it regularly during the spring and summer, and ensure that it is always moist by misting its leaves frequently. Reduce the amount of water that you give it during the winter, but don't let the compost dry out.

Feed this plant every two weeks during the summer.

Repot it in early spring and prune it lightly to prevent it from becoming leggy.

Propagate the plant in spring by taking stem cuttings, treating them with a growth hormone, and providing them with heat from below.

# Callistemon

*Callistemon citrinus*, a native of Australia, is an evergreen shrub that has fine, narrow, leathery leaves and attractive flower spikes.

These flower spikes grow abundantly near the end of the branches from April to June (in the northern hemisphere). The flowers have vivid scarlet, yellow-tipped stamens that stick out from the spikes like bristles from a bottlebrush, which is why *Callistemon* plants are commonly called bottlebrush plants. When the flowers die, woody seed capsules take their place and the stems continue to grow.

*C. citrinus* is an easy plant to care for, but before buying one, make sure that there are no dead leaves at its base because this is a sign of poor watering.

## Cultivating *Callistemon Citrinus*

*C. citrinus* enjoys bright light or full sun and can be placed outside during the summer. Although it prefers temperatures ranging from 50 to 75°F (10 to 24°C), it can survive in temperatures as low as 46.4°F (8°C) in winter. A specimen plant, it can be trained into a standard.

Water regularly from spring to fall, but sparingly during winter, allowing the compost to dry out between waterings.

Feed every two weeks during the growing season.

Pot on in spring, using John Innes No. 3 compost, and maintain the plant's bushy shape by pruning it in spring.

Propagate *C. citrinus* by taking stem cuttings in spring, treating them with rooting hormone, providing heat from below, and then placing the cuttings in a bright situation.

Its leaves may turn yellow if you give it too much fertilizer, but this plant is rarely bothered by pests.

# Camellia

*Camellia japonica,* which, as its botanical name suggests, originates in Japan, is an evergreen, bushy shrub with dark-green, shiny leaves and large flowers that often bloom in winter (although this depends on the variety). This species includes plants that have single, semidouble, or double flowers and that bloom in a huge variety of colors.

## Cultivating *C. Japonica*

If it is kept in a shady position whose temperature is no higher than 64°F (18°C), this colorful plant will thrive, but it dislikes being in a warm, centrally heated environment. It is therefore a good choice for a large container in a cool or unheated conservatory. After it has flowered, it enjoys

spending the summer outside, but bring it inside as fall aproaches. *C. japonica* can be grown as a bonsai or standard plant.

Always keep its compost moist--with rainwater if possible--but do not allow it to become waterlogged. Increase the humidity around the plant by standing it on a pebble tray. You could also mist its leaves, but not when the buds have appeared because they rot very easily when they become wet.

When new shoots appear, start to give the plant a weak acidic feed once a week, but stop when it begins to produce buds.

Once buds have appeared, do not move the plant lest they fall off. If it becomes necessary to repot the plant, do so after it has flowered, using an ericaceous or acid compost. If pruning is required, do this lightly during the fall, before any new shoots are visible.

Propagate in spring by taking stem cuttings, treating them with rooting hormone, and providing heat from below.

Scale insects, mealy bugs, and aphids can all beset this plant. If the leaves fall off or rust appears, the temperature around the plant is probably too high.

# Canna

*Canna indica* (Indian shot), which originates in central and South America, is a big, bold plant whose oval leaves range from bright green to bronze in color. Its tubular blooms, which are carried in stalks that reach heights of between 20 in and 5 ft (50 cm and 1.5 m), flower in shades of yellow, orange, or red.

Cannas are grown from rhizomes, which multiply quickly. If you are buying one as a rhizome, check that it is firm to the touch. Otherwise, do not buy a canna that is flowering and instead ensure that a tight bud is forming.

## Cultivating *Canna Indica*

 A specimen plant for a large room or conservatory, *C. indica* likes a warm, bright, sunny position, but not midday sun.

Water *C. indica* frequently, allowing the compost to dry out between waterings. When it has ceased flowering, water it sparingly before leaving the rhizomes to dry out almost completely.

A greedy feeder, this plant will need to be fed weekly while it is in bloom, which is usually until the end of summer.

In spring, place the rhizomes in moist peat in a warm position, potting them on in good-quality compost when shoots appear. After it has flowered, let the leaves die back before removing the rhizomes and overwintering them in dry peat at a temperature ranging between 50 and 53.6°F (10 and 12°C) until spring.

Propagate in spring by division.

Note that aphids can afflict this plant, and that its rhizomes will rot if they are stored when damp.

# Capsicum

*Capsicum annuum*, a Peruvian plant, is closely related to the chilli peppers (*C. acuminatum*) that are used in cooking, itself bearing fiery hot, edible fruits. It is a neat, bushy plant that has small, oval, deep-green leaves and little white blooms that appear in the leaf axils during the summer. The flowers are followed by green fruits that soon turn cream, then orange, and, finally, red.

Although many are sold at Christmas time (which is why they are often called Christmas peppers) when their fruits are red, it is best to buy plants whose fruits are in their green or cream phases. Note that if the plant is positioned in a sunny, but cool, spot, its fruits will last for several months.

### Caution
C. annuum's green parts (apart from the immature, green fruits) are poisonous.

## Cultivating *C. Annuum*

*C. annuum* is an ornamental plant that is suitable for a light, cool room. It needs a bright, airy, sunny position (but not midday sun) and temperatures ranging between 50 and 59°F (10 and 15°C).

Water regularly to keep the compost just moist and to prevent the fruits from shriveling. As an extra precaution against this, stand its pot on a pebble tray. Mist the leaves occasionally.

Feed weekly.

Discard the plant when the leaves and fruits have died back because it rarely flowers or produces fruits in its second year.

Propagate from newly bought seeds in spring, supplying the seeds with some heat from below. Do not save the seeds of a plant that you have been cultivating as a houseplant because they will rarely produce satisfactory results when propagated.

If the plant is kept in conditions that are too wet, it may fall prey to gray mold (botrytis) and aphids. Its leaves may drop off if its conditions are too warm.

# Carex

*Carex morrowii* 'Variegata' originates in Japan (hence its common name, Japanese sedge). It is a hardy, tufted, grassy plant that has green-and-white-striped, arching leaves that grow to lengths of between 8 and 16 in (20 and 40 cm). Its catkinlike flowers are not particularly decorative, and the plant is primarily grown for its attractive foliage. It is a very easy-going plant that requires no special care.

## Cultivating *Carex Morrowii* 'Variegata'

This ornamental foliage plant is suitable for most positions and can be grown in a terrarium. Although it can be placed in any sort of light--including full sun or shade--it thrives in a bright position. It prefers a temperature of about 50°F (10°C) in winter.

Keep the root ball moist all year round. If you feel that the plant would benefit from more humidity to keep its root ball damp, mist it occasionally or position its pot on a pebble tray.

Feed it with a dilute fertilizer once a month.

Repot the plant every two or three years in spring, using well-draining compost.

Propagate in spring by division.

This plant is usually only bothered by the occasional visiting spider mite.

# Celosia

*Celosia argentea plumosa* (plume flower), a native of tropical Africa, has upright, feathery, plumed, red or yellow flowers, while *C. argentea cristata* (cockscomb) has crested flowers that are flattened into a fan shape resembling a cockscomb (which you could dry to use as a long-lasting decoration). Both plants are annuals that should be thrown away after they have finished flowering.

## Cultivating *Celosia Argentea*

A colorful plant that is ideal for a conservatory, *C. argentea* likes a light and sunny position (but plants should be shaded from the heat of the midday sun), temperatures ranging from between 50 and 59°F (10 and 15°C), and plenty of fresh air.

Keep its compost moist by watering it all year round. Mist its leaves occasionally, but do not let its flowers get wet.

Feed every two weeks.

Although propagating the plant is never very successful, you could try growing it from seed in spring, encouraging germination by providing some heat from below.

*C. argentea* is vulnerable to attack by aphids.

# Chamaerops

*Chamaerops humilis* (European fan palm or dwarf fan palm) is the only palm that is native to Europe. It has several stems and suckers measuring up to 5 ft (1.5 m) high, with spiny stalks carrying blue-green leaves that form deeply lobed fan shapes measuring 24 to 36 in (60 to 90 cm) across. Its small yellow flowers are replaced by little datelike fruits that range from yellow to brown in color.

## Cultivating *Chamaerops Humilis*

 Place *C. humilis* in a light or sunny position--perhaps a conservatory or unheated porch--but ensure that it is not exposed to direct sunlight (which can scorch its leaves) or drafts. It requires a minimum temperature of 50°F (10°C) in winter.

Water it generously in summer, letting the water drain through the compost, but keep its compost merely moist in winter. Mist it regularly to help to keep red spider mites and aphids at bay.

Feed every two weeks during spring and summer.

Because this plant dislikes being disturbed, repot it only when it has become really pot-bound. Like all palms, its roots will rot if they are permanently wet, which is why it is essential to pot it into free-draining compost. Sponge mature leaves to remove any dust.

It is difficult to propagate this plant from seed, but if you decide to try, ensure that you keep the seeds at a temperature of 82°F (28°C) and note that it will take three to four months for them to germinate--if at all. Removing and potting on the parent plant's suckers is a more successful propagation method.

Aphids and red spider mites will descend upon this plant if its conditions are too dry. Its roots will rot if its compost is too wet during the winter.

# Chlorophytum

*Chlorophytum comosum* 'Vittatum', better known as the spider plant, is one of the most popular of all houseplants. Originating in South Africa, it adapts to most conditions. Its green-and-cream leaves arch from dense rosettes, while small, white, star-shaped flowers appear at the end of long, yellow shoots, followed by airborne plantlets. These plantlets can be removed for propagation or left to grow on the parent plant to give an impression of a curtain of greenery.

## Cultivating *Chlorophytum Comosum* 'Vittatum'

Although it requires bright light if its leaves are to retain their coloring, this plant will happily grow in a semishaded position. It requires a temperature ranging from 50 to 64°F (10 to 18°C) during its growing season, and not less than 44°F (7°C) during the winter. This plant is good for hydroponics and looks attractive in a hanging basket or on top of a shelf, when its plantlets can be seen to best advantage. It enjoys the company of other plants and is very good at removing indoor pollutants.

This plant needs a lot of water during its growing season, but do not allow it to become waterlogged because its roots rot easily. In winter, let its compost nearly dry out between waterings. It also benefits from being misted.

Feed every two weeks throughout the year, especially once it has produced plantlets.

Repot it when roots appear on the surface of the compost. Don't plant it too deeply, otherwise stem rot will occur.

Propagate in a variety of ways. Peg down a plantlet that is still attached to its parent plant in compost and sever the stem when it has rooted. Divide the plant when you are repotting it. Remove a plantlet from its parent plant, place it in a jar of water so that its base is just touching the water, leave until it roots, then pot it up.

This plant is generally pest-free, but can be attacked by aphids. If the tips of the leaves turn brown, you are probably not feeding it enough.

# Chrysanthemum

Some members of the *Chrysanthemum* genus of flowering plants can be grown as houseplants. Although *C. morifolium* has glorious blooms (which are available in every color apart from blue), the pot specimens that are sold all year round have been treated with growth retardants and artificial light to encourage out-of-season flowering, which means that their flowers won't last long in the home. Before buying this plant, ensure that it has plenty of buds and that its leaves are firm and not drooping.

   *C. morifolium* 'Charm', a native of North Africa that has a mass of small blooms, has recently become very popular. *C. frutescens* (which is also known as *Argranthemum frutescens*) is a subshrub with finely serrated, gray-green leaves. In summer, it is covered with small, white, pink, or yellow, daisylike flowers, each with a yellow central disk.

## Cultivating *Chrysanthemum*

Chrysanthemums like a cool position in a temperature range of between 50 and 59°F (10 and 15°C) and plenty of bright light, but not too much sun. They make attractive standard or windowsill plants.

Keep the compost moist throughout the year.

Feed weekly.

Prolong a chrysanthemum's flowering period by removing dead blooms. When the plant has finished flowering, either throw it away or plant it in the garden, where it will revert to its natural size. To promote bushy growth in a *C. frutescens*, regularly pinch out dead flowers and perhaps even prune it hard. Unlike other chrysanthemum species, *C. frutescens* can be overwintered in a cool position and watered sparingly before being repotted and fed in the spring.

Except in the case of *C. frutescens*, whose stem cuttings root readily during the spring or summer, propagating a chrysanthemum is a professional's job.

This plant is prone to being attacked by aphids and red spider mites.

*C. frutescens.*

# Cissus

Three species of *Cissus* are sold as houseplants, all of which are very different in both appearance and requirements.

The Australian *C. antarctica* (kangaroo vine) is the most popular species. It grows vigorously, to heights of nearly 10 ft (3 m), and its oval, glossy leaves, which have serrated edges, can often be seen climbing up trellises.

*C. discolor,* a native of Cambodia, has green leaves with red, purple, pink, cream, or white markings that resemble those of begonias (which is why it is commonly called begonia vine). Although it can climb, it is best used as a trailing plant in hanging baskets.

*C. rhombifolia* (which is known as grape ivy) has shiny green leaves, with matte red undersides, that grow in groups of three. This species has more of a trailing habit.

## Cultivating *Cissus*

All species of *Cissus* should be positioned in bright light, but out of direct sunlight. Do not let the temperature around *C. antarctica* drop below 44.6°F (7°C), or that around *C. discolor* and *C. rhombifolia* fall below 60°F (16°C). *C. antarctica* can be pressed into service as a "green screen," while *C. discolor* is more suitable for hanging baskets, and *C. rhombifolia* should be regarded as an ordinary pot plant.

Water *C. antarctica* freely during the summer, but keep its compost merely moist during the winter. *C. discolor* requires plenty of water and regular misting to keep its foliage looking attractive. *C. rhombifolia's* compost should be kept moist throughout the year; this plant also benefits from the occasional misting.

Feed all species monthly from spring to fall.

Pot plants on in spring, into free-draining compost.

Propagate in spring by taking stem cuttings.

The pests that target *Cissus* include aphids, whiteflies, and red spider mites. If the air is too dry, all species of *Cissus* will shed their leaves.

# Citrus

Oranges (or sweet oranges, *Citrus sinensis*), lemons (*C. limon*), grapefruits (*C. paradisi*), and tangerines (*C. reticulata* and *C. deliciosa*) are members of the *Citrus* genus of plants, which originates in Southeast Asia.

The very fragrant, white, star-shaped flowers borne by *Citrus* plants that are grown as houseplants are followed by miniature fruits, which are green at first, but later turn orange. Note that the fruit produced by home-grown plants is edible, but sour, and is therefore best used in cooking.

Because they germinate easily, it is very tempting to grow *Citrus* plants from pips, but these plants soon become too large and straggly and rarely bear fruit. Growing their pips is nevertheless an enjoyable activity to carry out with children, but if you require a plant to produce fruit, you must acquire a specially cultivated tree. Orange plants are very unreliable fruit-producers when grown in this way, but lemons and grapefruits often flower and grow small fruits that never mature.

## Cultivating *Citrus*

*Citrus* plants prefer a cool, airy atmosphere, a minimum temperature of 44°F (7°C), and good light (but not direct sun, which may damage the foliage). They are ideal plants for a cool conservatory, but it is important to position them outside, in a sunny, sheltered location, during summer.

In summer, water the plants generously with rainwater--and mist them regularly, too--but keep their compost only slightly moist during winter. Don't ever let the root ball dry out, especially during summer.

Feed the plants once a week during spring and summer, but not during winter.

Pot plants on in spring, using an acid-based compost. Prune plants in March to remove weak, straggly growth.

Propagate by taking stem cuttings, but you will rarely be successful. (See also above for propagating from seed, or pips.)

The plants are often attacked by mealy bugs, scale insects, and aphids. If the leaves start to turn yellow, add more feed to the water before watering. Brown leaves are a sign that a plant is too cold; its foliage will drop, but will grow again the next spring.

# Clivia

*Clivia miniata* (kaffir lily), a native of South Africa, is the most popular species of *Clivia*. It has dark-green, leathery, straplike leaves, which arch to long lengths. A tall stalk bearing up to twenty orange-to-red, funnel-shaped blooms, rises from the center of the leaves.

Note that you should avoid moving this plant once its flower buds have formed because it will then shed them. It is best to buy a specimen whose buds are forming and that is not in full flower.

## Cultivating *Clivia Miniata*

Although *C. miniata* is tolerant of shade, it requires good light if it is to flower, but should be protected from direct sunlight. To encourage flower buds to form, keep it at a temperature somewhere between 44 and 50°C (7 and 10°C) for two months from fall to early winter, after which it will enjoy temperatures ranging between 59 and 70°F (15 and 21°C). This ideal specimen plant is suited to hydroponics.

Water the plant well during its growing season, but keep its compost almost dry during its resting period.

Once its flower stalk has been established, feed it once a week.

This plant dislikes being disturbed, so repot it only when its roots are falling over the top of its pot and otherwise top-dress it each year. When it has withered, remove the flower stalk.

Propagate this plant either by dividing it or by removing offsets that have three or four leaves.

Mealy bugs can afflict this plant. Its leaves may rot if its conditions are wet.

### Caution
The latex (white fluid) that *C. miniata* produces is poisonous.

# Ccocos

Keeping *Cocos nucifera*--better known as the coconut palm--healthy inside is a challenge because it generally dies after a couple of years. It is often sold as a large, decorative plant because of its attractive, slender, green-ribbed leaves and potential height of 8 ft (2.5 m). The leaves grow directly from the coconut, which should be positioned on top of the compost. There is some doubt regarding *C. nucifera*'s country of origin, but the most likely candidate is Malaysia.

## Cultivating *Cocos Nucifera*

An unusual plant for a large, light, warm room, *C. nucifera* requires an airy, very bright position in full sun (except at midday during the summer) and thrives on a constant temperature of between 64 and 75°F (18 and 24°C) during the day and a minimum temperature of 64°F (18°C) at night.

Place the plant's pot on a pebble tray, water it regularly with soft water, and mist it frequently. Do not allow it to become waterlogged, but keep the compost moist.

Feed with a weak fertilizer every two weeks.

Be warned that any disturbance can prove fatal, so pot it on only if absolutely necessary, and then into well-draining, sandy soil that has been enriched with lime and potash.

Although you are unlikely to be successful, you could try propagating *C. nucifera* by placing a coconut in moist peat and keeping it at a temperature of between 78.8 and 86°F (26 and 30°C).

Spider mites may occasionally attack this plant. If its conditions are too dry, its leaves may turn brown.

# Codiaeum

*Codiaeum variegatum pictum* (croton or Joseph's coat), a Malaysian plant, is the commonly sold variety of the *Codiaeum* genus. The foliage varies widely in color (it can be red, purple, yellow, orange, and pink, and occasionally all of these colors appear on one plant) and shape (the leaves can be oval or resemble those of oaks), but all have glossy, leathery leaves, veining in contrasting colors, and sometimes wavy or twisted edges. New leaves are green, but change color as they mature, and bright light is necessary to maintain the colors.

Before buying a *Codiaeum* plant, inspect it carefully to ensure that its leaves have not been damaged or turned brown.

## Cultivating *Codiaeum*

*Codiaeum* needs as much light as possible all year round, but not direct sunlight. Highly sensitive to sudden changes in temperature, it will tolerate a minimum temperature of 59°F (15°C), but prefers a temperature as high as 80°F (27°C). A plant that can be cultivated using hydroponics, eco-friendly *Codiaeum* helps to remove chemical vapors from the surrounding atmosphere.

Keep its compost moist by regularly watering it with warm rainwater, but water it less during the winter. In summer, frequently mist or sponge its leaves with warm water. A plant that enjoys being grouped together with other plants to form a microclimate, it can be positioned on a bed of moist gravel equally successfully.

Feed weekly from spring to fall, but do not use a foliar feed.

Repot the plant in late spring, using free-draining compost. To encourage new growth from the base, cut back the top shoot in spring.

Propagate in spring by taking stem cuttings, planting them in a peat-based compost, storing them in a plastic bag, and supplying heat from below until new growth is visible.

Spider mites and scale insects can plague this plant. Overwatering can cause the stem and roots to rot.

### Caution
The latex produced by *Codiaeum* is slightly poisonous and may irritate the skin.

# Coleus

*Coleus blumei* (flame nettle) is a foliage plant with square stems and unusually colored leaves in hues of citron-green, white, apricot, pink, brown, purple, or scarlet, all of them patterned. Its blue, insignificant-looking flowers (which resemble those of nettles) are best removed in order to encourage a more bushy growing habit. This plant, which grows to a height of 23 in (60 cm), originates in tropical Africa and Asia.

## Cultivating *Coleus Blumei*

*C. blumei* is suited to a light spot or a mixed planter. Keep it in conditions that are as light as possible all year round, but shade it from the midday sun. It requires a minimum temperature of 50˚F (10˚C).

Water the plant regularly with soft water from spring to fall, but keep its compost fairly dry throughout the winter. Mist its leaves during the summer.

Feed once a month.

Repot the plant whenever it outgrows its pot, which could be as often as two or three times a year. Prune it back drastically in spring and note that pinching out will help to create a more compact-looking plant.

Propagate either by taking stem cuttings in spring or late summer or by sowing its seeds in spring.

This plant is vulnerable to aphids, spider mites, and whiteflies. If its leaves fall off, its conditions are too cool. If its growth becomes leggy, its position is too dark.

# Columnea

A native of tropical America, *Columnea* x *banksii* has evergreen, dark-green, glossy leaves held on arching stems that extend to lengths of 23 in (60 cm). In winter and early spring, scarlet, tubular flowers with extended, hoodlike upper lips bloom from upper leaf axils that resemble the mouth of a fish (which is one of the reasons why the plants that belong to the *Columnea* genus are commonly called goldfish plants). These plants are sold by stores and garden centers relatively rarely.

*C. gloriosa,* whose stems can grow to lengths of 3 ft (1 m), is a much more pendulous plant whose leaves are covered with fine down.

## Cultivating *Columnea*

*Columnea* needs a lightly shaded position and a temperature ranging from between 59 and 64°F (15 and 18°C). It requires a winter resting period, during which the temperature around it should be 59°F (15°C), to stimulate bud growth. It is an ideal plant for a hanging basket positioned in a warm room, and is also a perfect subject for hydroponics.

Its compost must be kept permanently moist during the growing season, but water the plant less during the winter. Because it requires conditions of high humidity, place its pot on a wet pebble tray and mist it often.

Feed the plant an acid fertilizer every two weeks during spring and summer.

The plant should be potted on into acid, peat-basted compost every two or three years in spring. Once the buds have formed after its resting period, move it to a warmer position. Trim back the stems in the spring, after they have flowered.

Propagate the plant in spring or summer by taking cuttings from nonflowering stems, planting them in peat-based compost, and providing heat from below.

If its conditions are too wet, the plant will contract gray mold (*botrytis*).

# Cordyline

*C. terminalis* 'Rededge'.

*C. australis.*

Plants belonging to the *Cordyline* and *Dracaena* genuses are often confused and labeled with the wrong name. Members of the *Cordyline* genus have white, fleshy, knobbly roots, while those of the *Dracaena* genus have deep-yellow, smooth roots.

*Cordyline australis* (cabbage tree or grass palm), whose botanical name is sometimes given as *Dracaena indivisa,* is a native of New Zealand. It has a single trunk that can grow to a height of 3 ft (1 m), and it is crowned with a fountain of long, narrow, evergreen, green or bronze leaves.

*C. terminalis* 'Rededge' originates in tropical Asia and has small, red leaves streaked with green. It is a very popular variety that is often used to make a ti tree (the lower leaves are stripped from the stem to leave a "head" of leaves).

## Cultivating *Cordyline*

An attractive foliage plant, *Cordyline* is suitable for both a warm room and hydroponic cultivation. It needs a minimum temperature of 44°F (7°C) and good light, but should not be positioned in direct sunlight.

Water the plant regularly during the summer to keep the root ball moist, and less during the winter (but ensure that its compost does not dry out). Mist it often and sponge its leaves to remove any dust (and, in the case of *C. terminalis* 'Rededge', to reveal its attractive coloring).

Feed once a week during the spring and summer and once a month for the rest of the year.

Repot in spring every two or three years.

Propagate either by taking stem cuttings and planting them horizontally in free-draining compost or by air-layering its crown.

*C. terminalis* 'Rededge'.

If its conditions are too dry, the plant is vulnerable to attack from spider mites and scale insects.

# Crassula

The plants that belong to the *Crassula* genus are succulents. *Crassula argentea* (jade plant or money tree), a native of South Africa, has thick, branched stems carrying thick, fleshy, oval, green leaves with red edges. Its pink, starlike flowers bloom in spring. The gray, red-edged leaves borne by *C. arborescens* are more rounded.

## Cultivating *Crassula*

*Crassula* likes to receive plenty of light and sunshine all year round. Although it can be stationed outside during the summer, it must be protected from rain. In winter, it requires a minimum temperature of 50°F (10°C). It is a perfect plant for a sunny room or dish garden.

Water sparingly during the summer by soaking the root ball, but do not water it again until it has almost dried out. Keep the compost nearly dry during the winter.

Feed with a high-potassium fertilizer once a month during the spring and summer.

Pot the plant on only when it becomes pot-bound, and then into free-draining compost to which some grit has been added.

Propagate in spring or summer by taking leaf or stem cuttings and leaving the cut edges to dry out before planting them. Do not cover the cuttings and keep their compost almost dry.

If its conditions are too wet, this plant may be attacked by mealy bugs, and its roots and stems may rot.

# Crossandra

*Crossandra infundibuliformis* (which is often given the incorrect botanical name *Crossandra undulifolia*) comes from India. The foliage of the firecracker plant, as it is commonly called, consists of neat, compact sets of spear-shaped, deep-green leaves that are shiny and slightly waxy. Its long-lasting, lobed, pale-orange flowers bloom from spring to fall and grow to lengths of 1 in (2.5 cm) on spikes that are 4 in (10 cm) long.

## Cultivating *Crossandra Infundibuliformis*

During its growing period, *C. infundibuliformis* thrives best in bright light, but should be shaded from direct sunshine. In winter, it again requires a bright position, as well as a minimum temperature of 59°F (15°C). Suitable for a humid room, it is also a good subject for hydroponic cultivation.

During its growing season, water it regularly with soft water. In winter, keep its compost almost dry. Mist the leaves frequently in both summer and winter.

Feed weekly from midwinter to summer.

The plant should be repotted in spring into a nutrient-rich compost, perhaps John Innes No. 3. In spring, pinch out the tips of the stems to promote bushiness. Encourage the plant to bloom from spring to fall by removing dead flowers.

Propagate by either planting its seeds or taking stem cuttings in spring, in both cases then providing heat from below.

The plant's leaves will roll up if its conditions are too dry.

# Cuphea

*Cuphea ignea* (cigar plant) is a small, evergreen, bushy plant that originates in Mexico. It has little, pointed leaves and red, drooping, tubular flowers measuring ¾ to 1 in (2 to 3 cm) in length, whose white-and-purple tips resemble a glowing cigar. These flowers bloom prolifically from spring to the end of summer.

When buying this plant, choose one that has plenty of buds rather than flowers.

## Cultivating *Cuphea Ignea*

*C. ignea* likes a light position, but not full sun, and can be placed outside during summer. It requires a temperature ranging from between 41 and 50°F (5 and 10°C) in winter. It should thrive in a conservatory or on a bright windowsill.

Always keep the plant's compost moist, except during winter, when it should be allowed to dry out between waterings.

Feed every two weeks during its growing season.

Repot the plant in good-quality compost every spring and prune any straggly stems. Promote a bushier plant by pinching out new growing tips and prolong its flowering season by removing dead blooms.

Propagate either from seed in spring (the new plants will flower during their first year) or by taking stem cuttings in spring or summer.

*C. ignea* is rarely attacked by pests.

# Cycas

Despite its common name of sago palm, *Cycas revoluta* is actually a cycad rather than a palm (cycads have one thick trunk, while palms have many stems), which originated millions of years ago in Japan. Its woody trunk, which can grow to a height of 5 ft (1.5 m), holds a rosette of arching, fernlike leaves that develop vibrant-green fronds of great length. It can take *C. revoluta* up to two years to produce one circle of stem-bearing fronds on the trunk, each measuring 29 in (75 cm) in length.

Note that *C. revoluta* is an expensive plant, and that you should check that its leaves are undamaged and display a healthy color before buying one.

## Cultivating *Cycas Revoluta*

*C. revoluta* needs an airy, bright position (with no direct sun) all year round. Although it should not be exposed to too much rain, it can be placed outside during summer. It requires a temperature ranging from between 50 and 53°F (10 and 12°C) during the winter. Make sure that it is not positioned in a drafty spot. This statuesque foliage plant makes a decorative specimen plant for a large room. It is a suitable subject for hydroponics.

During its growing period, keep the plant's compost moist, letting it almost dry out between waterings, but barely moist during winter. (Be warned that being waterlogged will kill this plant.) Mist or sponge its leaves frequently during summer.

Feed weekly once new growth has appeared in spring. Do not feed in winter.

Repot every three to five years in spring, into a nutrient-rich compost mixed with an equal quantity of sand.

Although you could try to propagate this plant from seed in spring, when you should heat the seeds from below to a temperature ranging from 86 to 95°F (30 to 35°C), note that the seeds of cycads do not germinate easily.

This plant can be attacked by scale insects. If its conditions are too wet, its roots may rot.

### Caution
*C. revoluta* is poisonous to both humans and animals.

# Cyclamen

*Cyclamen persicum* is a popular, winter-flowering plant that originates in the southeastern areas of the Mediterranean. Its heart-shaped, dark-green leaves bear silver markings, and it can bloom in a variety of colors. Growing on tall, fleshy stems, its flowers start as downward-curving, pointed buds, whose petals then unfurl and sweep back to reveal white, pink, red, or maroon blooms. In favorable conditions, cyclamen can flower from October to February or March (in the northern hemisphere).

When buying a cyclamen, never choose a plant that has been standing outside, check the leaves for basal rot, and buy one that has a lot of buds, but few flowers. Cyclamens that are bought in fall flower much longer than those bought at Christmas time.

## Cultivating
## *Cyclamen Persicum*

To prolong its flowering period, place *C. persicum* in a light, cool position that receives no direct sunlight, is free from drafts, and has a temperature between 50 and 64°F (10 and 18°C). It can either be displayed as an individual specimen or be included in a mixed planter or indoor garden.

Water using the immersion method (see pages 36 to 37). Allow excess water to drain away and let the compost dry out between waterings. (Root rot as a result of waterlogging is the most common killer of this plant.)

Feed every two weeks, even in the growing season.

Once it has finished flowering, position the pot on its side, in a cool, sheltered spot until fall. Then repot into a clean pot three-quarters filled with peat-based compost, positioning the corm so that its top third is above the surface. Then bring the pot inside, place it in a cool, light spot, and keep its compost merely moist. When new growth appears, begin to feed the plant.

Propagate by sowing its seed in late summer. Any plants grown from seed can take two or three years to flower.

Although this plant is not troubled by pests, it may be plagued by gray mold (*botrytis*) if its conditions are too wet.

# Cymbidium

*Cymbidium*, which horticulturalists regard as the beginner's orchid, originates in tropical Asia and Australia. Its attractive, long-lasting flowers appear toward the end of summer, each erect flower spike holding twelve or more blooms. *Cymbidium*'s flowers can be a variety of colors, with the lip's color generally contrasting with that of the main petals.

Choose a miniature *Cymbidium* variety to start with because standard ones can grow to a height of 3 ft (1 m). The guidelines below will give you some indication of how to care for this plant (and see also pages 71 to 72), but always follow any growing instructions provided with the plant when you bought it.

## Cultivating *Cymbidium*

This orchidaceous plant should receive bright light (but not direct sunlight) for up to fifteen hours a day in both summer and winter. It is important that *Cymbidium* is exposed to a daytime temperature ranging from 72 to 82°F (22 to 28°C)--although it can tolerate temperatures as high as 100°F (38°C)--and a minimum temperature of 50°F (10°C) at night. Like many orchids, it will suit a terrarium or bromeliad tree, and makes an interesting specimen plant for a hot and humid room. It will also remove chemical pollution from the atmosphere.

Water this plant regularly throughout the year, allowing excess water to drain away and leaving it almost dry in winter. Regularly mist its leaves (but not its flowers) with tepid water and place its pot on a pebble tray to increase the humidity of the air around it.

Give the plant a half-strength feed once a month during its growing season

Pot on (into compost formulated specially for orchids, available from garden centers) only when it is completely pot-bound and there is no more room for its roots in the pot (usually in spring).

Propagate by division when you are repotting it.

Aphids and scale insects can target this plant, but root rot due to overwatering is a more common problem.

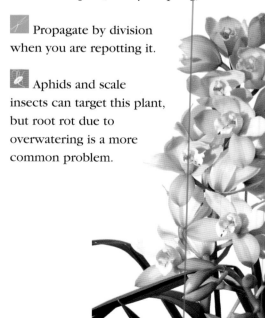

# Cyperus

Being a marsh plant, *Cyperus alternifolius*, a native of Mauritius, cannot be overwatered. The narrow, grasslike leaves that grow at the top of each of its long, thin, three-sided stems form an "umbrella" (which explains the plant's common name, umbrella plant), and its flowers appear as brownish spikelets at the top of each umbrella. *C. papyrus* (papyrus plant), which originates in tropical Africa, is a fast-growing species that can attain a height of 10 ft (3 m) and is crowned by a dense cluster of hairlike leaves.

When choosing an umbrella plant, make sure that you select one that has lush, green leaves and is free of pests.

## Cultivating *Cyperus*

Although the plant requires a light position, it will tolerate some shade. It needs a temperature ranging from between 50 and 70°F (10 and 21°C) during its growing period, and slightly cooler conditions in winter. It makes an attractive specimen plant, but is particularly suited to an indoor water or bog garden or group humidity-loving plants around it.

Stand the pot in a container that is half full of water to keep its roots saturated, and change the water daily. Mist regularly.

Feed by pushing a fertilizer tablet well down into the compost and replacing it every two months. (Don't add fertilizer to the water that you replace daily).

When potting up, which you should do in spring each year, include some charcoal in the compost to keep it fresh.

Propagate by division in the spring.

This plant is vulnerable to attack by red spider mites. If the air around it is too dry, the tips of its leaves may turn brown.

# Cytisus

*Cytisus canariensis* (commonly called genista broom) and *C. racemosus,* which originate in the Canary Islands, have arching, gray-green stems that are covered with racemes (numerous-stemmed, single flowers on a long stalk) of very fragrant, bright-yellow flowers in winter and spring. Unless they are pruned every year, they can grow to a height of 5 ft (1.5 m).

Buy *Cytisus* when its buds are just beginning to take on some color.

## Cultivating *Cytisus*

*Cytisus* requires a cool, light position--perhaps in a conservatory--all year round, but must be positioned outside after it has finished flowering in summer.

Water it well during spring and summer, especially when it is flowering. Mist the foliage when the weather is warm.

Feed this plant every month during its growing season.

Pot on in May and June (in the northern hemisphere) into multipurpose compost. After it has flowered, pinch out some growing shoots to maintain the plant's shape, but do not cut into old wood because this will discourage growth. Stand it outside during summer and bring it back inside and keep it cool and almost dry during fall before moving it to its winter and spring display position and then gradually increasing the amount of water that you give it.

Propagate by taking stem cuttings when it has finished flowering.

Aphids and red spider mites can afflict this plant.

# Datura

A native of Central America, *Datura candida* (whose common name is angel trumpet, and is sometimes also called *Brugmansia*) is an impressive plant with large, trumpet-shaped flowers. The beautifully fragrant, early-flowering blooms are usually white, although pink, yellow, and orange varieties are available. This plant can grow up to 20 ft (6 m) in height and therefore needs careful pruning if it is to remain manageable.

## Cultivating *Datura Candida*

In summer, *D. candida* needs sun or partial shade and can be placed outside. In winter, it requires a bright position (although out of direct sunlight) and a temperature between 40 and 50°F (4 and 10°C). It is probably best planted in a tub and displayed in a conservatory.

Water it regularly during the summer, but allow the compost to become fairly dry in winter. It can be misted, but don't let water come into contact with the blooms.

Feed once a week during its growing season, but stop feeding in winter.

Repot in spring (into a pot of the same size as its previous one if you are anxious to minimize the plant's growth). Remove dead blooms to promote prolonged flowering. Prune back in fall. Note that *D. candida* will withstand a major cut-back if it has grown too large, but may flower a little later than normal as a result.

One way of propagating it is to take stem cuttings in late spring or summer, apply a rooting hormone, and supply heat from below; the resulting plants should flower in their first year. Or sow its seeds in spring. It may take three years for plants germinating from these seeds to flower.

*D. candida* is very prone to whitefly infestation.

### Caution
**All parts of *D. candida* are poisonous.**

# Dicksonia

A native of eastern Australia, *Dicksonia antarctica* (commonly called soft tree fern) is both difficult to obtain and a real talking point when on display. Over time, its thick, treelike trunk grows to a length of 16 ft (5 m), and it is covered with a mass of rusty-brown roots. Long, divided, bright-green fronds arch from the top of the trunk.

Before buying this plant, consult a reputable nursery for professional advice on how to acquire a specimen that has been correctly grown.

## Cultivating *Dicksonia Antarctica*

*D. antarctica* requires cool conditions of 41 to 50°F (5 to 10°C) and good, indirect light (but not direct sunlight, which would scorch its young fronds) all year round. It also needs plenty of space, making it a suitable specimen for a large, cool conservatory.

During its growing season, keep the plant's compost moist, but not soggy (which would rot its roots). In winter, allow the surface of the compost to dry out between waterings. Mist it regularly whenever the temperature rises above 50°F (10°C).

Feed with a weak solution of fertilizer every week. It will also like a foliar feed once a month during its growing season.

When it is pot-bound, repot it at any time of year into free-draining compost.

Don't even think about propagating this plant because you will be doomed to failure!

Although this plant is rarely attacked by pests, its trunk may rot if it becomes waterlogged.

# Dieffenbachia

The Brazilian *Dieffenbachia picta* (also called *D. maculata,* while its common names include leopard lily and dumb cane) is one of the most popular of all houseplants. Its thick, fleshy, upright stems bear large, smooth, oval leaves that are dark green in color, with creamy-white variegations and prominent, midrib veins. Unless the plant is kept at a constant temperature, its flowers rarely appear.

## Cultivating *Dieffenbachia*

Although *Dieffenbachia* is tolerant of shade, it requires bright, indirect light, especially during the winter. It should be kept out of drafts and prefers a year-round temperature of 70°F (21°C), but can stand temperatures as low as 59°F (15°C). A superb foliage plant for a warm, humid room, it is also a suitable subject for hydroponics. Its ability to remove polluting vapors from the atmosphere makes *Dieffenbachia* an eco-friendly plant.

Because its roots rot easily, water it with care, allowing the compost to dry out between waterings. Using the immersion method (see pages 36 to 37) is the best way of watering this plant, and remember to let any excess water drain away before returning it to its usual postion. The plant likes a very humid atmosphere, so set its pot on a pebble tray, and also group it with other plants to increase the humidity. When the atmosphere is dry, mist its foliage and carefully sponge mature leaves with water.

Feed with a weak solution of fertilizer every time that you water it.

Pot on each year in summer, adding a layer of grit to the bottom of the pot before filling it with free-draining compost.

Propagate either by taking suckers from the base of the plant or by taking stem cuttings (complete with leaves), and keeping them in warm, humid conditions.

If the air around it is too dry, red spider mites and aphids may attack. If its conditions are too cold, the plant will lose its lower leaves.

### Caution
All parts of *Dieffenbachia* are poisonous, and because its sap can irritate the skin, take care when tending it and wear gloves when taking cuttings.

# Dionaea

A North American carnivore, *Dionaea muscipula* (Venus flytrap) is a fascinating plant that children, in particular, find hugely entertaining. Each of its leaves consists of a broad, winged stalk that culminates in an oblong blade divided into two lobes, with stiff bristles positioned along its edges and three highly sensitive, trigger hairs on its surface. Up to eight of these leaves, which measure 3 to 6 in (8 to 15 cm) in length, form a rosette. When a trigger hair on the blade is touched by an insect that has been attracted to the plant by its scent, the blade rapidly snaps shut, trapping the insect, to be digested at the plant's leisure and contribute to its nitrate requirements. (The plant has evolved this feeding habit in response to its nutrient-poor natural habitat.) After the insect has been digested, the leafy trap opens again, ready for the next victim. *D. muscipula* may produce white flowers during the summer.

## Cultivating *Dionaea Muscipula*

*D. muscipula* dislikes direct sunlight and prefers temperatures ranging from between 41 and 50°F (5 and 10°C).

The roots need to be constantly wet, so stand its pot in a container half-filled with water and top it up when necessary.

This plant feeds itself.

It's best to regard this plant as a short-lived source of entertainment and simply to throw it away when it is past its best.

The plant can be propagated by division (if you manage to keep it alive that long).

This plant eats the pests that usually feed on houseplants.

# Dipladenia

*Dipladenia sanderi* 'Rosacea', which originates in tropical South America and is sometimes sold as *Mandevilla*, is a vigorous climbing plant with glossy, dark-green, pear-shaped leaves. From summer through fall, it bears large, showy, trumpet-shaped flowers that are rose-pink in color.

When buying *D. sanderi* 'Rosacea', select a plant that is in bud rather than flowering.

## Cultivating *Dipladenia Sanderi* 'Rosacea'

*D. sanderi* 'Rosacea' requires a bright position, but not direct sunlight, all year round. It should be protected from drafts and prefers temperatures ranging from between 59 and 64°F (15 and 18°C). This attractive climbing plant is suitable for a conservatory.

Water it regularly during the spring and summer, but keep its compost relatively dry during the winter. Mist its foliage frequently with warm water.

Feed this plant once a week during the spring and summer.

Repot into multipurpose compost in spring, when you can also train any immature stems up bamboo canes or trellises. To encourage bushiness, prune back its stems after the plant has finished flowering.

Scale insects and mealy bugs will readily attack the plant. Being exposed to drafts will cause its foliage to turn yellow.

# Dizygotheca

Originally from Australasia, *Dizygotheca elegantissima* is a dainty-looking foliage plant. It usually has a single stem, which is rarely branched, but carries regularly spaced, slender stalks, each ending in a mass of thin leaves that have a spider- or fingerlike appearance (hence one of its common names, finger aralia, another being false aralia). When immature, its foliage is reddish in color, but as the plant ages, it becomes a deep olive-green or bronze.

## Cultivating *Dizygotheca Elegantissima*

*D. elegantissima* thrives in a bright position--and requires plenty of light during the winter--but should receive no direct sunlight. It prefers a temperature of 68°F (20°C), but will tolerate temperatures no lower than 55°F (13°C). It makes a graceful addition to a light, warm room and is suitable for hydroponic cultivation.

During spring and summer, water this plant only when the surface of the compost has dried out. During the winter, keep the compost almost dry. Mist the foliage regularly during the warmer months of the year.

Feed the plant every two weeks during the spring and summer.

Pot on into multipurpose compost in spring, but only when it is pot-bound.

Propagate in spring by taking stem cuttings, treating them with rooting hormone, and providing them with heat from below.

This plant is vulnerable to being attacked by red spider mites and scale insects if its conditions are too dry. If its conditions are too cold or wet, it will shed its lower foliage.

# Dracaena

The *Dracaena* genus originates in tropical Africa. When young, their ribbonlike leaves are arranged in a rosette, but as they age, their stem lengthens to form a short, thick trunk.

*D. fragrans* 'Massangeana' (corn plant), has broad, deep-green leaves bearing stripes that are dark-cream to gold in color.

*D. marginata* 'Tri-color' (Madagascar dragon tree or rainbow tree) is an attractive, upright, slow-growing variety with green, cream-striped leaves with reddish edges.

*D. draco* (dragon tree), grows slowly, but potentially to an enormous size. It has stiff, bluish-green leaves.

When choosing a plant, make sure that its leaves are not damaged or discolored as this can be a sign of mealy-bug infestation.

## Cultivating *Dracaena*

*Dracaena* should receive fairly bright light all year round, but no direct sunlight. (*D. draco* in particular requires good light, and although all tolerate temperatures as low as $44\,°F\,(7\,°C)$ in winter, they should be protected from drafts.) This plant is suitable for hydroponic cultivation, and is also very effective at removing polluting vapors from the surrounding atmosphere.

Water it well during the spring and summer, but keep the compost moderately dry in winter, without ever letting the root ball dry out. Mist when the weather is hot and, if necessary, place the pot on a pebble tray to increase the humidity of the air it.

Feed every two weeks during the growing season. It is best to top-dress the plant, and to repot it only when it is pot-bound, and then into John Innes No. 3 compost. If it becomes too tall, cut it back at any time of year.

After pruning, you can propagate the stem cuttings and heat from below.

If its conditions are too dry, mealy bugs and red spider mites may attack this plant.

# Duchesnea

*Duchesnea indica* (which, despite its Eastern European origins, is commonly called Indian strawberry tree) bears bright-yellow flowers in summer, followed by attractive, red fruits that look like strawberries, which are edible, but tasteless. Its trailing, long-branched runners are covered with pale-green leaves.

## Cultivating *Duchesnea Indica*

Position *D. indica* in bright light, but not direct sunlight. It prefers temperatures ranging from between 41 and 50°F (5 and 10°C) and therefore makes a suitable trailing plant for a cool conservatory.

Keep the plant's compost moist during its growing season, but do not let it become waterlogged. During winter, allow its compost to become nearly dry between waterings. Mist its leaves, but stop doing so once its fruits have appeared because exposure to water will make them rot.

Feed every two weeks during its growing season.

Repot every spring, using good-quality, multipurpose compost. As an alternative to allowing the stems to trail downward, you could train them around a trellis.

Propagate in spring, either by division or by pinning down its runners into the compost and waiting for them to root.

Although the plant is not attacked by pests, gray mold (*botrytis*) may take hold if its conditions are too wet.

# Echinocactus

*Echinocactus grusonii* (golden barrel), which originates in central Mexico, is a globular cactus armed with short, dense, brownish spines. This desert cactus can grow to 3 ft (1 m) in diameter. It has twenty or more prominent, green ribs, which form a large areole (sunken area) at the top from which wooly hairs grow. The silky yellow flowers only bloom when the plant is mature.

## Cultivating *Echinocactus Grusonii*

*E. grusonii* likes full sun all year round, and a temperature of 64 to 68°F (18 to 20°C) for most of the year, but a cooler temperature of 50°F (10°C) in winter. It is a good choice for a sunny windowsill or cactus garden.

Keep its compost barely moist, and in winter almost dry, and never allow water to come into contact with its hairs.

Feed once a month with a fertilizer that has been specially formulated for cacti.

The plant should only be repotted when it is growing out of its pot, and then into sandy, free-draining compost in spring.

This plant is never easy to propagate, but you could try doing so from seed.

Mealy bugs, scale insects, and red spider mites may all attack this plant.

# Eucalyptus

*Eucalyptus gunnii* (cider gum) is an evergreen tree, a native of Australia, that can reach 10 ft (3 m) in height. Its rough, blue-green or blue-gray leaves give off a characteristic whiff of aromatic eucalyptus oil when crushed. Because this plant's young leaves are more attractive than its older ones, it's advisable to prune it hard every year. The bark of older specimens naturally peels off in patches, so worry not when this happens, and instead admire the attractive patterns that are created.

## Cultivating *Eucalyptus Gunnii*

In summer, place it outside, either in full sun or partial shade. In winter, position it in a bright, airy spot inside, with temperatures ranging between 35 and 50°F (2 and 10°C).

Water well during spring and summer. Ensure that its compost stays almost dry in winter.

Feed occasionally with an acid fertilizer.

Repot in spring, into nutrient-rich compost. The plant grows rapidly, so to slow its growth, top-dress only. Promote bushy growth by pinching out growing tips and prune severely in spring.

It is easily propagated from seed.

Rarely attacked by pests or diseases.

# Eucomis

A member of the genus of plants whose common name is pineapple lily, *Eucomis comosa,* which originates in South Africa, needs plenty of space because it can grow to a height of 3 ft (1 m) within a season. Broad, shiny, green leaves measuring up to 5 ft (1.5 m) in height grow from its large bulb, and racemes (many-stemmed single flowers on a long stalk) of star-shaped flowers are carried on stalks measuring 19½ in (50 cm) in length. These blooms range from yellow-green to nearly white in color, and are flushed with purple, each flower also having a dark-purple ovary. Crowning them all is a tuft of green leaves.

## Cultivating *Eucomis Comosa*

*E. comosa* needs full sun and plenty of warmth--ideally a temperature ranging between 64 and 68°F (18 and 20°C)--when it is in bloom, but should be left in a cool, dry place to rest after it has finished flowering. It can be placed outside during the summer as long as it is protected from strong winds.

Water regularly during its growing season, ensuring that any excess water drains away. After it has ceased flowering, stop watering it and let its compost dry out. Start watering it again--but sparingly--during the spring to promote new growth. Note that its leaves will benefit from being misted or sponged with water if they become dusty.

Feed every two weeks during its growing season.

Repot every year, into nutrient-rich compost that drains well.

Propagate in spring, either by removing and planting its offsets or by sowing its seeds (which will take about five years to produce blooms).

Although this plant is rarely bothered by pests, its bulb will rot if its compost drains inadequately.

# Euphorbia

The *Euphorbia* genus of succulent plants consists of over four-hundred subtropical species that grow in a wide variety of shapes and sizes.

*E. milii* (crown of thorns, sometimes also known as *E. splendens*) is a small shrub. Its bright-green leaves cluster sparsely at the top of its stems. Its flowers, which consist of two bright-red, rounded bracts, appear in clusters on short, red stems in spring, and can bloom until the fall if the plant is situated in a light position.

*E. obesa* (Turkish temple) is a gray-mottled, spherical succulent whose eight ribs each produce tiny yellow flowers at their apex.

## Caution
*Euphorbia's* milky sap is poisonous.

## Cultivating *Euphorbia*

Although it can tolerate some neglect, *Euphorbia* needs good light all year round, as well as plenty of sunlight and a minimum temperature of 50°F (10°C). It is suitable for hydroponic cultivation.

Water regularly when in flower, allowing any excess water to drain away. Keep its compost almost dry in winter.

Feed every two weeks with a fertilizer that has been specially formulated for cacti.

Repot every two years in spring, into well-draining compost to which clay has been added.

Propagate by taking stem cuttings and leaving the cut areas to dry out before planting them in sandy compost.

This plant is rarely attacked by pests. Too much water results in leaf drop.

*E. milii.*

# Exacum

A prolific generator of blooms, the flowers produced by *Exacum affine* resemble violets (hence its common name, Arabian--or Persian--violet), having mauve petals with yellow centers and the added attraction of an exquisite, spicy scent.

If this plant, a native of India, is bought when it is starting to flower at the beginning of summer, it may bloom until the end of fall. In order to create a bushy effect, grow several *E. affine* plants in one pot.

## Cultivating *Exacum Affine*

An attractive flowering plant for a warm room, *E. affine* needs a light position (but not direct sunlight) and a temperature ranging from between 50 and 70°F (10 and 21°C).

Keep the plant's compost moist by watering it regularly with soft water.

In the spring, feed it weekly with diluted fertilizer. When it is flowering, give it an occasional full-strength feed.

Do not repot this plant, but instead treat it like an annual and throw it away after it has finished flowering. If you require a bushy plant, pinch out its growing tips in spring.

Propagate in fall by sowing its seeds and leaving them to germinate on a warm windowsill. When the seedlings are large enough to handle, pot them on and keep them cool, and they should flower in the same year. (Pinch out the central growing top to promote bushiness.)

Aphids can plague the plant, and gray mold (*botrytis*) will take hold if the plant's conditions are too wet.

# X Fatshedera

X *Fatshedera lizei*, which originates in France and is commonly called ivy tree, is an exotic, hybrid cross between *Fatsia japonica* and *Hedera helix* that makes an excellent plant for cool conditions. It starts out as an upright bush, but then tends to sprawl. In contrast to x *F. lizei*'s shiny, dark-green, evergreen leaves, the leaves of x *F. lizei* 'Variegata' are patterned with white and require bright light to maintain their variegation (so it's best to place it outside, but out of direct sunlight, in summer).

When buying a x *F. lizei* plant, make sure that you choose one that has glossy leaves because any sign of browning may indicate the presence of red spider mites.

## Cultivating x *F. Lizei*

X *F. lizei* thrives best in temperatures ranging from between 53 and 57°F (12 and 14°C), but will withstand a minimum temperature of 40°F (4°C). Although it can tolerate a shady location, it requires bright, indirect light in winter. (X *F. lizei* 'Variegata' dislikes drafts.) A fast-growing plant, x *F. lizei* can be cultivated using hydroponics.

Water regularly from spring to fall, allowing the compost to dry out between waterings, but give it less water during the winter. Mist or sponge the leaves frequently with water.

Feed once a week during the spring and summer.

Young plants should be repotted into multipurpose compost every year in spring. In the case of older plants, either repot them every two or three years or top-dress them every spring. The plant will not form branches until it has been pruned, and can become top-heavy; it is easily trained up canes or trellises, however, while regularly pruning an older plant will keep it bushy.

Propagate in spring or summer from stem cuttings taken when pruning.

Red spider mites may trouble x *F. lizei* if the atmosphere is dry.

# Fatsia

A native of Japan, *Fatsia japonica* (commonly called false castor-oil plant) is a tough, slow-growing, foliage plant that can reach 6 ft (2 m) in height. It has shiny, deep-green leaves made up of five to nine wavy-edged lobes carried on tall, thin stalks. A mature plant will produce milky-white flowers, followed by glossy black berries.

## Cultivating *Fatsia Japonica*

*F. japonica* will tolerate a bright to semishaded position during the summer, but needs to receive bright light during the winter. Although it prefers a cool temperature of around 50°F (10°C) all year round, it will cope with warmer conditions as long as it is misted frequently. It makes a good plant for a cool room.

Water regularly from spring to fall, allowing the compost to dry out slightly between waterings, and then reduce your watering regime during winter. Sponge its leaves with water frequently to highlight their shiny surfaces.

Feed this plant once a week from spring to summer.

Repot in spring each year, in multipurpose compost and, because the plant can become top-heavy, a fairly weighty pot. To encourage a more bushy growing habit, prune in spring.

Propagate this plant in summer by taking stem cuttings.

Pest and diseases rarely target this plant, but note that its leaves will fall off if the atmosphere is too dry or its roots are waterlogged.

# Ficus

F. benjamina.

The *Ficus* (fig) genus of plants--which originate in tropical Asia--comprises around eight-hundred species of trees, shrubs, climbing and trailing plants, most of which are impressive foliage plants that are capable of growing into quite large specimens. Although their growth is more controlled when their roots are confined to pots, the downside is that they then rarely flower or fruit.

*F. benjamina* (weeping fig) is a graceful, treelike shrub that can grow rapidly to a height of 6 ft (2 m) when housed in a pot. An attractive plant, its long, oval leaves taper to a point and are held on arching, pendent stems that grow from a single trunk. Young plants' leaves are pale green, changing to dark green as the plant matures. The leaves of the variegated variety, *F. benjamina* 'Variegata', have cream midribs and edges.

The slow-growing rubber plant *F. elastica* 'Decora' can reach a height of 10 ft (3 m) when grown in a pot. A single stem bears the oval or elliptical leaves, which measure 6 to 12 in (15 to 30 cm) in length. These leaves are mainly a dark, glossy green, with paler central veins, but while the top leaf is developing and unfurling, it is surrounded by a reddish sheath, the midribs of young leaves being a similar color.

As its common name--creeping fig--suggests, *F. pumila* is a climbing or creeping plant that clings to walls or supports rather like an ivy does. Its heart-shaped leaves, which have prominent veins, are pale brown at first, later becoming light green and then darkening with age.

*F. carica*, the common fig, is a fruit-bearing, deciduous shrub that is often grown in gardens. It has gray-green branches and vivid-green leaves made up of three to five lobes. After a sunny, warm summer, the flowers are enveloped by the developing fruits.

When choosing a fig plant, make sure that the leaves are undamaged and check the stem to see if any leaves have dropped off, which is a sign that the plant has been cultivated in poor conditions.

## Cultivating *Ficus*

All figs enjoy good light, but not direct sunlight because this will scorch their leaves. During the summer, place *Ficus* in a sunny position whose temperature is

F. carica.

around 64 to 75°F (18 to 24°C); in winter, move it to a shady spot whose temperature is around 41°F (5°C). (*F. pumila* requires a temperature of between 64 and 70°F (18 and 21°C) in summer, and a minimum temperature of 59°F (15°C) in winter.) Figs make good specimen plants for large rooms and warm, sunny conservatories. They are also suitable subjects for hydroponic and bonsai cultivation. All effectively remove chemical vapors, especially formaldehyde, from the atmosphere, too.

Water freely in summer, but sparingly in winter. The lower the temperature, the less water the plant requires. (Although some treelike *Ficus* species will benefit if you allow their compost to dry out between waterings, do not let *F. pumila's* root ball dry out and keep its compost moist during the winter.) Mist and clean the leaves of F*icus* plants, especially *F. elastica* 'Decora', regularly to remove any dust.

Feed every two weeks during the spring and summer, and if new growth continues to appear, also during the fall and winter, but then with diluted fertilizer.

In May (in the northern hemisphere), repot it if it has become pot-bound, or if it has grown too large to repot, top-dress it with nutrient-rich compost. Spraying a leggy plant with a foliar feed in summer can induce new shoots to sprout from a bare stem.

Propagate by air-layering or by taking stem cuttings and providing heat from below.

Mealy bugs and scale insects can plague *Ficus*. Its leaves will fall off if its conditions are too wet or too cold, if it has been positioned in a draft, or if it has experienced an abrupt change in temperature.

F. elastica 'Decora'.

# Fittonia

*Fittonia verschaffeltii argyroneura* 'Nana' is commonly known as snakeskin plant. It is a native of tropical South America, where it is most commonly seen as a low-growing, trailing plant. Its oval-shaped leaves are olive-green in color, with delicate white veining.

Never buy a plant whose stems are curling or whose leaves are dropping.

## Cultivating *Fittonia Verschaffeltii Argyroneura* 'Nana'

A shade-loving plant, *F. verschaffeltii argyroneura* 'Nana' cannot tolerate direct sunlight or, indeed, too much direct light of any kind. It should be kept out of drafts and at a temperature ranging from between 64 and 70°F (18 and 21°C) all year round. It suits hanging baskets and is ideal for a warm conservatory, a humid room, or a terrarium.

Keep the plant's compost moist throughout the year by watering it with soft, warm water. Because it is a plant that relishes very humid conditions, place its pot on a pebble tray and mist it frequently.

Feed the plant a weak liquid fertilizer every time that you water it, but stop feeding in winter.

Pot on every spring into peat-based compost and a shallow pot.

Propagate by taking stem cuttings either in spring or when conditions are humid and encouraging them to root by providing heat from below, at a temperature of 73°F (23°C).

Although this plant is rarely attacked by pests, its stem may rot if it becomes waterlogged.

# Fortunella

*Fortunella margarita*--a kumquat that originates in China--is a much-branched, evergreen shrub or tree that grows to heights of 3 to 6 ft (1 to 2 m). The fragrant white flowers that bloom amid lustrous, deep-green, oval leaves (which measure 2 to 3 in (4 to 8 cm) in length) are followed by acidic, but edible, oval fruits that vary in color from orange to red.

## Cultivating *Fortunella Margarita*

Place the plant in a position that receives plenty of direct light, and, if possible, full sun. It can be stationed outside during the summer. It requires lots of light and temperatures no lower than 41°F (5°C) in winter. Ideal for a light conservatory, *F. margarita* can be cultivated as a bonsai or standard plant.

Water frequently with soft water all year round, and never let the root ball dry out.

Feed every two weeks.

When it is still small, repot every year in spring, into good-quality, multipurpose compost. When it is larger, either top-dress it annually or repot it every three years.

Propagate either by sowing its seeds in spring or by taking stem cuttings in summer, enclosing them in a plastic bag to increase the humidity around them, and providing heat from below until you can see signs of growth.

This plant can be attacked by red spider mites and scale insects.

# Fuchsia

*Fuchsia* is a deciduous subshrub with branched, arching shoots. Its bell-shaped, pendent flowers have four upward-pointing petals and four downward-pointing petals. It blooms in a variety of colors, and its flowers are sometimes multicolored. It originates in the mountainous regions of tropical Central and South America, and there are around a hundred species and ten-thousand varieties. Fuchsias are usually available as trailing bushes or standard plants.

*Fuchsia* x *hybrida* plants have been cultivated for the houseplant market.

## Cultivating *F.* X *Hybrida*

In summer, *F.* x *hybrida* needs a cool spot and one in partial shade––it thrives when placed outside. In winter, it should be kept in a light, airy position, at a temperature between 40 and 46.°F (4 and 8°C). (Too high a temperature, and the plant will start to produce shoots, which is not desirable during its resting period.) Perfect for a cool conservatory, this is an ideal plant to train as a standard, but you may need to provide it with support because its head can become very heavy.

From spring to fall, keep its compost moist, watering it regularly, but let it become almost dry in winter. Mist it regularly, especially if the air is dry.

Feed weekly during its growing season.

If it is to flower the following year, this plant requires a winter rest period. In winter, prune the old stems to maintain the desired shape. In early spring, either pot it on into nutrient-rich compost or, if it's too large to move, top-dress it. Mist with warm water to kick-start its spring growth. Pinch out growing tips to encourage bushiness.

Propagate in summer by taking soft-stem cuttings.

Vulnerable to aphids, red spider mites, whiteflies, gray mold (*botrytis*), and fuchsia rust, it is also sensitive to changes in temperature and humidity, when it will shed its leaves.

# Gardenia

*Gardenia jasminoides*, a native of southern China, is a difficult plant to grow as a houseplant. A shrub that can reach 5 ft (1.5 m) in height, it has shiny, dark-green leaves that measure 4 in (10 cm) in length, are narrow at both ends, and grow in whorls of three. Its foliage provides a superb background for its creamy-white, scented flowers, which can grow to a length of 3 in (8 cm). The glistening white petals of these summer-blooming flowers turn ivory with age.

Before buying this plant, make sure that its leaves are glossy and that it has plenty of tight buds. Also check the leaves' undersides for scale insects.

## Cultivating *Gardenia Jasminoides*

*G. jasminoides* prefers a consistent temperature of between 60 and 68˚F (16 and 20˚C); although it will tolerate lower temperatures, it will not then flower. To encourage it to form buds, ensure that it receives bright light, but not midday sun, and that its daytime temperature is at least 64˚F (18˚C). This beautiful, fragrant plant, which can be trained into a standard, is best suited to a warm room or conservatory.

Keep its compost moist all year round by watering it with rainwater or soft water. Mist frequently, but don't allow water to touch the buds, or they will rot.

Feed with diluted, nonalkaline fertilizer at fortnightly intervals from winter to spring.

Pot on into acid-based compost each spring.

Propagate in spring by taking stem cuttings from new stalks (but not from woody stems, which won't root) and providing heat from below.

Scale insects and red spider mites can afflict this plant, especially if the air is dry. Watering with hard water or feeding the wrong type of fertilizer can make its leaves turn yellow. Too low a temperature will cause its leaves and buds to drop.

# Gerbera

*Gerbera jamesonii* (Barbeton or Transvaal daisy), which originates in South Africa, has upright, dull-green leaves with white and wooly undersides. These narrow leaves form rosettes, near the base of which long, leafless flower stalks emerge, each with a single, daisylike flower measuring 4 in (10 cm) in diameter. Both single- and double-flower varieties are available, in yellow, orange, pink, white, or red; *G. jamesonii* 'Happipot' is a dwarf variety.

Although they usually flower in summer, gerberas are sold all year round. And if a plant is well cared for, its blooms can last for a very long time.

## Cultivating *Gerbera Jamesonii*

*G. jamesonii* needs a light, sunny position and will tolerate temperatures ranging from between 44 and 73°F (7 and 23°C), making it an attractive flowering plant for a sunny windowsill or conservatory. As a reward for being looked after, it will efficiently remove chemical pollutants from the atmosphere.

Water regularly during its flowering season, but otherwise keep its compost fairly dry. When conditions are hot and dry, mist its leaves occasionally.

Encourage new flower growth by feeding once a month.

Repot into well-draining compost every spring.

Propagate by sowing its seeds, by division, or by taking cuttings from nonflowering shoots in spring.

Aphids, whiteflies, and red spider mites can all home in on this plant. It is also susceptible to powdery mildew and root rot caused by overwatering. If its conditions are too hot, its leaves will wilt, which is a signal to move it to a cooler position.

# Glechoma

A native of Europe and Asia, *Glechoma hederacea* 'Variegata' (ground ivy) is a fast-growing, evergreen, creeping or trailing plant whose nodes will root when they come into contact with damp compost. Its kidney-shaped leaves, which are green tinged with white, smell fragrant when touched, and its small, mauve, two-lipped flowers grow from leaf axils.

*G. hederacea* is an all-green species, but is not often available.

## Cultivating *Glechoma Hederacea* 'Variegata'

This plant prefers a well-lit position, although it will tolerate some shade. It thrives best at temperatures ranging from between 59 and 64°F (15 and 18°C) during its growing season, and at around 50°F (10°C) during the winter. It makes an attractive ground-cover plant for large planters and can also be planted in hanging baskets.

Water regularly from spring to fall, but give it less water during the winter. Instead, just ensure that the root ball is moist.

Feed every two weeks.

Repot every year in spring. Its trailing stems dry up in winter, when you should prune them right back, which will also encourage new shoots to grow the following year.

Propagate by division in spring or by taking stem cuttings in fall, making sure that a node is attached to each cutting.

It is rarely attacked by pests.

## Caution
All parts of *G. hederacea* 'Variegata' are poisonous.

# Guzmania

*Guzmania lingulata*, a bromeliad relative of the pineapple, originates in the West Indies. Its thin, narrow, shiny, yellow-green leaves, which grow to lengths of 17 in (45 cm), form a central rosette that acts as a water-collection area. When *G. lingulata* is about to flower, its central leaves become brightly colored. Sprouting from the middle of these leaves are orange-red bracts that protect the cluster of white flowers within and give the plant its common name, scarlet star.

## Cultivating *Guzmania Lingulata*

*G. lingulata* requires a semi-shaded spot and a temperature of at least 59°F (15°C) all year round. It can be positioned in a humid conservatory or included in a bromeliad tree and is very suited to hydroponic cultivation.

Water this bromeliad freely with rainwater or soft water, topping up the central water-collection area when necessary (but not when the flower spike is visible). To increase the humidity around it, mist it frequently with warm water and place its pot on a pebble tray.

Feed both the compost and water-collection area with half-strength fertilizer every month.

Rarely needs to be potted on because it dies soon after flowering, leaving offsets.

Propagate by planting its offsets in compost that has been specially formulated for bromeliads.

This plant is occasionally plagued by scale insects and red spider mites.

# Gynura

A native of Malaysia, *Gynura aurantiaca* (velvet plant) is a bushy, trailing plant that becomes a climber as it ages, when it requires support. The dark-green, spear-shaped leaves, which measure around 5 in (13 cm) in length, are toothed along their edges. Both the stem and leaves are covered with a mat of purple hairs. The orange flowers, which appear in March (in the northern hemisphere), are best removed on account of their rather off-putting odor.

## Cultivating *G. Aurantiaca*

*G. aurantiaca* prefers an airy, slightly shaded situation in summer, but benefits from plenty of light in winter and requires a year-round temperature of 55°F (13°C). This rapidly growing plant makes a useful addition to a hanging basket.

Water this plant frequently from spring to fall, but give it less water during the winter, when you should allow its compost nearly to dry out between waterings. Although it requires conditions of high humidity, misting its leaves will cause brown spots to develop, which is why it is best placed on a pebble tray.

Feed once a week in the spring and summer.

Repot in spring, into multipurpose compost, but discard the plant after two or three years, when it will have become very straggly and will have lost its lovely color. Any trimming or cutting back is best done at the same time as repotting. To maintain the plant's bushy shape, continually pinch out the main shoot. If it is being grown in a hanging basket, allow its shoots to grow freely. Because its leaves are quite heavy, provide plenty of support when training it to climb.

Propagate at any time of year by taking stem cuttings, which will root very easily.

Pests and diseases rarely trouble this plant. If its conditions are too cold, it will lose its leaves, however.

# Haworthia

The various species of the *Haworthia* genus of succulents display a wide variety of leaf markings. Originally from South Africa, *H. margaritifera* (pearl plant), for example, is a low-growing, rosette-forming plant. Its long, thickened, dark-green leaves are triangular in shape, with upward-curling tips and toothed edges. Their surfaces are covered with pearl-white tubercles (rounded nodules). Its small, white flowers are borne on long, thin stems.

## Cultivating *Haworthia*

*Haworthia* requires a bright, but sun-free, position all year round. In summer (when it can be placed outside), it enjoys temperatures ranging from 59 to 64°F (15 to 18°C), but should be kept at a temperature of 50°F (10°C) during the winter to encourage it to flower. (Keep winter-growing *Haworthia* in as light a position as possible, such as on a south-facing windowsill.) *Haworthia* is a suitable candidate for a succulent dish garden.

Water thoroughly during its growing season, allowing its compost to dry out between waterings, but never leave its pot standing in water because this will rot the plant's roots. Ensure that water doesn't come into contact with the center of the rosette of leaves either. Water it less during its resting period, when its compost should remain almost dry.

During its growing season, feed it every two weeks with a high-potassium fertilizer like tomato fertilizer.

Pot on only when it is pot-bound at the beginning of its growing season, and then into a shallow container filled with sandy, free-draining compost. When repotting, don't worry if its roots look shriveled--this is quite normal--new ones will grow later.

Propagate by taking stem or leaf cuttings, side rosettes, or offsets, all of which should be left to dry out before being planted in sandy, free-draining compost. Do not cover them and water them sparingly.

Rarely plagued by pests or diseases.

# Hebe

*Hebe* x *andersonii* is an evergreen shrub native to New Zealand, with small, green, leathery leaves arranged in couplets. Its numerous little tubular flowers, which are violet, fading to white, in color, are carried on spikes and appear in the axis of the plant's top shoots between April and September (in the northern hemisphere). *H. pinguifolia* 'Papagei' has deep-blue leaves.

## Cultivating *Hebe*

*Hebe* likes a very light position that receives full sun, and a winter temperature ranging from 43 to 50°F (6 to 10°C). During its summer flowering period, it prefers to be outside, and its blooms will not last very long if it is stationed inside. It is also best positioned outside when it is not in flower. A good compromise home for large, attractive species is therefore an airy conservatory, while smaller species should be regarded as only temporary houseplants.

Keep its compost moist from spring to fall, and give it just enough water to keep its leaves firm during the winter. Do not let this plant become waterlogged. Mist it occasionally.

Feed every two weeks in summer.

When it becomes pot-bound, repot it in spring, into nutrient-rich, free-draining compost. After it has ceased flowering, trim back its stems to maintain the plant's shape. This is also a plant that you could train into a standard.

Propagate by taking stem-tip cuttings at any time of year.

*Hebe* is rarely bothered by pests or diseases.

# Hedera

The *Hedera* (ivy) genus consists of foliage plants that vary widely in size, shape, and leaf color. A typical leaf comprises three to five leathery, green lobes, often with cream-and-white variegation and silvery edges, and, long, pointed, wavy or rounded tips.

The common *H. helix*, which is native to Europe, is a vigorous climber whose aerial roots attach themselves to any surface, and whose stems and branches become woody.

Before buying an ivy, always ensure that it has plenty of leaves because a leafless stem usually indicates a pest infestation.

> ### Caution
> *Hedera's* berries are very poisonous.

## Cultivating *Hedera*

Although *Hedera* is tolerant of shade, variegated ivies need plenty of light to prevent their leaves reverting to green. *Hedera* grows best in temperatures ranging from 50 and 59°F (10 and 15°C), but can cope with higher daytime temperatures and a minimum winter temperature of 41°F (5°C). A good choice for a cool spot, it is not suited to a heated room, where it will soon drop its leaves. *Hedera* can be used as a ground-cover plant in pots, planters, indoor gardens, and atriums. An excellent plant for topiary and hanging baskets, it is also good for both hydroponic cultivation and training into a standard. It effectively removes chemical vapors, especially formaldehyde, from polluted atmospheres.

Water well during the spring and summer, but allow the compost almost to dry out between waterings. In winter, keep the compost barely damp. Mist regularly.

Feed every two weeks during the spring and summer.

Repot in spring, into John Innes No. 3 compost, only if pot-bound. Keep growth in check by trimming its foliage at any time of year; give it a major prune in spring. Remove dead and dying leaves regularly.

Propagate at any time of year by taking stem cuttings that include some aerial roots. Alternatively, if you place the cuttings in water, they will generally develop roots.

Red spider mites and scale insects may target this plant if the atmosphere is too hot and dry.

# Heliotropium

Commonly called cherry pie, *Heliotropium arborescens,* which originates in Peru, has long, wrinkled, dull-green leaves that are oval in shape, with pointed tips, and can grow to a length of 23 in (60 cm). This heliotrope normally grows as a low bush, but can be trained into a standard plant. Its violet stems bear many star-shaped, purple and lavender flowers, which exude a superb, vanillalike fragrance.

When choosing a *H. arborescens* plant, make sure that it has plenty of flower buds and that there is no mold at the base of the stem.

## Cultivating *Heliotropium Arborescens*

*H. arborescens* needs a light position and some sunlight--but should be protected from the midday sun--and thrives best at temperatures above 46.4°F (8°C), when it will continue to flower throughout the winter.

Keep its compost moist all year round, making sure that any excess water drains away because its stems will rot if they become waterlogged.

Feed with diluted fertilizer every two weeks during spring and summer. Do not feed it too often, or with full-strength fertilizer, because it may then grow leaves rather than flowers, and its flowers are its main attraction.

Repot in spring into multipurpose compost. Remove dead flower heads to encourage further flowering. Note that older plants can become rather straggly and may not produce good flower heads, and that the best floral displays are staged by plants that have been grown from cuttings (the parent plant then being discarded).

Propagate in spring or late summer either by taking stem cuttings and planting them in moist sand or by sowing its seeds in winter (any plants that grow from the seeds will bloom the following year).

Whiteflies can plague this plant.

# Helxine

*Helxine soleirolii* (mind your own business), which is often sold as *Soleirolii soleirolii* (baby's tears), is a native of Corsica and Sardinia. Its tiny, round, glossy green leaves, which are carried on thread-like stems that are purplish-pink in color, form a dense, prostrate mat. *H. soleirolii* 'Aurea' has golden foliage, while *H. soleirolii* 'Argentea' is a silvery variation. These plants root spontaneously from their stems, which means that they can be invasive if planted with other genuses.

## Cultivating *Helxine Soleirolii*

*H. soleirolii* will grow in a slightly shady or brightly lit position, and prefers a cool temperature of at least 41°F (5°C). Cultivate it as a ground-cover plant, in a wall pot or hanging basket or at the edge of a trough. Do not plant it in a terrarium with other plants, however, because it will quickly take over.

Its compost should be kept moist, but should never be allowed to become waterlogged. So water it from below and allow any excess water to drain away to ward off root rot. It is essential to mist it frequently in hot weather.

Feed with half-strength fertilizer every two weeks during the summer.

Because this plant grows vigorously, it may be necessary to repot it in spring in multipurpose compost. Trim its foliage with scissors to maintain its shape. It will have become straggly after two years, however, and it is best to throw it away at this point.

Propagate by division in spring, making sure that each section has plenty of roots. They will soon root and produce leaves that cover the entire surface of the compost.

This plant is rarely bothered by pests, but conditions that are either too wet or too dry can prove fatal.

# Hibiscus

*Hibiscus rosa-sinensis* (rose of China), from tropical Asia, makes an ideal houseplant, not least because it bursts into full bloom when it is only 15 in (38 cm) high. Its woody stems bear glossy, evergreen leaves, and it produces a succession of superb, funnel-like flowers from summer to fall. *H. rosa-sinensis* varieties can display single or double blooms that are pink, yellow, white, or crimson. It is commonly plagued by aphids, so check the undersides of its leaves for these pests before buying one.

## Cultivating *Hibiscus Rosa-sinensis*

If it is to produce flowers, *H. rosa-sinensis* needs very bright light, but not direct sunlight. It is happy at a year-round temperature of between 55 and 64°F (13 and 18°C), but should be shielded from drafts because any sudden change in temperature will cause its buds to drop. It is suited to hydroponic cultivation, can be trained as a standard, and makes an attractive addition to a conservatory.

Water it regularly to keep the compost moist, allowing the surface to dry out between waterings. When in bud, mist it frequently and place its pot on a pebble tray to increase the humidity around it.

During its growing season, feed it with a weak solution of fertilizer every time that you water it.

Pot on in spring, into nutrient-rich, free-draining compost. Some leaves will fall off during winter, but new ones will grow in spring. Prune only if the plant is becoming straggly, and after it has stopped flowering.

Propagate from late spring to late summer by taking stem cuttings and providing heat from below.

Red spider mites and aphids can afflict it. Its buds will drop off if its conditions are too cold or its position is changed radically.

# Hosta

Commonly called plantain lilies, the members of the *Hosta* genus of plants originate in Asia. Grown mainly for their decorative foliage, their elegant, broad leaves of varying textures, colors, and variegations form large clumps that can spread to widths ranging from 1½ in to 5 ft (4 cm to 1.5 m). In summer, tall flower spikes rise above the foliage.

## Cultivating *Hosta*

*Hosta* requires a semishaded or shaded position and a temperature of around 59 to 64°F (15 to 18°C), and certainly no higher, during its growing season. But it can tolerate temperatures as low as 37.4°F (3°C) during the winter, when it should ideally be kept at 41°F (5°C). The perfect plant for a cool room or an indoor water garden, it can also be added to a hanging basket.

Ensure that its compost is constantly moist from spring to fall, and that any excess water drains away. In winter, keep its compost barely damp, but mist it regularly if the atmosphere is dry.

Feed every two weeks during its growing season.

Pot on into multipurpose compost every spring, when it is still dormant, after which it should be watered sparingly until shoots appear. Its leaves will shrivel and die in winter, when it should be stored in a cool, shady place until spring.

Propagate in spring by division.

When it is inside, the plant is rarely troubled by pests, but if it is placed outside, it will be feasted on by snails.

# Hoya

An Australasian plant, *Hoya carnosa* (wax plant) belongs to a genus of easy-to-cultivate, climbing and trailing plants that have very long stems. Its shiny, evergreen leaves are thick and spear-shaped. The plant flowers from spring to fall, and its white or rose-pink, waxy, star-shaped flowers are carried in clusters of about twenty blooms. The flowers' sweet fragrance is especially noticeable at night.

## Cultivating *Hoya*

*Hoya* grows best in bright light, but not direct sunlight, at a temperature ranging from between 59 and 64°F (15 and 18°C) during its growing season; during winter, it should be kept at 50°F (10°C) to help it to bloom in spring. Very useful as a climbing plant for a conservatory, it can also be planted in a hanging basket.

Water it generously from spring to fall. In winter, allow its compost nearly to dry out between waterings. Mist it regularly during its growing season.

Feed it monthly when it is growing.

This plant dislikes being disturbed, so repot it in spring only when it is pot-bound, into free-draining compost. Prune it drastically in spring to keep its shape. When you see buds, don't move the plant or they will drop off. *Hoya* requires plenty of support to climb, so train it to grow up a trellis or preshaped wires.

Propagate in spring by taking stem cuttings and heating them from below.

This plant is rarely plagued by pests and diseases, but if conditions are too cold or wet, its leaves may turn yellow, curl up, and eventually drop off.

# Hyacinthus

Hyacinths, as members of the *Hyacinthus* genus of flowering plants are usually called, have Mediterranean origins. They look tender, but are actually tough plants. They are grown for the heady fragrance of their large, multibloomed spikes, which flower from December to April (in the northern hemisphere) in a variety of colors, and not for their light-green leaves.

When buying a *Hyacinthus* bulb, pick a big, solid one. If you want it to flower at Christmas time, buy a specially prepared bulb and plant it in bulb fiber by the beginning of September. If they are planted before the end of October, ordinary hyacinth bulbs will flower in February. If you are planting a number of bulbs in a bowl, ensure that they flower at the same time by using the same cultivar. *Hyacinth* bulbs can also be grown over pebbles, sand, or water (see pages 60 to 61).

## Cultivating *Hyacinthus*

The brighter and cooler its position, the longer a hyacinth's blooms will last when it is flowering, making it a superb plant for a windowsill.

Always keep its compost moist, but not too wet as this will cause its bulb to rot.

There is no need to feed this plant.

Pot up the bulb into bulb fiber, or else place it above water in a hyacinth glass, in late summer or fall, and then keep it in a cool, dark place until it has produced shoots that measure 2 in (5 cm) in length. Then move it to a light room with a temperature no higher than 60°F (16°C). *Hyacinthus* grows toward the light, so remember to turn its pot frequently. Hyacinths rarely bloom as spectacularly again after their first year, so it's best to plant the bulb in the garden after it has finished flowering.

You could try propagating it by removing its bulbils, or offsets, but this method is not always successful.

If it flowers poorly, this is probably because it spent insufficient time in darkness beforehand.

# Hypocyrta

*Hypocyrta glabra*, which originates in tropical America, is a summer-flowering, low-growing, bushy plant, whose slightly arching stems hold pairs of dainty, shiny, bright-green leaves measuring just over 1 in (3 cm) in length, rather like a box (*Buxus*) plant's. Its numerous, tubular-pouched, orange flowers develop from leaf axils and are often described as looking like feeding goldfish or Dutch clogs (hence *H. glabra*'s common name, clog plant).

## Cultivating *Hypocyrta Glabra*

This plant enjoys a position that is brightly lit (in winter) to semishaded (in summer), and a minimum year-round temperature of 59°F (15°C). It is useful for slightly shady locations and looks attractive in a hanging basket.

Always keep its compost moist, but never overwater it. Mist it frequently.

Feed the plant at monthly intervals, being particularly careful to do so when new growth appears.

Pot on in spring, into a well-draining, peat-based compost after adding lots of crocks to the bottom of the pot.

Pinch out the growing tips in spring to produce a bushier plant. Prune it after it has flowered.

Propagate in spring or summer, either by division or by taking stem cuttings.

This plant is rarely bothered by pests, but if its conditions are too cool, or it has been overwatered, its foliage may turn yellow.

# Hypoestes

Members of the *Hypoestes* genus are commonly known as freckle-face or polka-dot plants. *H. phyllostachya* is a short, erect species and has branching stems that carry small, green, oval leaves that are smothered with white to pale-pink spots. (By contrast, *H. sanguinolenta* has red-veined leaves.) The quality of its leaf color depends on both the intensity and duration of the available light. The purple-and-white blooms are not particularly attractive.

Note that although these plants are usually discarded after a year, by which time they will have become very straggly, they will respond to pruning.

## Cultivating *Hypoestes*

*Hypoestes* enjoys a bright position and some sun (although it will tolerate a semi-shaded spot, its leaves may lose some of their coloring). It requires a minimum temperature of 59°F (15°C) throughout the year. With its attractive and unusual foliage, this plant is ideally suited to a light, warm room or terrarium. It

also makes a delightful addition to a hanging basket if its growing tips are not pinched out.

Water regularly during the spring and summer, and give it less water during the winter, but never let its root ball dry out. Because it thrives in a very humid atmosphere, it is best placed on a pebble tray and misted frequently.

Feed every two weeks in summer, and monthly in winter. It will also welcome the occasional foliar feed.

Pinch out its growing tips in spring to encourage the plant to become bushier. Even so, because its stems can grow to a height of 23 in (60 cm) within a season, it can end up looking unattractively straggly. It's best to discard this plant after a year, perhaps first taking cuttings from it to propagate.

This plant is easily propagated from seeds sown in spring (and any plants that grow from them will flower in the summer of the same year). Alternatively, take stem cuttings in spring.

Aphids and whiteflies may attack this plant. Its leaves may turn yellow if its conditions are too cold.

# Impatiens

*Impatiens walleriana* is just one of the six-hundred species that belong to the *Impatiens* genus of flowering plants (commonly known as busy Lizzies) that originate in tropical Africa and Asia. It has become a very popular houseplant, mainly because it is capable of flowering all year round. *I. walleriana petersiana* has burgundy-colored leaves and flowers. The recent *I.* x 'New Guinea' hybrids often have variegated leaves.

Before buying a busy Lizzie, make sure that it has plenty of buds, firm, bright-green leaves, and that it is aphid-free.

## Cultivating *Impatiens walleriana*

To produce flowers, *I. walleriana* must be placed in the lightest and airiest position, be protected from fierce sunlight and drafts, and live in a year-round temperature of 64°F (18°C). It is suitable for hydroponic cultivation and for hanging baskets.

Water regularly during the summer so that its compost is always moist, but not waterlogged. Misting will damage flowers, so instead position its pot on a pebble tray.

Feed regularly during the spring and summer, but only once a month during the fall and winter. Adding one teaspoon of Epsom salts to 17 fl oz (500 ml) of water will help its leaves to keep their color.

Pot on in spring, into ericaceous compost. Encourage bushiness by pinching out its growing tips. If it is a large plant, trim it back hard during fall to prevent it from becoming too straggly.

Propagate by taking stem cuttings, or sow its seeds in spring. Don't cover with compost until they have germinated; the new plants should flower in the same year.

Aphids can infest the plant, as can red spider mites and whiteflies. If its conditions are too wet, its stems will rot.

# Ixora Ixora

A difficult plant to cultivate, *Ixora coccinea* (flame of the woods), which originates in India, is an evergreen shrub that grows to 3 to 5 ft (1 to 1.5 m) in height. It has pointed, leathery leaves that are a glossy dark-green in color, and tubular flowers that appear in large, globular, terminal clusters from June to September (in the northern hemisphere). Typically scarlet, the flowers of some plants are pink, white, or yellow.

Buy *I. coccinea* just as its flower buds are forming because they will drop off if the plant is moved.

## Cultivating *Ixora Coccinea*

*I. coccinea* requires bright light--but not direct sunlight--all year round, as well as a temperature ranging from 64 to 68°F (18 to 20°C). Position it in a spot that is both warm and airy, but also free from drafts.

Keep its compost damp throughout the year by watering it regularly with rainwater or soft water, but less so during winter. To increase the humidity around it, mist it frequently and place its pot on a pebble tray.

Feed every two weeks during its growing season.

Repot in spring, in multipurpose compost, but only when it has become pot-bound. If it becomes leggy, prune it back after it has flowered (never cut back new shoots because flowers will later develop at the end of these stems).

Propagate in spring by taking stem cuttings, treating them with a rooting hormone, and providing heat from below.

If the air around this plant is too dry, scale insects may attack it. Its leaves will drop off if they are exposed to drafts, and will turn yellow if it is given hard water. Finally, it will shed its flower buds if it is moved.

# Jasminum

Members of the *Jasminum* genus of flowering plants are better known as jasmines. Originating in western China, *J. polyanthum*, which is commonly called pink jasmine and is often bought trained around a wire hoop, is a fast-growing, naturally twining and rambling, evergreen shrub that can reach a height of 16 ft (5 m). Its glossy, dark-green leaves are divided into four or five leaflets, while the petals of its white, starlike flowers are tinged with pink on the outside. These flowers have a powerful scent, grow freely in clusters from fall through to spring, and are followed by shiny, black berries.

## Cultivating *Jasminum*

*Jasminum* needs a light, airy position with some direct sunlight. It is best placed outside during the summer and requires a minimum temperature of 44°F (7°C) in winter. It is ideal for a conservatory or garden room, where it can be trained to grow around a wall and up a large trellis.

Its compost should always remain moist, so water regularly during its growing season, but less so in winter. Mist it often.

Feed every two weeks while it is flowering, and continue until the end of spring.

Repot in spring in multipurpose compost. Planting in a larger pot will cause it to grow larger, so you may instead prefer to top-dress it. As soon as its shoots have grown to a length of 4¾ in (12 cm), train them around wire shapes or up a trellis. It should be pruned and cut back after it has finished flowering.

Propagate by taking stem cuttings in March (in the northern hemisphere) and growing them on in a sunny position, at a temperature of around 60°F (16°C); these plants should provide a good display of flowers during their first winter.

Aphids may attack this plant if its winter conditions are too warm.

# Jatropha

A Central American plant, *Jatropha podiatrica* is a deciduous shrub whose thickened, bottle-shaped stem displays horny stipules (outgrowths from the base of a leaf stalk that look rather like scales) that contain water-storage tissue. It grows to a height of between 17 and 35 in (45 and 90 cm). The leaves—each of which is 7 in (20 cm) wide and consists of three or five lobes—grow in a cluster at the top of long stalks. Small, scarlet flowers develop on long, red stalks during the plant's winter resting period. This rather bizarre-looking plant, which is commonly called gout plant or nettle spurge, is both easy to care for and becoming increasingly popular.

## Caution
All parts of *J. podiatrica* are poisonous.

## Cultivating *Jatropha Podiatrica*

This unusual plant requires a light position all year round (but should not be exposed to the hot summer sun) and a temperature ranging from 53 to 70°F (12 to 21°C).

Always water sparingly, and keep its compost almost dry after its leaves have fallen.

Feed with cactus food once a month during winter.

When it has become too large for its pot, repot in spring, into free-draining compost.

Propagate either from seed in spring (note that the seeds should be heated from below) or by taking stem cuttings in summer (but be warned this method is rarely successful).

Although this plant is not attacked by pests, its roots may rot if its conditions are too wet.

# Kalanchoe

*K. blossfeldiana.*

*Kalanchoe blossfeldiana* (flaming Katy), a native of Madagascar, is a popular houseplant whose yellow, orange, pink, violet, or scarlet blooms provide an outstanding splash of color during the winter. Its short, branching stems support fleshy, oval, shiny, dark-green leaves with toothed edges, and its star-shaped flowers grow in clusters from long stems.

Two other species of the *Kalanchoe* genus of succulent plants are grown for their foliage. *K. tomentosa* (panda plant) has long, thick leaves covered in silver hairs that lie together to form a feltlike layer and have red-brown edges. A slow-growing plant, *K. beharensis* (felt plant) has hairy leaves that are olive-green in color; if a stem breaks, it has the ability to form a new plant at the point of fracture.

## Cultivating *Kalanchoe Blossfeldiana*

A position that receives good light is essential for *Kalanchoe*, while sunlight enhances the appearance of its leaves. It prefers an airy atmosphere, but dislikes drafts, and will tolerate temperatures ranging from 55 to 73°F (13 to 23°C). This plant is suitable for hydroponic cultivation.

Water thoroughly all year, ensuring that excess water drains away, and allowing the surface of the compost to dry out between waterings.

Feed every two weeks from March to August (in the northern hemisphere) to build up its flower power.

Repot in spring in multipurpose compost.

Propagate by taking leaf cuttings, allowing the edges to dry out, and laying them on a bed of moist sand.

Aphids and mealy bugs can afflict this plant, congregating especially on the underside of its leaves. Erratic watering may cause the edges of its leaves to turn brown, while gray mold (*botrytis*) may appear if its conditions are too wet.

*K. tomentosa.*

# Llachenalia

*Lachenalia aloides* (Cape cowslip), which originates in South Africa, is a bulbous plant that has strap-shaped, red-spotted, dull-green leaves that measure 1 in (2 cm) in width. In spring, bell-shaped flowers that are yellow to greenish-yellow and tinged with orange in color, and that grow to a length of 1 in (2.5), bloom on leafless spikes above the leaves.

## Cultivating *L. Aloides*

*L. aloides* requires a sunny, airy position, a temperature ranging from between 50 to 59°F (10 and 15°C) in summer, and a winter temperature of 41 to 50°F (5 to 10°C). It suits a windowsill or conservatory.

Water carefully, keeping the compost barely damp during winter, but giving it more water once shoots have appeared so that the compost remains quite moist.

Feed once a week until it starts flowering.

When its leaves start to turn yellow, rest the bulb in warm and dry conditions. In fall, place the bulb in sandy compost, positioning it so that its tip lies just below the surface. Place it in a cool, bright room, water it well, and then leave it until you can see shoots, at which point you should start to water it more often and move it to a sunny spot.

Propagate by removing offset bulbils when you pot up the bulb in fall and planting each in its own pot.

Although this plant is rarely attacked by pests or diseases, its bulb may rot if it is overwatered.

# Lactuca

Lettuce, or to give it its botanical name, *Lactuca sativa,* a northern European native that is thought to have originated in England during the fourteenth century, can be grown inside. The recent "cut-and-come-again" varieties are especially suitable for indoor cultivation, and it's best to choose 'Kendo', 'Little Gem' or any variety that has colored leaves.

## Cultivating *Lactuca Sativa*

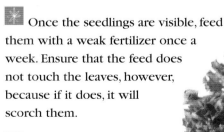 Sow individual *L. sativa* seeds in preformed pots at any time of year and then keep them in a light position at a temperature ranging from between 59 and 64°F (15 and 18°C).

When the seedlings appear, water the young plants frequently.

Once the seedlings are visible, feed them with a weak fertilizer once a week. Ensure that the feed does not touch the leaves, however, because if it does, it will scorch them.

When the leaves are about five weeks old, or 4 in (10 cm) long, cut them back to their stumps, leaving about ¾ to 1 in (2 to 2.5 cm) of growth. The leaves will now sprout again, and harvesting them regularly in this way will ensure a constant supply for eight to ten weeks. Once the leaves show little sign of regrowth, throw the plants away.

Ensure that you are never without this home-grown salad ingredient by planting new seeds every two months.

Indoor lettuce should not be troubled by pests, but the stems may rot if the plant becomes waterlogged.

# Lantana

*Lantana camara* (yellow sage), which originates in tropical America, can remain in flower for nine months of the year. A shrubby plant that grows from 3 to 6 ft (1 to 2 m) in height, its upright, rough, prickly stems are covered with egg-shaped, crinkled leaves with toothed edges. The small, tubular flowers, each of which consists of five spreading lobes, form dense, globular flower heads measuring 2 in (5 cm) in width. The flowers change color as they age, with the outer rows of petals becoming darker, so that the flower heads can appear yellow, orange, pink, and white.

When buying this plant, choose one that has a mass of buds rather than flowers.

### Caution
All parts of *L. camara* are poisonous, so wear gloves before taking cuttings.

## Cultivating *Lantana Camara*

*L. camara* really enjoys sunshine, so provide it with as much natural light as possible. But it needs protection from the midday sun, and also ensure that it is exposed to a minimum temperature of 43°F (6°C) during the winter. It makes a good plant for a large container positioned in a conservatory, and can be trained as a standard.

Water regularly from spring to fall, allowing its compost partially to dry out between waterings; in winter, keep its compost nearly dry. Its leaves benefit from being misted, but make sure that the water doesn't wet its flowers.

Feed every fortnight.

Repot in early spring in multipurpose compost, when you can also prune any unwanted stems and perhaps propagate them.

Propagate by taking stem cuttings in early spring or late summer and providing heat from below. Alternatively, sow its seeds in spring.

This plant is vulnerable to attack from whiteflies.

# Laurus

The bay tree, or *Laurus nobilis*, a native of most Mediterranean regions, is grown for its decorative foliage, as well as for the delicious use to which its leaves can be put in the kitchen. If you place a fresh bay leaf in a flour container, it is also supposed to ward off flour weevils. Its narrow, oval leaves, which are a glossy green, release a strong, aromatic fragrance when crushed. Flowers grow from its leaf axils in spring, and may be followed by dark fruits if the plant is not pruned.

When choosing a *L. nobilis* plant, check that its leaves are shiny and not discolored.

## Cultivating *Laurus Nobilis*

The bay tree relishes both shade and direct sunlight, preferring a cool and airy position outside during the summer. Although it thrives best when the temperature is around 59°F (15°C), it can tolerate temperatures as low as 32°F (0°C) during the winter. It makes an excellent specimen for a pot or tub, and can be easily trained to grow as a standard or around a preshaped framework.

Keep the root ball moist in spring and summer, but allow its compost to dry out between waterings during the winter. Mist it regularly to keep scale insects at bay.

Feed weekly.

If the plant grows too large, either repot it or top-dress it in spring using John Innes No. 3 compost. It can be pruned or cut back drastically from spring to summer.

Propagate in summer by taking stem cuttings.

If conditions are too warm during winter, it may be attacked by scale insects. Do not over-water in winter, as the stem will rot.

# Lisianthus

A native of the U.S.A. and Mexico, *Lisianthus russelianus* (commonly known as prairie gentian, and sometimes sold as *Estoma grandiflorum*) is a slow-growing, upright plant that can reach a height of 23 in (60 cm) and whose deep-green, lance-shaped leaves measure up to 3 in (8 cm) in length. Its flowers, which may be pink, purple, blue, or white, appear in bowl-shaped clusters of satin-textured, five-petaled blooms that measure 2 in (5 cm) across when open and resemble poppies.

When buying this plant, look for one that has plenty of buds and fresh-looking, firm leaves. Be warned that prairie gentians are not easy to cultivate, however, because they require a constant temperature and draft-free position and hate being too wet or too dry, and that the plants that are offered for sale have often been treated with growth retardants and won't therefore flower well the following year.

## Cultivating *Lisianthus Russelianus*

The plant requires a brightly lit position that receives some sunshine, as well as a constant temperature of around 64°F (18°C). It is best regarded as a short-term plant for a windowsill.

Water regularly, but allow its compost nearly to dry out between waterings. Mist the leaves, but not the blooms, which can be damaged by water.

Feed every two weeks while it is flowering.

Discard this short-lived plant after it has finished flowering.

Propagate either by sowing its seeds in spring or by dividing it after it has finished flowering, then keeping its compost nearly dry during winter.

Aphids may attack this plant.

# Lithops

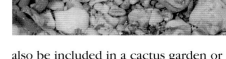

A member of the *Mesembryanthemum* family, the South African succulent *Lithops salicola* mimics the appearance of stones, which is why its common name is living stone. The plant consists of a short, single stem, which grows beneath the surface of the compost, from which protrude two thick leaves that press closely together to form a head. Their flattened tops can be gray, brown, or fawn and often bear a mottled or spotted pattern rather like a stone's. Yellow or white, daisylike flowers emerge from the cleft between the leaves during summer and fall.

## Cultivating *Lithops Salicola*

*L. salicola* needs a brightly lit position that receives full sun all year round, and although it will thrive best when placed outside during the summer, it must be protected from rain. During the winter, it prefers a temperature ranging from 41 to 46.4°F (5 to 8°C). This unusual succulent is ideal for a very sunny position and can

also be included in a cactus garden or succulent dish garden.

Keep its compost dry during the winter resting period. When the old leaves have shriveled up and new ones are developing, start watering it by standing its pot in water and then allowing excess water to drain away. Do not water it again until the compost has dried out.

During its growing season, feed it with a weak high-potassium feed, such as tomato fertilizer, every two weeks.

Although it is extremely slow-growing, it will eventually form a clump that fills its pot. At this point, pot it on--at any time of year--into very free-draining compost to which you've added a little grit.

Propagate either by separating plants that have clumped together and potting them on individually or by sowing its seeds in spring.

Its roots may rot if it is overwatered.

# Lycopersicon

*Lycopersicon esculentum* (or *L. lycopersicum*), which originates in Mexico and is better known as the tomato, is not usually thought of as a houseplant. Some beautiful and edible varieties can be grown in hanging baskets, however, so why not give it a try? Suitable varieties include 'Tumbler', a trailing plant; 'Sweet Million', a very sweet, cherry-type tomato; and 'Tiny Tim' and 'Supersweet 100', also cherry-type tomatoes, but semisweet ones.

## Cultivating *Lycopersicon Esculentum*

Either buy young *L. esculentum* plants from a garden center or sow their seeds in early spring and leave them to germinate in a warm, light place. When they are large enough to be handled, plant them in either a hanging basket or a large pot filled with lots of multipurpose compost. If you are growing them in a pot, tie their stems to vertical canes at regular intervals. These plants will thrive in a sunny conservatory.

Water regularly to ensure that the compost is constantly damp. Mist regularly, too, to encourage the fruits to set.

When the first fruits start to swell, feed the plants with a high-potash tomato fertilizer once a week.

Nip out the lower branches' side shoots to promote good fruiting. Discard the plant once you have picked all its fruit.

Indoor tomatoes are prone to infestation by whiteflies, which you should deal with as soon as you spot them.

# Maranta

*M. leuconeura* 'Kerchoveana'.

*Maranta leuconeura,* which originates in tropical America, is called the prayer plant because of the way in which it folds up its leaves and holds them erect when darkness approaches. With their chocolate-colored blotches and prominent, red or white veins, these pale-green, lightly ribbed leaves, which are oval in shape and blunt at the ends, are striking. The leaves of *M. tricolor* (herringbone plant) have a silvery central zone and dark-green veins, with other, crimson veins curving out to the edges.

These plants never recover from being badly treated, so check its leaves carefully for discolored tips before buying one.

## Cultivating *Maranta*

Because sunlight damages its foliage, *Maranta* must have a shady position (the color of its leaves also deepens in the shade). It is happiest at 70°F (21°C), but will tolerate temperatures as low as 64°F (18°C), but not drafts. This attractive

foliage plant, which responds well to hydroponic cultivation, is thus suitable for a warm, shady area. It will also remove chemical vapors from the atmosphere.

It is essential to water it regularly with warm water, but make sure that the surface of the compost feels slightly dry before thoroughly soaking it and then leaving it to drain. Because it likes a very humid atmosphere, mist it regularly and occasionally sponge its leaves with water. It is also best to position its pot on a pebble tray or to group it with other plants.

During its growing season, feed it with a weak solution of fertilizer every time you water it, but stop feeding in winter.

Repot only when it has grown too big for its pot. In spring, snip off any dead leaves.

Propagate in spring by division.

Red spider mites and aphids are the only pests to target this plant. If its leaves roll up during the day, it is a sign that its conditions are either too cold or too dry.

*M. tricolor.*

# Mentha

There are many varieties of *Mentha* (mint), including those that have apple-, spearmint, ginger-, and lemon-flavored leaves. *Mentha spicata* (spearmint), which originates in Mediterranean regions, grows well on any windowsill because it doesn't mind whether its position is sunny or shady, just as long as it receives plenty of light.

A useful culinary herb to have to hand on the kitchen windowsill, *M. spicata* also makes an attractive addition to a hanging basket. Not only that, but its scent will keep aphids away from neighboring plants. Mint is said to repel mice, too, so if you think that these little pests are haunting your house, leave sprigs of mint around any areas that you suspect are harboring them.

## Cultivating *Mentha Spicata*

There are two ways of growing a *M. spicata* plant: in compost or in water. If you want to grow it in compost, place plenty of drainage material, such as crocks, in the bottom of its pot, ensure that you pack multipurpose compost tightly around its roots, and then place the pot in a container. If you prefer to grow it in water, wash the soil from its roots and place it in a glass jar filled with water, ensuring that the water level is below its leaves.

If your mint is growing in a pot, keep its container one-third full of water. If it is growing in water, top up the water when necessary and perhaps add a piece of charcoal to keep it smelling fresh.

If the plant is growing in water, add a few drops of plant food to it once a month. Regularly cutting off sprigs from the top of the plant will promote renewed growth.

Propagate by division at any time of year except winter.

This plant is untroubled by pests or diseases.

# Mimosa

*Mimosa pudica*'s primary attraction is its habit of folding up its leaves whenever they are touched--which is why its common name is sensitive plant--any further disturbance prompting its leaf stalks to collapse, so that the plant looks wilted or even dead. If it is subsequently left alone, it will slowly return to its normal position, a process that could take thirty to sixty minutes. It also folds its leaves at night without any external interference. These leaves, which have a slight resemblance to the fingers of a hand, are composed of small, feathery leaflets, at the base of which is a pale, raised spot (this is the touch-sensitive organ). Its small, pink, pompom-like flowers bloom in late summer. This native of tropical American regions is easy to cultivate.

When selecting a *M. pudica* plant, remember that the older the tree, the less likely it is to react to touch.

## Cultivating *Mimosa Pudica*

*M. pudica* prefers a bright, airy position that receives some direct sunlight and an average temperature of 64°F (18°C), but not less than 55°F (13°C) during the winter. It makes an interesting plant for a light, warm room.

Keep its compost moist all year round, watering it less in winter, but making sure that the root ball never dries out. It will benefit from being misted occasionally, too.

Feed every two weeks during its growing season.

If it has become pot-bound, repot it in spring in multipurpose compost. To preserve its bushy shape, prune it after its flowers have faded, but note that these plants tends to become straggly with age.

Propagate in spring, either by taking stem cuttings or by sowing its seeds (soak the seeds in tepid water overnight before sowing them to speed up the germination process considerably).

Although red spider mites may attack this plant, they rarely do so.

# Monstera

A native of Mexico, *Monstera deliciosa* (Swiss cheese plant) is a tough, hardy plant with glossy leaves. A mature plant can reach a height of 19 ft (6 m). Its heart-shaped, leathery leaves are deeply serrated and become perforated with age. Brown, cordlike, aerial roots hang from the stems in search of water. A mature plant can produce creamy, arumlike flowers that bloom in groups of two or three, developing into fruits that resemble pale-green pineapples. *M. deliciosa* 'Variegata', which grows more slowly, has leaves that are variegated with white.

Before buying this plant, make sure that its leaves are glossy and undamaged.

## Cultivating *Monstera*

This plant requires plenty of space and a bright position (but not direct sunlight, which will scorch its leaves). Although it can tolerate some shade, if it is situated in too shady a location, its leaves will lose their serration. A constant temperature ranging from between 59 and 70°F (15 and 21°C) is perfect. This bold specimen plant is suitable for hydroponic cultivation.

Water it often to keep its compost constantly damp. Because it thrives in a moist atmosphere, mist it frequently during the spring and summer and sponge older leaves carefully with a damp cloth (but not young leaves, which are easily damaged).

When it is actively growing, feed every week. In winter, feed once a month.

Pot on at any time of year, and into well-draining compost. If it has become too big to move, top-dress it instead. Train any stray aerial roots back into the compost or else into a water container. This plant requires a sturdy support, and a moss stick is ideal. If you want, you could limit its growth by cutting off its growing tip, which will encourage side shoots. If you then pot on the tip part, it will root and grow quickly.

Propagate by air-layering or taking stem cuttings (see above).

Scale insects sometimes attack this plant. If the edges of its leaves are turning brown, the compost is too wet.

# Musa

A native of Southeast Asia, the banana plant, *Musa coccinea*, is a large, rapidly growing plant that requires a lot of space to accommodate its fast-spreading habit. Its trunklike stem, which can reach a height of 3 ft (1 m), is sheathed with leaf stalks that are shed as the plant ages. Note that when *M. coccinea* is kept in a pot, it rarely produces fruit

Before buying a *M. coccinia*, take note of where it is being displayed because these plants respond badly to drafts and cold conditions. Ensure that its leaves are firm and upright, too, because these are signs that the plant is healthy.

## Cultivating *Musa Coccinea*

*M. coccinia* needs plenty of bright light, but should be protected from the hot, midday sun (and do not let its leaves come into contact with a windowpane during the summer either because they will end up being scorched). It should be kept at a minimum year-round temperature of 59°F (15°C), but is happier at 64 to 70°F (18 to 21°C). A majestic-looking plant for a large room or conservatory, it will also remove polluting vapors from the atmosphere.

Although this plant requires plenty of water during its growing season, it should not be left standing in it, so ensure that any excess drains away. It needs less water during the winter, but never allow the root ball to dry out. Sponge its leaves with water frequently throughout the year.

Feed at the same time that you water it, except during the winter.

Pot on into free-draining compost in spring or summer every year. Remove its lower leaves when they turn yellow and die (don't worry--new ones will grow in spring).

Propagate by division or by taking suckers from the mother plant in spring, potting them on, and keeping them in a hot and humid atmosphere.

This plant may be attacked by red spider mites and mealy bugs.

# Myrtus

*Myrtus communis*, whose common name is myrtle or bride's plant, is an evergreen shrub that originates in western Asia and can grow to a height of 6 ft (2 m) when planted in a container. It has glossy, dark-green, leathery leaves and its masses of fragrant, white flowers are followed by long, purple-black berries. It is known as the bride's good-luck flower and many bridal bouquets contain a sprig of myrtle.

You'll probably find this plant in a garden center rather than in the houseplant section of a supermarket.

## Cultivating *M. Communis*

This plant requires a bright, sunny position and can be placed outside during the summer, but should be protected from direct midday sun. During the winter, it needs a light location whose temperature ranges between 41 and 50°F (5 and 10°C). *M. communis* is an ideal plant to train as a standard, and is also suitable for bonsai cultivation.

Keep its compost moist during the spring and summer by watering it regularly with rainwater or soft water. Allow the surface of the compost to dry out between waterings during the winter. Mist the leaves frequently.

Feed this plant once a week from spring to summer.

Repot every two or three years in spring in multipurpose compost, into a slightly larger container each time, ensuring that you do not position its trunk any lower than it was before. To encourage bushiness, pinch out young shoots. This plant can withstand pruning in spring, and can either be clipped into a variety of shapes or trained as a standard.

Propagate by taking stem cuttings in spring or summer and providing them with some heat from below.

Scale insects and aphids may attack this plant if its conditions are too warm during the winter, and its leaves will drop off, too. Its roots may rot if its compost remains too wet.

# Narcissus

Originally from North Africa, the members of the *Narcissus* genus provide welcome color in-winter and early spring. Most strains usually grown outside can be easily cultivated inside, such smaller varieties as *N.* 'Tête-à-Tête', *N.* 'Peeping Tom', and *N.* 'February Gold' generally proving the best.

*Narcissus* bulbs can be grown in gravel and water, as well as in bulb fiber (see pages 60 to 61). To enjoy *Narcissus* blooms at Christmas, you will need to buy specially prepared bulbs to plant by September.

## Cultivating *Narcissus*

When in flower, *Narcissus* requires a bright position and a temperature ranging from 5 to 8°C (41 to 46°F). Best in a cool room, it should be kept in a warm room for a short period only or its flowers will wilt. Turn its pot daily so that it grows evenly.

N. 'Paperwhite'/ 'Soleil d'Or'.

N. cyclamineus.

Keep its compost constantly moist, but not wet.

There is no need to feed this plant.

## Caution
**All parts of *Narcissus* are poisonous.**

Plant your *Narcissus* bulb in fall and then keep it in a cool, dark place until its shoots are 2 in (5 cm) high, at which point gradually move it to an increasingly light position. After the flowers have died, wait until the leaves have turned yellow and then plant the bulb in the garden.

Propagate by removing its offset bulbs.

Pests rarely attack this plant, but its bulb may rot if its conditions are too wet.

# Neathe

A native of Mexico, the common name of *Neathe bella* (also called *Chamaedorea elegans* or *Collinia elegans*) is parlor palm. This slow-growing plant, which reaches a maximum height of 3 ft (1 m), bears stiff, bamboolike stems from which grow graceful, leathery fronds. Its clusters of yellow flowers are followed by small, round fruits—best removed because they sap the plant's vigor. Before buying a parlor palm, check its leaves for red spider mites and damage or discoloration

## Cultivating *Neathe bella*

Bright light is important for *N. bella* (but not strong sunlight). It can tolerate semi-shade and can be put outside during the summer. It also likes temperatures between 60 and 70° F (16 and 21° C) during its growing season—but cooler conditions during winter—as well as a humid atmosphere. It makes a good plant for a terrarium when it is still small, and is suitable for hydroponic cultivation. *N. bella* is capable of removing chemical pollutants from the air.

Water its compost thoroughly and allow any excess to drain away (it will die if it becomes waterlogged). Mist its fronds regularly and occasionally sponge mature leaves with water to remove dust. Put its pot on a pebble tray to help humidity.

As soon as a young plant is established, feed it little and often during the spring and summer months.

Pot on only when it has become pot-bound, using multipurpose compost.

It is difficult to propagate from seed. It is easier to encourage its offsets to root, which require a warm, humid atmosphere during their first few months.

If the air around it is too dry, red spider mites and scale insects may infest this plant. Root rot caused by waterlogging is the biggest threat to the plant's wellbeing.

# Nephrolepis

All varieties of the *Nephrolepis exaltata* species of fern grow rapidly, with runners, rather than roots, and fronds that can be wavy, curly, or twisted. A native of the tropics, *N. exaltata* 'Bostoniensis' (Boston fern) is a popular houseplant whose bright-green fronds, which can grow to a length of 23 in (60 cm), form a tufted rosette.

When choosing a Boston fern, never buy one whose fronds have turned brown.

## Cultivating *Nephrolepis Exaltata* 'Bostoniensis'

*N. exaltata* 'Bostoniensis' likes a light position that receives filtered sunshine (but can tolerate a little shade as long as it is not exposed to drafts) and a minimum temperature of 50°F (10°C). It makes an ideal plant for a hanging basket or for displaying on a pedestal. Suitable for hydroponic cultivation, the Boston fern is also one of the most efficient of all plants at removing pollutants from the air.

Water frequently during the spring and summer, but allow its compost almost to dry out between waterings in winter. It should be misted frequently and, if possible, placed on a pebble tray to increase the humidity.

During its growing season, feed this plant every two weeks.

Repot in spring using multipurpose compost, making sure that you do not bury its crown any lower than it was previously, otherwise it will rot. Remove dead foliage.

Propagate by division, by taking offsets or by encouraging its spores to germinate in spring.

If its leaves are too dry, red spider mites may attack this plant and the tips of its leaves may turn brown. This may also happen if it becomes waterlogged (in which case plunging it in its pot into a bed of peat and leaving it for a few months will give its runners a chance to revive).

# Nerium

Perhaps better known as oleander, *Nerium oleander*, which originates in Mediterranean regions, grows both easily and rapidly to a height of 6 ft (2 m). An evergreen plant, *N. oleander*'s shiny, dark-green leaves resemble spears. Its fragrant, single or double, funnel-shaped flowers produce a superb display when it flowers from summer through fall.

## Cultivating *Nerium Oleander*

*N. oleander* prefers a hot, sunny place in summer, but should be moved to a light spot and exposed to temperatures as low as 37°F (3°C) in winter. It can be put outside in spring and summer, and is suitable for a spacious, sunny conservatory

Water regularly from spring to fall, but sparingly during the winter.

Feed once a week during the spring and summer.

Pot on in spring every year until it has grown too large to do so, when you should top-dress it. If it is becoming too large, prune it drastically--indeed, you could cut some branches back to compost level. To prevent it from becoming straggly, prune a smaller plant's growing tips. Note that any pruning must be done immediately after the plant has finished flowering, otherwise you will prevent it from forming buds the following year.

Propagate in summer by taking stem cuttings, standing them in water, and leaving them to root (these plants will flower in their third year).

Scale insects occasionally trouble this plant, and it is also susceptible to fungal diseases.

## Caution

*N. oleander*'s wood and sap are poisonous.

# Nertera

*Nertera granadensis*, a native of Southeast Asia and Australia, is a small, creeping evergreen from whose threadlike stems grow mounds of tiny, oval leaves. Its minute, greenish flowers are followed by a profusion of brilliant-orange, pea-sized berries that resemble beads (which is why its common name is bead plant). During fall, these berries, which last for about two months, almost cover the plant.

When choosing a *N. granadensis* plant, ensure that there is no mold on its leaves because this is a sign that it is waterlogged.

## Cultivating *Nertera Granadensis*

Along with a temperature of 55°F (13°C), *N. granadensis* requires a semishady position during the summer, but plenty of bright light during the winter if its flowers, which bloom in late spring, are to develop. It can tolerate temperatures as low as 33°F (1°C) during the winter. This small, attractive, fast-growing plant is therefore ideal for a cool position, and suits a shallow dish perfectly.

Keep the compost damp all year round by watering it from below. It must not become waterlogged. Mist frequently, but not when it is flowering.

Feed every two weeks.

Although this plant is often thrown away after its berries have died, it can flourish for several years. Extend its life by placing it in a cool position and keeping its compost barely moist during the winter. Increase the temperature once it starts flowering. Repot in multipurpose compost when new growth is just becoming visible in early spring.

Propagate either by division or by sowing its seeds (which germinate very easily) in spring.

This plant is occasionally attacked by aphids. If its conditions are too wet, gray mold (*botrytis*) will take hold.

# Ocimum

Basil, or *Ocimum basilicum,* to give this Mediterranean plant its botanical name, is a very useful herb to have growing on the kitchen windowsill, not least because it is supposed to keep flies at bay. When they are crushed or cut, its pale-green, oval leaves release their strong flavor, which, depending on the variety, can resemble cinnamon, lemon, or a sharp spice. The tiny, white flowers that bloom at the top of the plant's stems can also be used for flavoring food.

## Cultivating *Ocimum Basilicum*

Once it has become well established in its pot, *O. basilicum* likes a bright, sunny position and a temperature ranging from 59 to 75˚F (15 to 24˚C), making a kitchen windowill an ideal position. You could either display it on its own or position its pot with those of other herbs in a herb basket.

Basil will quickly wilt if its compost becomes dry (but will revive if the compost is then soaked), so ensure that it always remains damp, but do not let it become waterlogged. You could also mist the plant (see below), which may mark its leaves, but will not affect their flavor.

Feed it a weak solution of fertilizer every week.

When harvesting its leaves, pick off the top of the stem just above a leaf junction to ensure that it grows again (cutting off the whole stem will prevent its regeneration). Discard the plant once it has withered.

Propagate by sowing its seeds in a shallow container in late winter, keeping them at a temperature ranging from 70 to 75˚F (21 to 24˚C), and pricking them out into individual pots when they are large enough to handle. Once the seedlings have started to thrive, place them outside in a warm, sheltered position.

Aphids can infest the plant, so discourage them by spraying it with water,. But because this is a culinary herb, do not treat it with an insecticide.

# Olea

A native of the Mediterranean areas of Europe, *Olea europaea*--commonly known as the olive tree--is a slow-growing, open-branched, evergreen shrub that can grow to a height of 10 ft (3 m) when cultivated in a tub. Its willowlike, dark-green leaves, which are lancet- (spear-) shaped, measure ¾ to 3 in (2 to 8 cm) in length, and have gray-green surfaces and silvery-gray undersides. Clusters of tiny, fragrant, white flowers appear in late summer, and are followed by small, glossy, plumlike fruits that start life green and then turn black.

## Cultivating *Olea Europaea*

*O. europaea* needs full sun and a temperature between 64 and 82.4°F (18 and 28°C) during its growing season, but a light, airy position and a temperature between 41 and 50°F (5 and 10°C) during its winter resting period (it requires this dramatic variation in temperature if it is to bloom the following year). A good container plant for a sunny conservatory, it can be placed outside during summer. *O. europaea* is an ideal subject for bonsai cultivation.

Water regularly during the spring and summer, making sure that any excess water drains away. Keep the compost dry during the winter.

Feed every two weeks during the spring and summer.

Plant a young olive tree in John Innes No. 3 compost, in a pot to which you've added drainage material, such as crocks. Thereafter, only pot the plant on in spring when it has become pot-bound, into a container that is just one size larger than its previous one. Top-dress it when it has become too big to move. If necessary, prune it in late spring to maintain the desired shape.

Propagate by taking stem cuttings in late summer and encouraging them to root by providing heat from below.

This plant is untroubled by pests, but will rot if it becomes waterlogged.

# Opuntia

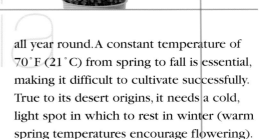

Two members of the *Opuntia* genus of desert cacti, *Opuntia microdasys* and *O. robusta,* are particularly popular houseplants.

A native of northern Mexico, *O. microdasys* branches freely. The "pads" that grow on top of one another, lending the plant its common name of bunny ears, are light green, fleshy, and dotted with areoles (sunken areas) containing clusters of barbed bristles, which may be yellow, white, or brown. Its yellow flowers are followed by red fruits. *O. robusta* (the prickly pear) bears bright-yellow flowers.

When buying *Opuntia,* remember that these cacti should have a fresh, clean-looking appearance. Any that are shriveled is an indication that they have been cultivated in unsuitable conditions.

## Cultivating *Opuntia*

*Opuntia* needs a position that gets bright light, full sun, and plenty of fresh air all year round. A constant temperature of 70° F (21° C) from spring to fall is essential, making it difficult to cultivate successfully. True to its desert origins, it needs a cold, light spot in which to rest in winter (warm spring temperatures encourage flowering).

Water thoroughly from spring to midfall, making sure that any excess water drains away and allowing the compost to dry between waterings. Keep the compost almost dry in winter, but give *Opuntia* a little water if it appears to be shriveling up.

Feed a cactus feed once a week.

When pot-bound, repot using free-draining compost in spring.

To propagate, remove an offset or "pad" in spring and let the cut surface dry out before planting it in free-draining compost or peat, where it will root easily.

This plant is vulnerable to attacks by mealy bugs, scale insects, and red spider mites.

## Caution
Take care when handling *Opuntia* because its barbed hairs will irritate the skin.

# Osmanthus

*Osmanthus heterophyllus* 'Variegatus', which originates in Japan, is an evergreen shrub that can reach a height of up to 6 ft ( 2 m). Its green, leathery leaves are edged with yellow and resemble holly leaves in shape, which is why its common name is false holly. Although its small, white, fragrant flowers bloom in clusters during the fall when it is growing in its natural conditions, it rarely flowers when it is kept inside. The leaves of *O. heterophyllus* 'Purpureus' are nearly black.

## Cultivating *Osmanthus Heterophyllus*

*O. heterophyllus* enjoys a bright position (and can tolerate both some sun and partial shade) and a temperature of 59°F (15°C). It can be placed outside during the summer and otherwise makes a good container plant for a cool conservatory, where it can be trained into a standard.

Water carefully during its growing season to ensure that it does not become waterlogged, allowing its compost almost to dry out between waterings. During the winter, let its compost become nearly dry. Mist during its growing season.

Feed once a month.

Repot in spring only if it is pot-bound, using multipurpose compost. To maintain its shape, prune it in spring.

Propagate in spring by taking stem cuttings.

This plant is rarely attacked by pests, but can suffer from stem rot if it becomes waterlogged.

**Caution**
If you have children, think carefully about where best to position *O. heterophyllus* because its spiky leaves may injure them.

# Pachyphytum

*Pachyphytum oviferum* is a succulent from Mexico that is similar to *Echeveria* in that it has erect, thinly branched stems when it is young; these become prostrate with age. One of this plant's common names is sugar-almond plant (another being moonstones) on account of its thick, egg-like leaves that, although predominantly grayish-blue in color, have a lavender-tinted patina that gives them an almost smoldering appearance as they crowd together at the top of their stems. The rich-red flowers cluster together atop stalks from late winter to early spring.

## Cultivating *Pachyphytum Oviferum*

*P. oviferum* requires an airy, brightly-lit position that receives some full sun, and can be stationed outside during the summer. It prefers a temperature ranging from 60 to 68°F (16 to 20°C) in the spring and summer, but needs a temperature of 46.4 to 50°F (8 to 10°C) in winter if it is to flower the next year. It will happily grow on a hot, sunny windowsill, and will look very attractive in a succulent dish garden.

Its leaf tissue retains water, so water the plant thoroughly all year, letting any excess water drain away. Then do not water it again until the compost has dried out. Do not allow water to come into contact with its leaves.

Feed with a weak fertilizer once a month during its growing season.

Repot in spring, but only when it becomes pot-bound, and then into a shallow container using free-draining compost. Remove shriveled leaves as soon as you see them.

Propagate by taking stem or leaf cuttings in spring and leaving the cut edges to dry out before planting them in free-draining compost.

The plant will remain untroubled by pests, but its roots may rot if it becomes waterlogged, especially during the winter.

# Pachystachys

The easy-to-grow *Pachystachys lutea* (lollipop plant), a native of Peru, is an evergreen shrub that can reach a height of 3 ft (1 m) and is smothered in flowers from late spring to fall. Its stiff, upright stems bear spear-shaped, very thick, glossy, green leaves that are deeply veinedand grow to lengths of 4 to 7 in (10 to 18 cm). At the top of each stem grows a conical spike, 1½ to 2 in (4 to 5 cm) long, that consists of golden-yellow bracts from which the small, white flowers bloom.

Before buying this plant, ensure that it has plenty of flower buds, but not lots of flowers because it will then be past its best.

## Cultivating *Pachystachys Lutea*

*P. lutea* needs a brightly lit position and a temperature from 64 to 70°F (18 to 21°C), but can tolerate temperatures as low as 59°F (15°C). It must not be put in a drafty place and is perhaps best suited to a conservatory or garden room.

From spring to fall, keep the compost moist, allowing excess water to drain away. Water less during winter. The plant enjoys humidity, so place its pot on a pebble tray.

Feed every two weeks during the spring and summer.

Pot on each year in spring, using multi-purpose compost. Remove a young plant's stem tips in spring to promote bushiness. Prune in spring to maintain its shape and promote bract growth. After flowering, cut back the yellow bracts to half their length.

Propagate by taking stem or leaf cuttings or sowing its seeds in late spring or summer.

If conditions are too wet, this plant can be attacked by aphids, mealy bugs, and gray mold (*botrytis*). It will shed its lower leaves if its conditions are too cold.

# Passiflora

If its conditions are favorable, *Passiflora caerulea,* a native of tropical America and Asia, can grow at a considerable rate. The passionflower, as it is commonly called, is so named because missionaries thought that they could see elements of Christ's crucifixion in its flowers. Although the flowers do not last long individually, the continuous succession of blooms from early summer to fall makes up for that.

You can buy a passionflower at any time of year. Look for one that has green, fresh-looking leaves and plenty of buds. Note that although these plants are usually sold trained around wire hoops, they will soon outgrow these supports.

## Cultivating *Passiflora Caerulea*

*P. caerulea* likes the brightest and sunniest position possible. When situated inside, it prefers a well-ventilated room and a temperature ranging from 55 to 64°F (13 to 18°C). It can cope with higher temperatures, but then becomes vulnerable to attack by red spider mites. It makes an attractive addition to a conservatory or garden room, but will climb up almost anything, including other plants.

This plant needs plenty of water during the summer, so ensure that its compost is always very moist. Water less often during winter, but don't let its compost dry out. Mist the leaves frequently.

Encourage this plant to flower by giving it a high-potash feed once a week in summer, and then once a month for the rest of the year.

This plant flowers more readily when slightly pot-bound. If you do need to repot it, do so carefully in spring as it resents having its roots disturbed. Use John Innes No. 3 compost, making sure that its roots are firmly anchored within it. Prune it hard in fall, after flowering.

Propagate by taking stem cuttings in summer or sowing its seeds in spring, which will then take a few years to flower.

This plant is targeted by voracious aphids, red spider mites, and whiteflies.

# Pelargonium

Ivy-leaved pelargonium.

There are so many species and varieties of the *Pelargonium* genus of flowering plants (whose members are often commonly called geraniums) that it is impossible to describe them all in this book. They have become popular houseplants because they are so easy to care for and often flower freely from spring to fall. They can take the form of delicate trailers, exquisite miniatures, or lovely, big, and blowsy plants, rounded flower heads that bloom all year. Some varieties are grown for their attractive, variegated foliage rather than for their flowers.

As their name suggests, the stems of ivy-leaved pelargoniums bear ivy-shaped leaves. These trailing plants are particularly suitable for hanging baskets, and although their flower heads are more open and delicate, they can bloom just as well if regularly fed.

Scented-leaved pelargoniums, which have very delicate flowers, are grown for their fragrant leaves, which, when crushed,

Regal pelargonium.

Regal pelargonium.

Regal pelargonium.

and their single or double flowers, some of which are heavily scented, bloom in every color (apart from yellow and blue).

Zonal pelargoniums are the most common. These plants are bushy and densely branched, with leaves that are soft and velvety to the touch and big,

release scents reminiscent of rose, lemon, mint, or peppermint.

The woody stems of regal pelargoniums bear large, serrated leaves. Although they produce fewer flowers than zonal varieties, their flower heads are larger and have bright markings or patterns.

Scented-leaf pelargonium.        Scented-leaf pelargonium.

## Cultivating *Pelargonium*

To flower well, it requires an airy, dry position in full light with plenty of sun that is not exposed to drafts. It will tolerate any temperature between 50 and 68°F (10 and 20°C) in its growing season, and should be kept at 50°F (10°C) in winter. It is vital to feed it sparingly if you're hoping for a good display of flowers. Too much fertilizer will prompt foliage to grow, not blooms.

Repot young plants every spring; older ones should be top-dressed as they flower better when pot-bound. Always use good-quality compost. Prune back the plant's top growth in the winter resting period.

During its growing season, soak its compost with water and let it dry out between waterings. Keep it fairly dry over winter. Do not mist or its flowers will rot.

Provide a weak feed once a month when in bud.

Propagate by taking stem cuttings in late summer. New plants will flower the following year.

Almost all pests attack pelargoniums, including aphids, vine weevils, mealy bugs, and whiteflies, and it's vital to treat an infestation quickly. The plants can also suffer from stem rot, rust, and, if the atmosphere is too cold and moist, gray mold (*botrytis*).

Zonal pelargonium.

# Pentas

*Pentas lanceolata*, originally an east African plant, is a subshrub that grows to a height of 23 in (60 cm) and has hairy, spear-shaped, light-green leaves that measure 2 to 3 in (4 to 9 cm) in length. The appearance of its pink, white, red, or violet, star-shaped flowers explains why this plant's common name is Egyptian star cluster, being held as they are at the end of the stems in dense clusters measuring 2 in (4 cm) in diameter.

When buying this plant, select a specimen that has plenty of buds rather than flowers.

## Cultivating *P. Lanceolata*

A flowering plant that will brighten the winter months, *P. lanceolata* likes a light, airy position that receives some sun and a year-round temperature ranging from between 59 and 68°F (15 and 20°C).

Water regularly during its growing season to ensure that its compost is always moist. During the winter, allow the compost to dry out between waterings. Once the flower buds have set, mist

Feed once a week during its growing season.

Pot on after it has finished flowering, and prune it hard to maintain its shape. The plant has a tendency to become straggly, so promote bushiness by regularly pinching out its growing tips.

Propagate in spring either by taking stem cuttings or by sowing its seeds and providing some heat from below.

Pests rarely attack this plant. If its leaves turn yellow, this a sign that the plant has become waterlogged.

# Peperomia

Three species of the *Peperomia* genus of foliage plants are usually grown as houseplants.

*Peperomia caperata*, a native of Brazil, is a bushy plant with small, corrugated, glossy, deep-green leaves. It bears a profusion of upright, tail-like catkins, or "mouse tails," on pinkish stems from spring to winter.

*P. scandens* 'Variegata', which originates in Peru, is a trailing variety making it useful for hanging baskets. It produces pink leaf stalks with small, green-and-cream, heart-shaped leaves.

*P. magnoliifolia* , a West Indian plant commonly called the desert privet, displays cream-and-green variegation on its glossy leaves. As the plant ages, its leaves turn green.

*Peperomia caperata.*

Before buying this plant, check its stems for signs of rot, which is irreversible.

## Cultivating *Peperomia*

*Peperomia* requires a humid atmosphere and prefers temperatures ranging from 55 to 64°F (13 to 18°C). Its ideal position is in an airy, light, draft-free spot to discourage mold. Depending on its growing habit, it can be put on a windowsill, in a hanging basket, on a bromeliad tree, or in a terrarium, while all species and varieties are suited to hydroponic cultivation.

This plant stores water in its leaves, and will rot if overwatered, so water it carefully all year round with soft water or rainwater. Allow its compost nearly to dry out between waterings, but never let the plant become so dehydrated that it wilts. Never mist the leaves.

Feed every two weeks in spring and summer, and monthly during fall and winter, always with half-strength fertilizer.

It dislikes having its roots disturbed, so pot it on only every two years in spring, into peaty, gritty, free-draining compost. After potting on, water very cautiously to prevent its stem from rotting.

Propagate either by dividing its crowns in late spring or by taking stem cuttings in spring or summer.

Red spider mites can attack, but gray mold (*botrytis*) and stem rot due to overwatering are far worse threats.

# Petroselinum

*Petroselinum crispum*, which originates in Mediterranean regions, is better known as parsley. Both a useful kitchen herb and an attractive foliage plant, its leaves may be curled or flat (flat-leaved varieties often have more flavor).

*P. crispum* can be planted in a strawberry pot or hanging basket or be grown in a pot on the kitchen windowsill.

## Cultivating *Petroselinum Crispum*

Propagate *P. crispum* by sowing its seeds at any time from spring to the end of summer. Sow them in a deep pot filled with multipurpose compost, making sure that they are covered by a layer of compost up to ½ in (1 cm) deep. Place the pot in a moist and warm place--ideally in a propagator set at 64°F (18°C)--and then wait for them to germinate, which can take up to six weeks. Once this has happened, there may be too many seedlings crowding the pot, in which case thin them out and plant the surplus seedlings in separate pots. Thereafter, position them in a sunny spot, such as on a windowsill, perhaps moving them outside on sunny summer days.

When the plant is established in its pot, always keep its compost moist.

To encourage more leaves to grow, cut back the plant's stems hard. Discard it when it has stopped sending up new shoots.

Sowing its seeds in rotation as described above will ensure that you have a year-round supply of this herb.

This plant is unaffected by pests and diseases.

# Phalaenopsis

A native of tropical Asia, *Phalaenopsis*, or the moth orchid, is one of the most beautiful of the orchidaceous plants. It has strong, aerial roots that grow outside the pot, and it produces only a few thick, leathery leaves at a rate of one a year. Its pink-and-white flowers appear as long, arching sprays, sometimes blooming twice in one year.

The guidelines below provide general information on how to care for this orchid (see also pages 71 to 72), but always follow any growing instructions provided when you bought it.

## Cultivating *Phalaenopsis*

*Phalaenopsis* should be exposed to bright light (but not direct sunlight) for up to fifteen hours a day in both summer and winter. It requires a temperature ranging from 70 to 80.6°F (21 to 27°C) during the day and a nighttime temperature of 50°F (10°C). It makes a good plant for a terrarium or bromeliad tree, as well as a striking pot plant for a hot and humid room. It will also efficiently remove chemical pollution from the atmosphere.

Water regularly, draining away excess water. Keep it dry during its resting period. Mist its leaves (but not its flowers) regularly with tepid water and place its pot on a pebble tray to increase the humidity

Feed weekly with orchid food in spring and summer.

Pot on after flowering (use orchid compost, available from garden centers), only when completely pot-bound. After flowering, cut the stalk just below the node that produced the first flower to encourage it to branch out and produce more flowers.

Propagate this plant by division when repotting it.

Aphids and scale insects may attack, but root rot caused by overwatering is a more common problem.

# Phoenix

*P. canariensis.*

*Phoenix canariensis,* the Canary date palm, which originates in the Canary Isles, has dark-green, feathery leaves when young that arch with age and spread to form a dense crown. A North American native, *P. dactylifera* (the date palm) is not as graceful as other species of *Phoenix*, and has slightly more upright, gray-green leaves.

## Cultivating *Phoenix*

*Phoenix* likes a light, airy, sunny position all year round. It is important that it receives enough light, although not strong sunlight, and it can be positioned outside during the summer. It will, however, tolerate semi-shady conditions. Temperatures ranging from 60 to 70°F (16 to 21°C) in its growing season, and cooler temperatures in winter, are needed. Suitable for hydroponic cultivation, it can play a useful role in removing chemical pollutants from the air.

Water its compost from the top and ensure that any excess drains away Mist its fronds regularly, and sponge mature leaves with water occasionally to remove dust.

As soon as a young plant is established, feed little and often in spring and summer.

Like other palms, *Phoenix* dislikes having its roots disturbed, so pot on only when it has become pot-bound, making sure that the compost is firmly compacted around its roots.

This plant can be grown from a stone saved from a packet of dates (see page 50). Propagating from seed is difficult. Although offset reproduction is more successful, young palms need a warm, humid atmosphere for their first few months.

*P. canariensis.*

Red spider mites and scale insects can plague this plant. Its foliage becomes discolored if it is fed insufficiently. Root rot caused by waterlogging is the biggest threat to this plant.

P. depressa.

# Pilea

The foliage plants that belong to the *Pilea* genus are available in both upright and creeping forms. Two of the most popular species are *P. cadierei* and *P. depressa*.

*Pilea cadierei* (aluminum plant), the most popular species, is a native of Vietnam that grows to a height of about 12 in (30 cm). Its bushy, succulent stems hold spear-shaped leaves that are dark green in color, with raised, silver-gray blotches between rather sunken veins.

P. cadierei.

A native of Puerto Rico, *Pilea depressa* (creeping Jenny) has prostrate stems that will root if they come into contact with compost to form thick mats. Its leaves are an attractive bright-green color.

## Cultivating *Pilea*

*Pilea* flourishes in shady surroundings and should never be positioned in direct sunlight. It prefers temperatures ranging from 59 to 70°F (15 to 21°C) and should not be exposed to temperatures below 55°F (13°C) or to drafts. It is suitable for warm, humid rooms, hydroponic cultivation, and terrariums. *P. depressa* can be displayed to good advantage in a hanging basket.

Water in spring and summer with warm water from above, ensuring that any excess water drains away. Then let the surface of the compost dry out between waterings. In winter, allow the compost to become totally dry before watering it again.

Feed every time that you water it.

Pot on in spring, into ericaceous compost. Prune in spring, but remove any dead leaves when you spot them. The plant tends to become leggy after a few years, so pinch out its growing tips frequently to retain its bushiness. When it looks really messy, take cuttings for propagation and then throw the plant away.

Propagate in summer by taking stem cuttings, planting them in peat-based compost, and applying bottom heat.

Mealy bugs and red spider mites can plague this plant. If its conditions are too wet, especially during the winter, it will soon succumb to gray mould (*botrytis*).

# Pittosporum

*Pittosporum*, which originates in eastern Asia and Australia and is commonly called Japanese pittosporum, is an attractive genus of evergreen trees whose foliage is commonly used in floral arrangements. Of the available species, the most generally found are *Pittosporum tobira*, *P. tobira* 'Variegatum', and *P. tenuifolium.*

*P. tobira* is an evergreen tree or shrub that has dense foliage and can reach a height of 10 ft (3 m). Its shiny, leathery, oval leaves have smooth edges and are a deep-green color. Its creamy-white, star-shaped flowers, which are borne in clusters, have a strong fragrance. The blooms are followed by attractive, red seed capsules that are covered in an annoying sticky secretion.

The leaves of *P. tobira* 'Variegatum' have silvery-gray markings and cream margins.

*P. tenuifolium* makes an excellent foliage shrub. It has an erect tendency, grayish-green leaves, and red flowers.

## Cultivating *Pittosporum*

*Pittosporum* needs an airy position in bright light to partial shade all year round. It prefers temperatures ranging from 50 to 59 °F (10 to 15 °C) during the summer, when it can be stationed outside, and a minimum temperature of 41 °F (5 °C) during the winter. This decorative tub plant suits a bright conservatory.

Water regularly during the spring and summer, but keep its compost barely moist in winter. Mist its leaves all year round.

Feed once a week from spring to the end of fall, then once a month in winter.

Pot on into multipurpose compost every year in spring until it reaches the required height, when you should top-dress it instead. It can be pruned into any shape.

Propagate by sowing its seeds in spring or by taking stem cuttings in late summer, in both cases providing bottom heat.

Scale insects and red spider mites readily attack this plant. If the edges of its leaves turn brown, it has been receiving insufficient water. If it wilts, water it, and it should then quickly recover.

# Platycerium

Natives of Africa, Australia, and South America, the members of the *Platycerium* genus of evergreen plants are epiphytic ferns that have an unusual, commanding appearance. Each plant has both sterile and fertile fronds; the sterile ones specialize in taking up nutrients and water and create humus as they rot.

*Platycerium birfurcatum*, commonly known as stag's-horn fern, has evolved flat, sterile fronds, with which it attaches itself to trees. The leathery, dark-green, fertile fronds are antler-shaped and branch into narrow lobes. They can grow to a great size when the plant is mature. Their growing habit is both spreading and drooping.

The fronds of *P. grande*, the regal elk-horn fern, can grow to lengths of up to 6 ft (2 m). Its dark-green, fertile fronds are fan-shaped, deeply lobed, and both semierect and floppy in their growing habit.

## Cultivating *Platycerium*

*Platycerium* likes light to partial shade all year round. It prefers a constant temperature ranging from 59 to 70°F (15 to 21°C), but can tolerate temperatures as low as 55°F (13°C) in winter. It dislikes a dry atmosphere. It can be cultivated in a warm conservatory, displayed with other plants in a hanging basket.

Water regularly, with warm, soft water or rainwater, all year round so that its compost remains moist, but is never waterlogged. It enjoys a very humid atmosphere, so mist it frequently and perhaps position its pot on a pebble tray.

Feed with a weak fertilizer once a month from spring to the end of summer.

A young plant can either be tied to an epiphytic support or planted in orchid compost. Remove the fertile fronds when they die, but not the sterile fronds because these will provide nutrients to the parent plant.

Propagate by encouraging its spores to germinate or by dividing it in spring.

Scale insects may target this plant if the air around it is too dry.

# Plectranthus

The South African native *Plectranthus oertendahlii*, which belongs to a genus of plants whose common name is Swedish ivy, is an evergreen subshrub whose four-angled stems carry opposing pairs of leaves and clusters of spiky, tubular flowers that are pale lavender in color. A prostrate plant, its trailing stems, which grow to lengths of between 12 and 23 in (30 and 60 cm), root easily when they come into contact with damp compost. Its low-growing, rounded leaves are dark-green, with a cream-colored, scalloped edging and a purplish underside. The leaves give off a strong scent when rubbed.

Before buying a Swedish ivy, check its central foliage for mold.

## Cultivating *Plectranthus Oertendahlii*

A light, airy position out of direct sunlight is ideal for this plant all year round, as well as a temperature between 64 and 70 °F (18 and 21 °C) during its growing period and not lower than 50 °F (10 °C) in winter. It makes a good ground-cover container plant and looks eye-catching in a hanging basket.

During its growing season, water it regularly, keeping its compost moist, but never allowing it to become waterlogged. In winter, let the surface of the compost dry out between waterings. Mist regularly during spring and summer.

Feed every two weeks during its growing season.

Pot on in spring every year using multipurpose compost. Promote a more rounded shape when the plant is young by pinching out its growing shoots. It will have become very straggly after two or three years, however, when it is best thrown away.

This plant is easy to propagate, either by taking stem cuttings in late spring or summer or by dividing it in spring, in both instances encouraging growth by providing heat from below.

Scale insects may infest this plant if its conditions are too dry.

# Plumbago

*Plumbago auriculata* is a South African plant (common name Cape leadwort). It is a robust climber that produces clusters of slender flowers, resembling *Phlox* and bloom, from spring to fall. Its flower heads bear tubular blooms, while its dark, evergreen leaves are oval.

The flowers of most *Plumbago* plants are pale blue, but there is a white variety--*P. alba*--and you can create an interesting display by encouraging a blue- and a white-flowering plant to intertwine as they climb up the same support.

## Cultivating *Plumbago*

*Plumbago* likes light (but not direct sunshine) and temperatures ranging from 60 to 64°F (16 to 18°C) during its growing season. It should be kept in a cool position in winter, but a temperature higher than 41°F (5°C) will encourage it to flower in spring. This long-blooming plant is ideal for a cool conservatory, where it can show off its climbing ability to good effect.

Water regularly in spring and summer. In winter, keep its compost barely moist and allow the surface to dry out completely between waterings.

Feed once a week from the start of spring to the end of summer.

Pot on in spring into multipurpose compost. Deadhead frequently to extend its flowering period. If it is being encouraged to grow up a wall, provide support--either a trellis or canes. It responds well to pruning and can be cultivated as a pot plant for many years if reduced in size by two-thirds after flowering each year.

Propagate by taking stem cuttings in early summer or by sowing its seeds in March. Any plants that you raise from seed should flower in their first year.

It remains evergreen when its winter conditions are warm, but will quickly shed its leaves if it is too cold.

# Poinsettia

*Poinsettia pulcherrima* (or *Euphorbia pulcherrima*) is originally from Mexico. It is a very popular houseplant at Christmas time Its small flowers are outshone by its clusters of bright-red bracts--recent cultivars can be pink or creamy white

Do not buy a *Poinsettia* that has been displayed in a cold or drafty store as its bracts will drop as soon as you get it home.

## Cultivating *Poinsettia Pulcherrima*

If its bracts are to keep their color, *Poinsettia* requires plenty of bright light in winter. It dislikes sudden changes of temperature so much that it will shed its leaves, so do not place it in a drafty spot. It should have a constant temperature ranging from between 59 and 70°F (15 and 21°C) in fall and winter, but can tolerate cooler temperatures in the spring and summer. It provides a splash of color when few other houseplants are in flower. It suits a warm, light room. It is amenable to hydroponic cultivation.

Keep its compost moist in winter, or when flowering. After flowering, it's best to discard it. If you wish to keep it, reduce the amount of water you give it.

Feed every time that you water the plant in its flowering season.

When its bracts have died back, cut its stems to a height of 4 in (10 cm) and put the plant in a warm, dry position. When you can see new growth, repot into nutrient-rich compost and start watering and feeding the plant regularly.

Once new growth is visible in summer, propagate by taking cuttings, planting them in peat-based compost, and keeping them in humid conditions at about 70°F (21°C).

This plant is vulnerable to attack by whiteflies, gray mold (*botrytis*), and root rot if its conditions are too wet in winter. If its leaves are wilting, water it at once, and it should quickly revive.

# Polyscias

Perhaps the most popular member of the *Polyscias* genus of foliage plants is *Polyscias balfouriana* (dinner-plate aralia), which originates in tropical Asia. A bushy, evergreen shrub with distinctive foliage, it has heart- or kidney-shaped leaves that are a glossy, dark-green color, narrowly edged with white. Its twisted stems can reach a height of 5 ft (1.5 m) when it is grown in a pot.

## Cultivating *Polyscias*

*Polyscias* enjoys a light position, but not direct sunlight, and prefers a year-round temperature of 64°F (18°C). It is best in a light, warm, humid room or conservatory and can be cultivated using hydroponics.

Keep its compost moist in spring and summer, but water it less, and allow its compost almost to dry out between waterings, during winter. It requires a humid atmosphere if it is to thrive, so place its pot on a pebble tray and mist frequently.

Feed the plant once every two weeks from spring to the end of summer, and once a month during fall and winter.

Repot in spring, into nutrient-rich compost, until it becomes too large to do so, when you should top-dress it, again annually in spring.

Propagate by taking stem cuttings, but note that it is notoriously difficult to encourage such cuttings to root.

The plant is susceptible to scale insects and aphids if the atmosphere is too dry.

# Primula

The *Primula* genus of flowering plants consists of some four-hundred species of clump-forming, evergreen, and deciduous perennials, including the popular polyanthus and primrose. These plants originate in both northern Europe and Asia.

All varieties of *Primula* have a basal rosette of oblong-shaped leaves from which grow stalks with individual flowers or groups of flowers. All bloom in shades of pink, purple, red, yellow, or white.

Breeders have developed *P. vulgaris*, the common primrose, into an excellent, short-term pot plant that can tolerate chilly conditions. (Some can be forced to bloom in time for Christmas, but should be planted in the garden after flowering.)

The polyanthus *P.* x *tommasinii* is a hybrid with wrinkled leaves, whose large flowers bloom at the end of strong stems.

*P. malacoides*, which is named fairy primrose because of its dainty appearance, is the most popular *Primula* houseplant variety. Its oval, wavy-edged leaves form many rosettes, and its small, star-shaped flowers bloom in tiers in succession on thin stems that grow to lengths of between 11¾ and 13¾ in (30 and 35 cm).

*P. sinensis*, commonly called Chinese primrose, is a short-lived plant whose long, hairy leaves form a central rosette. This plant starts flowering in February and continues for many months, the blooms initially appearing in the center of the rosette, then growing higher as the stems develop, so that they are eventually held in whorls at the top.

*P. obconica* is commonly called poison primrose because of its allergenic properties. It produces flowers throughout the year in cool and moist conditions. It can also be cultivated as a houseplant for a second year.

✳ When choosing a *Primula*, look for one with plenty of buds, but few flowers. Check for mold at the base of the plant, and if you find it, don't buy the plant.

## Caution
**If handled, the leaves of both *P. sinensis* and *P. obconica* can trigger an allergic reaction.**

primula

## Cultivating *Primula*

During flowering, all varieties prefer moist, shady conditions (with no direct sunlight) and temperatures ranging from 50 to 60°F (10 to 16°C). The cooler the temperature, the longer the flowers will last and new ones will bloom.

While flowering, keep the compost moist by watering with soft water or rainwater. Do not let it become waterlogged or dried out, especially in hot conditions. Mist the leaves frequently, and ideally place the pot on a pebble tray.

Feed once a fortnight during the flowering season.

The tender *P. malacoides* and *P. sinensis* should be discarded after they have stopped flowering. Few species of *Primula* will need potting on, the exceptions being occasionally *P. obconica* and the hardy *P. vulgaris* and *P.* x *tommasinii,* which should be potted on in ericaceous compost. These hardy varieties should be returned to the garden after they have ceased blooming. Deadhead all *Primula* plants to promote prolonged flowering.

Propagate by sowing seeds in summer, into acid or ericaceous compost (which should not be covered). If they are to flower in the same year, the seeds of *P. obconica* and *P. siensis* are best sown in spring. As they dislike their roots being disturbed, it is important to pot on the resulting seedlings into the pot in which you intend them to remain for the rest of their lives, using ericaceous compost.

Aphids and red spider mites may attack these plants, but root rot or gray mold (*botrytis*)--due to overwatering, poor air circulation, or the root having been planted too deeply--are far more likely to cause the plant's death.

# Pseuderanthemum

*Pseuderanthemum atropurpureum* originates in Polynesia and is closely related to the *Eranthemum* genus of plants. It is erect and shrubby, and will grow to a height of 5 ft (1.5 m) if not pruned regularly. It is mainly cultivated for the attractive color of its foliage: purple flushed with green. Its slender, tubular-shaped, purple flowers consist of five petal lobes and have a red-purple eye. *P. atropurpureum* 'Tricolor' has deep-purple leaves splashed with white, pink, and green.

## Cultivating Pseuderanthemum atropurpureum

*P. atropurpureum* requires a position in light to partial shade, but no direct sun, and a year-round temperature of 60˚F (16˚C). It should not be exposed to drafts, which will cause its leaves to drop, and is best suited to a warm, humid conservatory.

Keep its compost moist throughout the year by watering it regularly with room-temperature soft water or rainwater. Allow it to dry out between waterings in winter. Mist the leaves in spring and summer.

Feed the plant every two weeks during its growing period.

When it becomes pot-bound, pot the plant on in spring, into nutrient-rich compost. Prune when new growth appears to maintain the plant's shape and size.

Propagate in spring or early summer by taking stem cuttings, treating them with a rooting hormone, and keeping them at a temperature ranging from between 68 and 77˚F (20 and 25˚C) until they have rooted.

Although this plant can fall victim to aphids, it is more prone to rotting if its compost is too wet.

# Punica

Better known as the pomegranate, *Punica granatum*'s place of origin ranges from southeastern Europe to the Himalayas. It is a deciduous shrub that can grow to heights of up to 6 ft (2 m), although the maximum height of the dwarf variety 'Nana', which is generally cultivated as a houseplant, is only 17 in (45 cm). This variety makes a neat bush with tiny, oblong, glossy leaves that are bright green in color and ¾ to 3 in (2 to 8 cm) long. Appearing in summer, its tubular-shaped flowers, which measure 1½ in (4 cm) across, are a brilliant, orange-red color and have cup-shaped, crinkled edges. The blooms are followed by leathery, miniature pomegranates (which are not edible), whose orange-brown color is tinged with red.

## Cultivating *Punica Granatum* 'Nana'

If it is to develop its inedible fruits, *Punica granatum* 'Nana' must be placed in a position that is light and sunny all year round. It can be situated outside during the summer, and can survive temperatures as low as 43°F (6°C) during winter, although it will then lose its leaves (they will quickly grow again in the spring, however). It makes a very attractive plant for a conservatory that can be cultivated as a small standard.

Water regularly from spring to the end of summer, making sure that any excess water drains away. During winter, water only when its compost is dry, especially if the plant suddenly drops all its leaves.

Feed the plant every two weeks during its growing season.

A young plant can remain in a pot whose diameter is 6 in (15 cm) for several years, when it should be top-dressed in spring. But when it becomes pot-bound, pot it on in spring using multipurpose compost. It is best pruned when its new leaves appear in spring, and it is easy to train into any shape, but ideally a standard.

It is easy to propagate this plant in spring by sowing its seeds; any young plants that result should flower in the same year. Alternatively, take stem cuttings in summer.

Pests and diseases rarely attack this plant.

# Rhapis

*Rhapis excelsa* (little lady palm), which is originally from southern China, resembles a bamboo on account of its erect, fibrous, nonbranching stem, which produces suckers freely and can grow to 5 ft (1.5 m) in height. Its leaves are composed of three to ten leathery, veined, dark-green leaflets that fan out like the fingers of an open hand.

Check that the leaves are undamaged before buying this palm.

## Cultivating *Rhapis Excelsa*

If *R. excelsa* is to thrive, it requires a position in good light--but not strong sunlight--although it can tolerate semi-shade. It likes a humid atmosphere, temperatures ranging from between 60 and 70°F (16 and 21°C) during its growing season (it can be stationed outside during the summer), and cooler temperatures during the winter. An attractive palm for a semishady position, it is suitable for hydroponic cultivation. Its ability to remove chemical pollutants from the air makes it an eco-friendly plant.

Water thoroughly throughout the year from the top of the pot, and ensure that any excess water drains away because being waterlogged will swiftly kill it. Stand its pot on a pebble tray to increase the humidity around it, regularly mist its fronds, and remove dust by sponging its mature leaves with water.

As soon as a young plant has become established, feed it little and often during the spring and summer months.

Pot it on into multipurpose compost in the spring, but only when it becomes pot-bound as it dislikes having its roots disturbed. To encourage new roots to grow, compact the new compost firmly around its existing roots and do not water.

Propagating by planting its offsets in spring is usually quite successful,

Red spider mites and scale insects can attack this plant if the air around it is too dry. Being fed insufficiently will cause its foliage to become discolored, but the biggest threat is the root rot that can set in.

# Rhoicissus

A native of India, *Rhoicissus rhomboidea* (which is sometimes wrongly named *Cissus rhombifolia*, both species sharing the common name of grape ivy) is a very tough, evergreen, climbing plant whose tendrils form at the tips of its stems. If it is allowed to climb or trail, it will reach a height or length of 10 ft (3 m), and although it is easy to train along any framework, it needs support or tying in.

When choosing a *R. rhomboidea* plant, look for one that has plenty of glossy, green leaves. Damaged or yellowing leaves are a sign that the plant is sick.

## Cultivating *Rhoicissus Rhomboidea*

This plant enjoys a position in bright light or shade (and can be situated in a shady spot outside during the summer), but cannot tolerate direct sunlight, which burns its leaves. It prefers temperatures ranging from between 59 and 70°F (15 and 21°C), but will cope with much lower temperatures as long as it is not in a direct draft. A robust plant that tolerates limited light, it is suitable for stairways and is also a good climbing plant to train up a room-divider or conservatory wall.

Water regularly all year, but do not allow its compost to become waterlogged because this will cause its leaves to drop and its roots to rot. Mist it frequently all year round.

Feed once a week during its growing season and once a month in fall, but not at all during the winter.

Every spring, either pot it on into multipurpose compost or if the plant has grown too large, top-dress it. Pinching out new growth in spring will make it bushier and curb its climbing habit. Trim back its foliage in fall. If necessary, support it with canes.

Propagate in spring or early summer by taking stem cuttings that have two or three leaves. (Bottom heat may speed up the rooting process, but is not essential.)

This plant's leaves and roots are very vulnerable to being attacked by mealy bugs, which should be removed as soon as you see them. The leaves turning brown or dropping are signs of overwatering.

# Rosmarinus

Rosemary, or to give it its official botanical name, *Rosmarinus officinalis*, is an evergreen Mediterranean shrub whose foliage's distinctive smell evokes the lazy days of summer and that can grow to a height of 3 ft (1 m) when cultivated in a pot. Its opposite pairs of fragrant, deep-green leaves resemble needles in shape and have hairy, silvery-gray undersides. Lavender-blue flowers measuring ¾ in (2 cm) in length bloom at the ends of the stems throughout the spring and summer; *R. officinalis* 'Albiflorus' has white flowers, while *R. officinalis* 'Roseus' has lilac-pink blooms.

Rosemary is a very useful culinary herb that is also reputed to aid the circulation (try adding some stem cuttings to your bath water).

## Cultivating
## R. Officinalis

*R. officinalis* thrives when it receives plenty of light (including full sun) throughout the year. In winter, it will survive temperatures as low as 35°F (2°C) as long as its compost is dry. It makes an ideal plant for a windowsill, not least because it enjoys the hot and sunny conditions (up to 82°F, or 28°C) that other plants would not easily survive.

Water sparingly all year round, allowing the surface of the compost to become dry between waterings, but never letting it dry out completely.

Feed once a month from spring until the middle of summer.

Pot it on in spring when it becomes pot-bound, into a loam-based compost like John Innes No. 2 or 3. If pruning becomes necessary, cut its stems back by one-third after they have flowered. Young, supple stems can be trained into a variety of shapes by tying them in, and this plant can also be trained as a standard. If any of the stems lose their leaves, cut them back to their base and they should then grow back.

Propagate by taking stem cuttings in spring and summer, which should root very easily.

This plant is rarely attacked by pests or diseases.

# Ruellia

A native of Brazil, *Ruellia mackoyana,* whose common name is monkey plant, has a shrubby shape and produces stems that grow to lengths of between 7 and 17 in (20 and 45 cm) and that can either be left to trail or can be attached to a support to create a more upright plant.

Its velvety, spear-shaped leaves measure 3 in (8 cm) in length and are deep green in color, with white veins and purple undersides. Its trumpet-shaped, purple-red flowers grow in clusters at the end of the stems throughout the year, but mainly in summer. *R. macrantha* has dark-green leaves and flowers whose color ranges from purple to rose-pink.

## Cultivating *Ruellia*

*Ruellia* likes a lightly shaded position out of direct sunlight and a constant temperature ranging from between 68 and 75°F (20 and 24°C). It is suitable for a warm and humid room.

Keep its compost moist all year round. To increase the humidity of the atmosphere around it, place its pot on a pebble tray. Mist its leaves regularly.

Feed every two weeks when it is flowering.

In fall, pot the plant on into ericaceous compost to which you've added some charcoal chips. Maintain an attractive shape by pruning it back after flowering.

Propagate in summer by taking root cuttings and providing heat from below.

Although this plant is generally untroubled by pests and diseases, its leaves will drop if its conditions are too cold.

# Saintpaulia

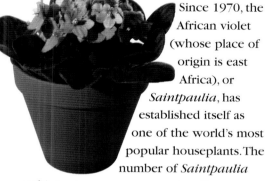

Since 1970, the African violet (whose place of origin is east Africa), or *Saintpaulia*, has established itself as one of the world's most popular houseplants. The number of *Saintpaulia* cultivars is now enormous, together offering flowers that range from white through pink, red, violet, and purple to bi-colored blooms, in single, double, and semidouble displays. Attractive minis have recently become available, too, which have very small leaves and flowers.

*Saintpaulia's* dark-green, velvety, rounded leaves sprout on short stalks from the plant's base to form a dense rosette.

When choosing a plant, check that it has not been kept in chilly conditions, that its leaves and stems are firm, not droopy, that there is no basal rot, and that it has few flowers, but plenty of buds.

## Cultivating *Saintpaulia*

*Saintpaulia* requires bright light and some direct sun, as long as it is not hot, midday sun. It must always be protected from drafts and prefers temperatures ranging from between 64 and 70°F (18 and 21°C). It is ideal for a bathroom or kitchen, and also for displaying in groups in a large container.

Water from below, using tepid, soft water or rainwater, and ensure that any excess drains away. It will survive cool temperatures if its compost is kept slightly dry. *Saintpaulia* enjoys very humid conditions, so position its pot on a pebble tray or pack its container with moist peat.

Feed it a weak solution of fertilizer every time that you water it.

Pot *Saintpaulia* on only when it becomes really pot-bound, and then into peat-based compost and a small plastic pot, both of which it prefers. Deadhead it regularly to prolong its flowering period, ensuring that you do not leave the stalk behind when removing the flower because this will encourage basal rot to set in.

Propagate this plant either by taking cuttings of a whole leaf and stalk or by dividing the crown in spring and providing a constant temperature of 70°F (21°C).

*Saintpaulia* may be attacked by mildew, gray mold (*botrytis*), aphids, and mites, but is more likely to be killed by root rot caused by overwatering.

# Salpiglossis

*Salpiglossis sinuata*, which is a member of a genus of plants whose common name is painted tongue, is a native of South America. Its erect stems, which grow to lengths of between 23 and 35 in (60 and 90 cm), branch at the top to display thin, oval leaves with wavy margins. (These leaves are largest at the plant's base and become smaller the farther up the stem they grow.) Its funnel-shaped, colorful flowers measure 2 in (6 cm) in length and 2 in (5 cm) in width and open to reveal five lobes that are either red, purple, blue, yellow, and/or cream in color, often with veins of contrasting shades.

## Cultivating *Salpiglossis Sinuata*

S. *sinuata* enjoys a bright position, with some direct sunlight, and temperatures ranging from between 50 and 62°F (10 and 17°C), making it suitable for a conservatory.

Keep its compost moist all year round, but never let it become waterlogged. Mist its leaves when the weather is hot, but do not allow water to come into contact with its flowers.

Stake *S. sinuata* if necessary, and deadhead regularly to prolong its flowering season. Throw it away after it has finished flowering because the plant will not flower in subsequent years.

Propagate by sowing its seeds in spring and then, when they have germinated, planting the seedlings in the pots in which they will remain for the rest of their lives (*S. sinuata* dislikes being disturbed). These young plants should flower in the summer or fall of the same year.

S. *sinuata* is not normally plagued by pests or diseases.

# Salvia

*Salvia officinalis*, whose common name is sage, is a herb that originates in southern Europe. This densely branched subshrub has square-shaped stems and wrinkled, oval, gray-green leaves that measure 1 to 2 in (2 to 6 cm) in length. In summer, its flower spikes bear tubular, two-lipped, blue blooms. *S. officinalis* 'Icterina' has golden, variegated leaves, while *S. officinalis* 'Purpurascens' has dark-purple leaves.

All varieties of *Salvia* can safely be used as culinary herbs, and also make attractive pot plants for a kitchen windowsill.

## Cultivating *Salvia*

*Salvia* likes plenty of light--including sunlight--all year round, and will flourish in summer temperatures of 82°F (28°C). As long as its compost is dry, it will survive winter temperatures as low as 41°F (5°C). It makes an ideal plant for a sunny windowsill.

Water sparingly throughout the year, letting the surface of the compost become dry between waterings, but never allowing it to dry out completely.

Feed once a month from spring until the middle of summer.

When the plant becomes pot-bound, pot it on in spring into a loam-based compost, such as John Innes No. 2 or 3. If it becomes necessary to prune it, cut its stems back by one-third after it has ceased flowering.

Propagate by taking stem cuttings in spring or summer (which should root very easily).

This plant is hardly ever attacked by pests or diseases.

# Sansevieria

The members of the *Sansevieria* genus of plants are natives of Africa and southern Asia. They will grow vigorously during the summer months if their conditions are favorable. If they are looked after correctly, clusters of small, green-white, fragrant flowers will appear in spring. Depending on the variety, they can be tall or small, but all have stiff, pointed leaves.

*S. trifasciata* 'Laurentii', whose common name is mother-in-law's tongue, is a tall, variety. *S. trifasciata* is commonly called the snake plant because its leaf markings (silvery-gray bands across a deep-green background) resemble those of a snake.

Before buying a *Sansevieria* plant, ensure that its leaves are not damaged and that their spiny tips are intact (their loss inhibits growth).

## Cultivating *Sansevieria*

This plant thrives in bright light, with some direct sun, but will also tolerate light shade. It prefers temperatures of between 64 and 80°F (18 and 27°C), and will survive temperatures as low as 55°F (13°C)--the lower the temperature, the dryer its compost should be.

Water regularly during spring and summer, allowing the surface of its compost to dry out between waterings. During fall and winter, ensure that its compost dries out fully between waterings.

Feed a weak fertilizer once every three or four weeks during its growing period; take care not to overfeed it.

*Sansevieria* prefers being pot-bound, so should only be repotted if it breaks out of its pot, in a loam-based compost like John Innes No. 3 and a massive pot to balance its tendency to become top-heavy.

Propagate in summer either by removing plantlets with plenty of roots from the parent plant or, if it is a green-leaved variety, by taking leaf cuttings. *S. trifasciata* 'Laurentii' should be propagated by division to prevent new plants' leaves from reverting to plain green.

Rarely attacked by pests, but can suffer if overwatered or put in too cold a spot.

# Saxifraga

A native of eastern Asia, *Saxifraga* is a genus of alpine plants that are grown for their attractive leaves and red runners, and have terminal plantlets with roots, hence its common name, mother of thousands.

*S. stolonifera* (which is sometimes called *S. sarmentosa*) is a creeping or trailing plant whose hairy, round- to kidney-shaped leaves have coarse-toothed edges. These dark-green leaves are threaded with silver veins and have reddish undersides. Its flower stems hold sprays of dainty, starlike, white flowers, which bloom in summer well above the leaf rosette. *S. stolonifera* 'Tricolor', which has cream-, yellow-, and pink-variegated foliage, is slightly smaller.

Before buying a *Saxifraga* plant, check that its leaves are undamaged and that there are no dead leaves in the center.

## Cultivating *Saxifraga*

*Saxifraga* prefers a light position (but not direct sunlight or drafts), although it will tolerate some shade. It thrives in cool conditions and likes temperatures as low as 40°F (4°C), but can also survive temperatures as high as 73.4°F (23°C). *Saxifraga* is suitable for a cool conservatory or an unheated room and can be grown to good effect in a hanging basket or trough or when positioned on a pedestal.

During spring and summer, water it regularly, allowing excess water to drain away and keeping its compost barely moist. During winter, water it only when its compost has dried out. The warmer its conditions, the more it will benefit from being misted.

Feed a weak concentration of fertilizer when you water it in spring and summer.

Pot it on in spring, into John Innes No. 2 or 3 compost to which you have added some grit. Regularly remove dead or dying leaves to avert mold. Remove flower stems after blooming, and trim back its foliage to curb its tendency to become straggly.

Propagate by detaching plantlets and planting them in individual pots in a 50:50 mix of John Innes No. 2 or 3 compost and grit. Water sparingly until they have rooted.

This plant is susceptible to being attacked by whiteflies and aphids. Its roots will rot if it is overwatered, which usually proves fatal.

# Schefflera

*Schefflera actinophylla* originates in Australia, and is sometimes sold as *Brassaia actinophylla*. It has been a popular houseplant for many years because of its attractive shape and evergreen leaves, although it rarely flowers when grown in pots. Its spear-shaped, leathery leaflets are glossy green in color. Growing at the top of long stalks, five to sixteen of these leaflets radiate from a central point like the spokes of an umbrella, which is why *S. actinophylla's* common name is umbrella tree. This robust plant is capable of growing to heights of between 6 and 9 ft (2 and 3 m).

Before buying a *S. actinophylla* plant, make sure that its leaves are undamaged and look a shiny, rich green.

## Cultivating *Schefflera*

*Schefflera* will tolerate most conditions, but is happiest when in bright light, but no direct sun. It prefers to be kept at a constant temperature of 64°F (18°C), but will cope with a few degrees lower or higher. Its tolerance makes it suitable for novice houseplant-growers or people who don't have much time.

### Caution
*Schefflera* can irritate some people's skin.

During spring and summer, water regularly to keep the compost barely damp. Water less in winter, when you should allow the surface of the compost to dry out between waterings. Mist it frequently during the summer.

Feed every two weeks from spring to the end of summer.

Repot in spring in multipurpose compost when it becomes pot-bound. Prune the main stem back to a node to reduce its height or prevent it from becoming too large. Keep its leaves shiny by regularly wiping them with a cloth moistened with water.

Propagate in spring, either by sowing seeds or by air-layering and then providing a temperature of 70° (21°C) from below.

This plant is vulnerable to rather a lot of pests, particularly aphids, red spider mites, mealy bugs, and scale insects.

# Scindapsus

A species native to Southeast Asia and China, *Scindapsus aureus*'s common name is devil's ivy. It is also sold as *Epipremnum aureum* (or golden Pothos). *S. aureus* sends out aerial roots that wrap around the nearest object, making it an ideal plant to grow up a moss stick or to train around a framework of canes. It can grow to a height or length of 6 ft (2 m) and has heart-shaped leaves, which are dark-green in color, with yellow variegation. *S. aureus* 'Marble Queen' has leaves that are darker green and marbled with white.

Before buying, check that its leaves are shiny, firm, and have no brown patches, usually a sign of gray mold (*botrytis*).

## Cultivating *Scindapsus Aureus*

Its leaves will lose their variegation if exposed to poor light for too long, so *S. aureus* should be placed in a bright situation, but not in direct sunlight. It requires a temperature ranging from 59 to 70°F (15 to 21°C) during its growing season, and 59°F (15°C) during its winter resting period. It is suitable for hanging baskets and hydroponic cultivation.

### Caution
*S. aureus*'s sap irritates the skin.

During its growing season, do not overwater it and ensure that its compost dries out between waterings. In winter, give it just enough water to keep its compost barely moist. If the atmosphere is dry, mist it frequently, and perhaps position its pot on a pebble tray and wipe its leaves.

Feed every two weeks during its growing season.

When it becomes pot-bound, pot on in spring, into nutrient-rich compost; when it becomes too large, top-dress it. To promote bushiness, prune back its main stems in spring.

Propagate in spring by taking stem cuttings and applying rooting hormone.

It is rarely attacked by pests or diseases.

# Sedum

The Mexican plant *Sedum morganianum* is commonly called donkey's tail, and as a member of the *Crassulaceae* family of succulents, is referred to as stonecrop. It is an unusual succulent subshrub because its branching, pendant stems can trail 3 ft (1 m) in length. They are also covered with fleshy, bluish-green, cylindrical leaves that are covered in a bloom. Small, red flowers cluster at the ends of the stems in spring.

Take care when handling this plant as its leaves fall off after the slightest of touches.

## Cultivating *Sedum Morganianum*

*S. morganianum* requires a light, sunny position all year round, but should be protected from the midday sun in summer, when it can be placed outside, or else near an open window, to enable it to enjoy plenty of fresh air. It prefers a cool temperature at night of 50°F (10°C) and needs to be exposed to a temperature of 50°F (10°C) in winter if it is to flower in spring. Its trailing stems make it suitable for a hanging basket, perhaps situated in a conservatory.

Water thoroughly in summer, allowing its compost to dry out between waterings. Water about once a month during the rest of the year, and then only sparingly.

Feed this plant once a month in spring and summer.

Pot on in spring, but only when it is pot-bound (it looks more attractive when it is spilling out of its pot), into free-draining compost and a pot to which you've added plenty of crocks.

Propagate by taking stem or leaf cuttings and letting the cut edges dry out before planting them in free-draining compost and watering them sparingly.

This plant is rarely attacked by pests, but easily develops root rot if overwatered.

# Selaginella

Members of the *Selaginella* genus of plants, whose common name is club moss, originate in tropical rainforests and so require a very humid, warm atmosphere. The foliage of these spore-bearing plants, which are closely related to ferns, consists of crowded masses of tiny, coarse leaves.

*Selaginella uncinata*, the rainbow fern, has densely tufted stems that radiate outward and bear bright-blue, metallic-looking leaves.

*S. kraussiana* is a prostrate, mat-forming variety and has bright-green, oblong leaves, the leaves of *S. kraussiana* 'Variegata' having creamy variegations.

*S. martensii* is an erect, fernlike plant that grows to a height of 11 in (30 cm).

*S. lepidophylla*, the resurrection plant, has branches that radiate inward to form a rosette. When its conditions are dry, it contracts to form a ball that expands again when it is remoistened.

## Cultivating *Selaginella*

*Selaginella* is ideal for a partially shaded position because the slightest direct sunlight burns its leaves. It prefers a temperature ranging from 64 to 70°F (18 to 21°C) for most of the year, and should be exposed to no lower than 60°F (16°C) in winter. It is suitable for bottle gardens, as well as for warm conservatories.

Water regularly with tepid, soft water or rainwater throughout the year so that its compost remains damp. It likes a very humid atmosphere, so mist it often with tepid water and place its pot on a pebble tray or surround it with moist compost.

Feed once a month all year round.

Repot in spring when pot-bound, in ericaceous compost. Remove any dead foliage to prevent mold spores setting in.

Propagate by division in spring or take stem cuttings from spring to fall.

This plant is not susceptible to pests, but can be attacked by mold.

# Sempervivum

Natives of the French and Spanish Pyrenean region, the *Sempervivum* genus of succulents (common name houseleeks) is easy to look after. Indeed, its Latin name means "always alive." The succulent leaves, which grow in a variety of colors, form tight, attractive rosettes

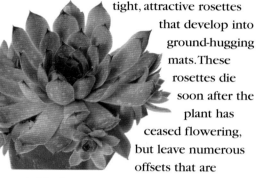

that develop into ground-hugging mats. These rosettes die soon after the plant has ceased flowering, but leave numerous offsets that are suitable for propagating.

*Sempervivum tectorum*'s common name is roof houseleek because it was often seen growing on the roofs of country buildings, which was thought to be a sign of good luck. This plant grows vigorously, producing clusters of star-shaped, reddish-purple flowers in summer.

The oval, fleshy leaves of *S. archnoideum*, which have tiny red tips, form an evergreen mat covered with a web of white hairs, hence its common name, cobweb houseleek. In summer, its star-shaped, rose-red flowers cluster at the ends of stems.

## Cultivating *Sempervivum*

*Sempervivum* requires a light, sunny position all year round. It can be placed outside or near an open window in summer (it thrives on fresh air). It enjoys cool night-time temperatures of 50°F (10°C), summer temperatures of 64.4 to 69.8˚F (18 to 21°C), and a winter temperature of 50°F (10°C) to encourage it to flower. It looks attractive in a succulent dish garden or an unusual container.

Water thoroughly in summer, allowing its compost to dry out between waterings. During the rest of the year, give it only a little water once a month.

Feed once a month in spring and summer.

Pot on in spring (when it becomes pot-bound as it looks attractive spilling over the edges of its pot), into free-draining compost and a pot with plenty of crocks.

Propagate by taking leaf cuttings and letting the cut edges dry out before planting them in coarse compost.

This plant is rarely targeted by pests. The main cause of death is root rot due to overwatering.

# Senecio

Consisting as it does of over three-thousand species, ranging from trees to succulents, *Senecio* is the largest genus of flowering plants. All have alternate leaves and daisylike, composite flowers.

*Senecio macroglossus*, which originates in South Africa and whose common name is Cape ivy, is a semisucculent, evergreen climber that can reach a height of 9 ft (3 m) or more. The leaves of *S. macroglossus* 'Variegatus' have cream veins and edges.

Although it is a member of the same genus as *Senecio*, *S. rowleyanus* is an entirely different plant whose place of origin is southwest Africa. Its bright-green, translucent, spherical leaves look as though they have been strung on their long, threadlike, hanging stems, which is why its common name is string of beads.

Its sweetly scented flowers have white florets and purple stamens that resemble miniature shaving brushes. This succulent will suit people who do not have much time to spend on looking after their houseplants.

*Senecio cruentus*--which is perhaps better known as cineraria--is a native of the western Mediterranean regions. Its large, green leaves, whose undersides are covered with gray hairs, surround a mass of daisy-shaped flowers. A plant that brings some color into the home during the winter months, *S. cruentus* is usually sold from December through to spring. It is best bought when its buds are beginning to show a little color.

Before buying this plant or positioning it with others, check it very carefully for pests.

## Cultivating *Senecio*

All varieties of *Senecio* like a light position, but will tolerate some shade as long as they are exposed to bright light during the winter and a minimum temperature of 46°F (8°C).

*S. macroglossus* and *S. rowleyanus* can be placed outside or near an open window in summer, and all enjoy warm temperatures of 60 to 68°F (15 to 18°C). The trailing varieties are suitable for hanging baskets in conservatories and garden rooms, where they will grow rapidly, enabling you to train their stems around the room. *S. cruentus* is ideal for a light, warm room.

Water thoroughly in spring and summer, letting the compost dry out between waterings. In winter, water sparingly once a month.

Feed *Senecio* once a month in spring and summer.

senecio

Repot *S. macroglossus* every two years in spring, into multipurpose compost, and remember, the bigger its pot, the larger it will grow. Once it has reached the required size, top-dress it once a year in spring. Because it grows so rapidly, it is best trained up a support or framework of canes. Alternatively, cut its stems back to a leaf joint in the spring and pinch out its growing shoots to create a more manageable, bushy plant.

*S. rowleyanus* is at its most attractive when it is spilling out of its pot, so pot on in spring, only when it becomes pot-bound, using free-draining compost and a pot containing lots of crocks.

*S. cruentus* should be regarded as an annual and thrown away after flowering. If properly looked after, it will flower for two or three months.

Propagate *S. macroglossus* by taking stem cuttings during the spring and summer.

Propagate *S. rowleyanus* by taking leaf cuttings in the spring and allowing the cut edges to dry out before planting them in coarse, gritty compost and watering them sparingly.

*S. rowleyanus.*

Propagate *S. cruentus* by sowing its seeds in late spring; the plants that result should flower in winter.

*S. macroglossus* is vulnerable to being infested by aphids and scale insects.

*S. rowleyanus* is rarely attacked by pests, but its roots may rot if it is overwatered.

*S. cruentus* is very vulnerable to aphids, fungi, and almost every known pest. If it appears to be wilting, place it in a cool, shady spot for a day, after which it should revive (don't be tempted to water it, though, because as strange as it may seem, this will make it wilt even more).

# Solanum

*Solanum* is a genus of shrubs and climbers that comprises about one-thousand six-hundred species, including the potato and tomato. The best-known houseplant species is *Solanum capsicastrum*, a native of Brazil, a bushy, evergreen shrub that grows to a height of 11 in (30 cm). Its

S. capsicastrum.

bright-red berries appear at Christmas time, hence its common name, winter cherry. It has oval, dark-green leaves with wavy edges and its berries are preceded by white, star-shaped flowers that bloom in summer.

Choose a plant whose foliage is deep green down to compost level--yellowing can indicate a root problem. Its berries should be starting to turn red or orange.

## Cultivating *Solanum*

*Solanum* needs plenty of light, with some direct sun, and will drop its berries in a shady spot. For lots of berries, place it in an airy situation with a temperature of between 50 and 59°F (10 and 15°C). It is suitable for a cool, light windowsill.

> ## Caution
> ***Solanum capsicastrum*'s berries are poisonous.**

During its growing season, water it regularly to ensure that its compost remains moist and never dries out. After its berries have died, let the compost dry out slightly between waterings and then start watering it frequently again once new growth shows. Misting it occasionally will encourage its berries to set.

Feed this plant once a week during its growing season.

When its berries have died, prune back its stems. In fall, pot it on into multipurpose compost, watering and feeding it regularly. Although this plant can be grown as a standard, this requires patience.

Propagate either by sowing its seeds in spring and providing heat from below to encourage a display of berries at Christmas time or by taking stem cuttings in spring.

This plant is targeted by whiteflies, aphids, and red spider mites. Gray mold (*botrytis*) can afflict it if its compost is too wet. If its foliage begins to turn yellow, water it with a solution of 1 teaspoon of Epsom salts to 17 fl oz (500 ml) of water.

# Spathiphyllum

*Spathiphyllum wallisii*, better known as the peace lily, originates in Colombia and is related to the *Anthurium* genus of plants. Its spear-shaped, glossy, dark-green leaves are carried on long, thin stems that grow in thick clumps to a height of 11 in (30 cm). Its cream-colored flowers, which bloom at the end of equally long stems from May to August in the northern hemisphere, change from white to green as they age.

S. x 'Mauna Loa' is a larger variety.

When choosing a plant, look for flowers that are in bud rather than in bloom, and don't buy a plant with drooping leaves.

## Cultivating *Spathiphyllum*

*Spathiphyllum* thrives best in a light situation that receives no direct sunlight, although it enjoys slightly shady conditions in summer. It prefers a year-round temperature of 64°F (18°C), and should be protected from drafts, which will kill it. It should do well in a bright, warm, and humid room. It is also an excellent subject for hydroponic cultivation.

Keep its compost moist all year round by watering it regularly with soft, tepid water, but do not allow it to become waterlogged. Because it likes a very humid atmosphere, mist its leaves frequently and perhaps position its pot on a pebble tray.

Feed this plant every two weeks when it is flowering.

Repot every year in spring, into ericaceous compost and a pot with plenty of drainage material. After all of its flowers have died, remove the flower stalks to avert the danger of basal rot setting in.

Propagate this plant by dividing it in spring.

It may be attacked by aphids, mealy bugs, and red spider mites if the atmosphere around it is too dry.

# Stephanotis

The flamboyant-looking *Stephanotis floribunda* (common names wax flower and Madagascar jasmine) originates in southern Asia. A natural climber, its twining stems grow to a height of 16 ft (5 m), and its masses of highly scented flowers are often included in bridal bouquets. Its thick, evergreen leaves are a shiny dark green and shelter its white, waxy flowers that emerge from May to October in northern climes.

When choosing a plant, look for one with shiny leaves, lots of flower buds, and only a few blooms.

## Cultivating *Stephanotis Floribunda*

*S. floribunda* needs a light position out of direct sunlight all year round. A temperature between 64 and 72°F (18 and 22°C) in summer, and one of 59°F (15°C) in winter, is ideal. But ensure that it never sinks below 50°F (10°C). It is suitable for a light conservatory, where its stems can be trained to grow around the room or tied into a wire hoop.

Water regularly in spring and summer with soft water or rainwater so that its compost remains moist. In winter, allow the surface to dry out between waterings. Mist its leaves in summer, but do not let water come into contact with its flowers.

When it is flowering, feed it with a weak solution of fertilizer when watering.

Repot in spring, into multipurpose compost. Prune in fall, after flowering, to maintain its shape.

Propagate either by sowing its seeds or by taking stem cuttings in summer.

This plant is targeted by scale insects, mealy bugs, and gray mold (*botrytis*).

# Strelitzia

Once seen, *Strelitzia reginae* is never forgotten, and yet its spectacular appearance belies the fact that it is easy to care for.

No description can do this South African plant justice. Its leathery, evergreen leaves are gray to blue-green in color, resemble a blunt spear shape, and grow at the top of long, thick stems. Its long-lasting flower is shaped like a bird's head--which is why *S. reginae*'s common name is bird of paradise--and consists of bright, sky-blue stigmas and three orange or yellow sepals, with one small, orange petal emerging at right angles from a boat-shaped bract.

## Cultivating *Strelitzia Reginae*

*S. reginae* should be placed in a light position that receives sunshine in winter, but no direct sunlight during the summer. It is vital that the temperature around it never drops below 50°F (10°C) in winter and 60 to 65°F (15 to 18°C) in summer. It makes a spectacular specimen plant for a light conservatory or large room.

Water this plant regularly during the spring and summer, ensuring that any excess water drains away and allowing the surface of the compost to dry out between waterings. Water sparingly during the winter. Mist its leaves occasionally.

Feed every two weeks during its growing season.

After it has ceased flowering, repot it into John Innes No. 3 compost. You can encourage it to flower by keeping it pot-bound or by adding superphosphate fertilizer when watering, to the top few inches of its compost.

Propagate by division in early spring, when you should cut through the roots with a sharp knife, which will do less damage than trying to pull them apart. Alternatively, sow its seeds and provide some heat from below, but be warned that any plants that result will not flower for three to five years.

Scale insects and aphids tend to attack this plant.

# Streptocarpus

*Streptocarpus rexii* (a native of South Africa that has clusters of blue, trumpet-shaped flowers) and *S. saxorum* (a hanging variety with small, rounded leaves) are members of a genus whose common name is Cape primrose. There are many hybrids available, such as S. x *hybridus* 'Concorde hybrid', which is a small plant that flowers in a wide range of colors from spring to late summer. Its clump-forming leaves lack stems and grow in a prostrate rosette formation. The leaves are narrow, hairy in texture, and easily damaged. Thin, wiry flower stalks rise above the leaves in succession and hold trumpet-shaped flowers that are white, pink, red, light or dark blue, and violet.

This plant is best bought in late spring. Look for one with leaves that bend upward, with plenty of buds and a few flowers. Do not buy one with limp leaves that hang over the edge of the pot.

## Cultivating *Streptocarpus*

If it is to flower throughout the summer, this plant requires a light position (but not one in direct sunlight) and a temperature ranging from 55 to 64°F (13 to 18°C). If its conditions are cooler, keep its compost almost dry. Keep it out of drafts to prevent its leaves from becoming limp. Its winter rest period should be spent in cool conditions to promote flowers the next spring.

Water regularly with soft water when it is flowering, using the immersion method. Rewater when the compost is dry. Water it less in winter. Mist it often if the air is dry.

When it is flowering, and only then, feed it weekly with a tomato fertilizer.

Pot on in spring, into nutrient-rich compost. To prolong flowering, deadhead and remove flowering stems regularly.

Propagate in spring, either by division or by taking leaf cuttings and keeping them at a temperature of 70°F (21°C).

It is vulnerable to attack by aphids and red spider mites, as well as gray mold (*botrytis*) if its compost is too wet.

# Streptosolen

*Streptosolen jamesonii* (marmalade bush), which originates in Colombia and Ecuador, is an evergreen, scrambling shrub that can grow to 6 ft (1.8 m) in height. Its alternating oval leaves are 1 in (3 cm) long, wrinkled, and deep green in color. Masses of bright-orange, tubular flowers, which grow to lengths of between 1 and 2 in (3 and 4 cm) and flare at the mouth to a width of ¾ in (2 cm), bloom at the ends of thin, weak stems during the spring and summer.

## Cultivating *Streptosolen Jamesonii*

A brightly lit position is essential for *S. jamsonii,* especially during the winter, but not one that receives direct sunlight. Although a year-round temperature of 59°F (15°C) is advisable, it will happily tolerate conditions that are a few degrees warmer or cooler. This plant is suitable for a conservatory, where it can either be trained as a standard or grown in a hanging basket.

When it is flowering, water it regularly and thoroughly to ensure that its compost remains damp. Allow it to dry out slightly between waterings during the winter. Mist its leaves occasionally, but try not to let any water come into contact with its flowers.

Feed every two weeks from spring to the end of its flowering season.

Repot into multipurpose compost when it has ceased flowering, when it can also be pruned to maintain its shape. Its weak, flexible stems can easily be tied into a framework or up a firm support if it is being trained as a standard. Its spreading stems also look attractive when the plant is grown in a hanging basket.

Propagate by taking stem cuttings in spring or summer.

*S. jamsonii* is rarely troubled by pests or diseases.

# Syngonium

*Syngonium podophyllum* (also sold as *Nephthytis triphylla*) originates in tropical America and is related to the *Philodendron* genus. A large climber, the leaves change shape as it matures, until they resemble a goose's foot (hence its common name, goosefoot plant).

When immature, it is a small, compact plant with triangular, arrow- or heart-shaped leaves, which, as the plant ages, divide into three- and then five-lobed leaflets. The leaves become paler as the plant matures.

*S. podophyllum* 'Green Gold' has arrow-shaped leaves that are a variegated yellow-green color. The leaves of *S. podophyllum* 'Imperial White' have a white-to-cream-colored, central rib.

## Cultivating *Syngonium Podophyllum*

If it is a variegated variety, the plant

should be positioned in a light, sunless position; if it is an all-green variety, it should be situated in a semishady spot. It should be exposed to warm temperatures all year round and to temperatures no lower than 53.6°F (12°C) in winter. It will thrive if grown in a warm conservatory and responds well to hydroponic cultivation.

During its growing season, water it regularly to keep its compost moist. During winter, allow the surface of its compost to dry out to a depth of 1 in (3 cm) between waterings. It relishes high humidity, so mist its leaves often with warm water and stand its pot on a pebble tray.

Feed every two weeks during its growing season, but not at all in winter.

When it is pot-bound, repot in multi-purpose compost in late spring, until it is the required size, then top-dress it annually. To promote bushiness, pinch back its shoots. Provide a climbing framework or a moss stick, or encourage its stems to trail by planting it in a hanging basket.

Propagate in summer by taking stem cuttings that have one or two leaves.

This plant is targeted by scale insects.

# Thunbergia

*Thunbergia alata* (black-eyed Susan) is an easily cultivated annual from tropical Africa. Its climbing stems, which rapidly reach a height of 9 ft (3 m), hold opposing, deep-green, triangular leaves with serrated edges. Its tubular, five-lobed flowers, which can grow to a length of 1½ in (4 cm), are carried on long stalks that grow from the leaf axils and are white to creamy-yellow or pale orange in color, with chocolate-colored centers. They bloom profusely from late spring into the fall.

Before buying one, check that the plant's foliage isn't turning yellow because this is a sign that it has become infested with red spider mites, to which it is particularly prone.

## Cultivating *Thunbergia Alata*

Position this plant in an airy, light, and sunny spot (but protect it from the midday sun) and maintain a temperature of 64°F (18°C) around it. It will flourish in a conservatory and is well suited to a hanging basket or large pot.

Water this plant regularly to keep its compost constantly moist, but do not allow it to become waterlogged because this will cause its stems to rot. If the atmosphere around it is dry, mist .

Feed it once a week when it is flowering. Deadhead it regularly to prolong its flowering period. Discard the plant once it has finished flowering.

Propagate from late winter to early spring by sowing its seeds in multipurpose compost. When the seedlings are large enough to handle, prick them out and plant them in pots, allocating three seedlings to each pot. As they grow, provide the young plants with climbing supports, such as canes, suspended strings, or preformed frames. To encourage a bushier growing habit, pinch out the tips of the young stems.

This plant is very susceptible to being attacked by red spider mites.

# Thymus

A native of southern Europe, thyme, or *Thymus vulgaris*, is a low-growing, shrubby herb whose tiny, evergreen leaves exude a wonderful, aromatic fragrance. Its foliage grows in a variety of colors, and it has dainty little pink, purple, or white flowers that bloom in summer.

The evergreen foliage can be cut all year round for culinary use.

habit. Trimming its leaves will create a bushier plant.

Propagate either by division or by sowing its seeds in spring.

This plant is invulnerable to pests and diseases.

## Cultivating *Thymus Vulgaris*

*T. vulgaris* requires a sunny and warm position throughout the year. This useful herb can be grown successfully in a hanging basket.

Water only when its compost is dry, when you should soak it and then let any excess water drain away.

Feed the plant a weak solution of fertilizer once a month.

When it is spilling out of its pot, and only then, pot it on into free-draining compost in spring, when it is best to divide it to encourage a more vigorous growing

# Tillandsia

The members of the *Tillandsia* genus are bromeliads that originate in South America.

*Tillandsi*a *caput-medusae* and *T. usneoides* are members of the epiphytic group. More commonly known as air plants, they can flourish on little more than the moisture in the atmosphere. In their natural environment, they secure themselves directly to trees or bare rocks, making them ideal specimens to cultivate on bromeliad trees or pieces of wood or rock. (And this is how they are often bought.) *T. caput-medusae* is an air plant with a large, bulbous base, while *T. usneoides* (Spanish moss) resembles a beard made up of dense, gray threads. *T. argentea's* very narrow, threadlike leaves are covered with white scales and emerge from a bulbous base.

*T. lindenii*, whose common name is blue-flowered torch, is an evergreen. Its basal rosette consists of long, grasslike leaves. Long, bladelike spikes grow above the leaves, bearing wide, deep-blue flowers that emerge in summer from green, pink-tinted bracts.

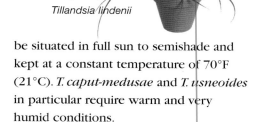

*Tillandsia lindenii*

## Cultivating *Tillandsia*

All varieties of *Tillandsia* should be situated in full sun to semishade and kept at a constant temperature of 70°F (21°C). *T. caput-medusae* and *T. usneoides* in particular require warm and very humid conditions.

Water regularly with tepid, soft water, allowing any excess water to drain away and letting the top third of the compost dry out between waterings. Mist its foliage with warm, soft water twice a day in spring and summer, and once a week in winter.

Feed once a month during spring and summer by misting with a very weak solution of soluble fertilizer.

It's rarely necessary to repot it, but if you do, it's important to use free-draining compost (perhaps one used for orchids) and to add lots of crocks to the pot.

Propagate by removing its offsets or, in the case of *T. usneoides*, its shoots at any time of year.

Although *Tillandsia* is untroubled by pests, it will die if its roots become waterlogged.

*Tillandsia argentea.*

# Tolmiea

*Tolmiea menziesii* originates in western parts of North America. The mounds of pale-green foliage that this clump-forming plant produces can grow to 23 in (60 cm) in height. Its leaves are slightly hairy, tooth-edged, and resemble a maple leaf in shape. In summer, spikes of greenish-white, tubular flowers grow on long flower stems. The interesting thing about *T. menziesii* is that perfectly shaped, miniature plants grow from the point where the leaf stalk joins the leaf, giving rise to the plant's several common names, which include piggyback (or pick-a-back) plant, mother of thousands, and youth on age. These plantlets can be removed and planted in pots.

When choosing a plant, select one that has bright-green leaves because yellowing foliage is a sign that it has been suffering in poor conditions.

## Cultivating *Tolmiea Menziesii*

A hardy plant that can adapt to most conditions (apart from direct sunlight), *T. menziesii* prefers a light position, but can survive in shade for short periods of time. Because it thrives in temperatures ranging from 44 to 59°F (7 to 15°C), it is particularly suitable for a cool room. Show off the plantlets that form at the end of its stems to their best advantage either by positioning its pot on a pedestal or by planting it in a hanging basket.

Water it regularly during the spring and summer to keep its compost moist (but less so during the winter), allowing it to dry out between waterings

Feed this plant a weak fertilizer every time that you water it during the spring and summer, but do so only occasionally during the fall and winter.

Repot every year in spring, into multipurpose compost. Remove any dead leaves as soon as you see them.

Propagate either by removing its offsets at any time of year or by dividing it in spring. (Note that the offsets will grow very quickly, and that you may therefore have to pot them on more than once a year.)

Red spider mites will attack this plant if its conditions are too warm, and aphids and mealy bugs can bother it, too.

# Tradescantia

The South American native *Tradescantia fluminensis* (wandering Jew) is a popular houseplant that is easy to cultivate. Its straggly growing habit makes it suitable for planting in a hanging basket, from which its stems can trail to a length of 11 in (30 cm). These stems carry small, oval, pointed leaves that are bluish-green in color, striped with white, and the plant's small, white, three-petaled flowers bloom from their axils. The leaves of *T. fluminensis* 'Variegata' display irregular, white-and-cream stripes, with purple tinting underneath, while those of *T. fluminensis* 'Tricolor' have white, green, and pink stripes.

## Cultivating *Tradescantia*

If its leaves are to maintain their variegation, *Tradescantia* requires a light, airy position, but should not be exposed to direct sunlight because this will scorch them. It prefers temperatures ranging from 50 to 59°F (10 to 15°C), and must be protected from drafts. It will look attractive when planted in a hanging basket or wall pot or when displayed on a pedestal or raised surface.

Water this plant regularly during the spring and summer to keep its compost moist, but allow it almost to dry out between waterings during the winter. Mist its leaves regularly, especially when the weather is hot.

Feed every two weeks during the spring and summer, and once a month during the fall and winter.

Pot this plant on in spring, into multipurpose compost. To create a bushier specimen, prune it severely in spring or pinch out its growing tips. Remove any shriveled leaves regularly.

Propagate in spring by taking stem cuttings (which should be broken off at a stem node) and then either planting them in compost or placing them in water, where they should root easily. Planting several cuttings in one pot will result in an attractive, bushy display.

This plant is vulnerable to aphids. If its leaf tips are turning brown, its conditions are either too wet or too dry. Shriveled leaves are normally a sign that it hasn't been watered sufficiently.

# Verbena

A native of North and South America, *Verbena* x *hybrida* is a slow-growing, perennial subshrub that is treated as an annual when cultivated as a houseplant. Its opposing pairs of oval, serrated, mid-green leaves grow to lengths of between 2 and 4 in (5 and 10 cm) on both prostrate and ascending stems 7 to 11 in (20 to 30 cm) high. Dense clusters of small, fragrant, tubular flowers bloom from summer through to fall. Depending on the variety, the flowers may be red, pink, blue, mauve, or white, with or without a central white "eye."

## Cultivating *V.* x *Hybrida*

*Verbena* x *hybrida* prefers a light and sunny, draft-free position with temperatures ranging from between 50 and 64°F (10 and 18°C). It suits a sunny conservatory or windowsill, and can be grown in a hanging basket.

Water it regularly to keep its compost damp, but never allow it to become waterlogged.

Feed once a week from spring until the end of its flowering period.

To prolong its flowering period, deadhead it regularly. The plant is usually discarded after flowering, but if you want to keep it for another year, trim back any straggly growth and keep its compost barely moist during winter. Pot it up in spring, into multipurpose compost, and start watering and feeding regularly again.

Propagate by sowing its seeds in spring and applying bottom heat. As soon as the seedlings are large enough to handle, prick them out and plant them in multipurpose compost in a pot in which you intend them to remain. Alternatively, take stem cuttings in late summer.

Aphids, red spider mites, and whiteflies all attack this plant.

# Vriesea

*Vriesea splendens* (flaming sword), which originates in tropical America, is a rosette-forming bromeliad whose strap-shaped, blunt-tipped, leathery leaves are dark-green in color, crossbanded with purple stripes. Its short-lived, yellow, tubular flowers are carried on tall, swordlike spikes of overlapping, scarlet bracts and retain their color for many weeks, dying back after it has flowered. *V. splendens* 'Major' is brighter colored and a more robust plant than *V. splendens*.

Before buying, make sure that it has been displayed in a warm, humid atmosphere, or the flower head will quickly perish.

*V. carinata* has bracts that resemble a yellow-and-red claw, giving rise to its common name, lobster claws.

## Cultivating *Vriesea*

If its flowers and colorful bracts are to look their best, *Vriesea* needs a year-round position in bright light (but not direct sunlight), humid conditions, and a temperature of around 77°F (25°C), although it will tolerate temperatures as low as 64°F (18°C). This colorful plant will respond to hydroponic cultivation.

Water by soaking its compost with soft water and then leaving it to become almost dry before rewatering. Mist it regularly, and fill its central "vase" with water every so often, too, but never when flower buds are visible, otherwise they will rot.

During spring and summer, feed with a dilute solution of fertilizer once a month, occasionally adding a similar feed to the plant spray before misting.

You should not need to repot it as its main rosette of leaves dies back after flowering.

Propagate by removing offsets that have four or more leaves, as well as some roots, planting them in seed compost, and keeping them in warm and humid conditions until they are established as independent plants.

This plant may be attacked by mealy bugs and scale insects. But this can usually be averted if it is kept in a humid atmosphere. If it does become infested, don't use chemical insecticides, but pick them off the plant by hand.

# Yucca

The members of the *Yucca* genus are natives of Mexico, where they are used to mark field boundaries. For Europe, the cut stems are shipped as small logs and placed in peat beds in humid conditions to encourage root and leaf growth.

   *Yucca elephantipes* grows as a single-stemmed plant from a thickened base and can reach 6 ft (2 m) in height. Its glossy, sword-shaped leaves have sharp points and are slightly serrated along their edges, and eventually form rosettes. When it is mature, it produces spikes of creamy, bell-shaped flowers. The leaves of *Y. elephantipes* 'Variegata' have creamy-white margins.

   When buying, look for firm, bright-colored leaves, the sign of a healthy plant.

## Cultivating *Yucca*

*Yucca* needs a very light position, and will tolerate full sun if its leaves don't have direct contact with a window. It can be placed outside in summer if it is fed and watered. Temperatures between 50 and 70°F (10 and 21°C) suit it when it is growing, but it prefers 50°F (10°C) in winter. It will thrive in a cool, bright room.

Water it regularly from spring to fall, but never let its stem stand in water. In winter, let its compost nearly dry out between waterings.

Feed each time you water in spring and summer, then once a month for the rest of the year.

*Yucca* should be potted on every two or three years in spring, into John Innes No. 3 compost and a heavy pot.

Propagate at any time of year either by removing and potting up offsets or by directly rooting bought cane cuttings that are 4 in (10 cm) in length.

This plant is sometimes attacked by scale insects. If its leaves turn yellow, this is due to a lack of bright light. Its stem will rot if it is overwatered.

# Zantedeschia

*Zantedeschia aethiopica*, which originates in South Africa, is better known as arum or calla lily. It is a flowering plant whose long-stalked, arrow-shaped leaves are a glossy, deep-green color and can reach 3 ft (1 m) in length. It produces a succession of white spathes, enclosing a yellow spadix, that bloom in midsummer. The spathes of *Z. aethiopica* 'Green Goddess' are striped with green, while *Z. aethiopica* 'Crowborough' is a more compact plant that bears fragrant flowers.

As its common name, yellow arum, suggests, *Z. elliottiana*'s spathes are bright yellow on the inside and tinged with green on the outside.

Before buying, check that the plant's compost is moist and that any flowers look clean and undamaged. However, it is best to buy a plant that is in bud rather than flowering.

## Cultivating *Zantedeschia*

*Zantedeschia* requires light to partially shady conditions all year round, as well as temperatures ranging from 59 to 64°F (15 to 18°C). It can be situated outside after flowering. An ideal plant for a cool and slightly shady room, it is suited to hydroponic cultivation.

When it is producing leaves, water it thoroughly and regularly. Once it has ceased flowering, cease watering.

Feed every two weeks as soon as you see the first signs of new leaves growing until it has finished blooming.

In spring or fall, pot up the rhizome-like roots into nutrient-rich, free-draining compost to which you've added some charcoal, water the compost thoroughly, and then keep it damp. After it has stopped flowering, place it outside to rest, when its leaves will gradually turn yellow.

Propagate in spring, either by planting its offsets or by division.

This plant is rarely troubled by pests or diseases.

# Zebrina

A native of Mexico, *Zebrina* is a trailing, evergreen plant that resembles *Tradescantia*. Its green leaves have a silvery sheen (which is why its common name is silvery inch plant) and undersides that are a rich shade of burgundy. *Zebrina* grows quickly, and can become straggly if it is not fed and watered sufficiently.

The best-known variety is *Zebrina pendula*, whose trailing or prostrate stems grow to 23 in (60 cm) in length and carry alternating oval, green leaves, each striped with two broad, silvery bands and having bright-red to purple undersides. Its tubular flowers, which are rose-purple in color, nestle amid each pair of leaves.

When buying, choose a compact specimen that has no straggly stems.

## Cultivating *Zebrina Pendula*

A light, airy position is essential if *Z. pendula*'s leaves are to maintain their variegation. But it should not be exposed to direct sunlight because this will scorch its foliage. It requires a draft-free spot and a temperature ranging from 50 to 59°F (10 to 15°C). It is suitable for a hanging basket or wall pot, and also looks attractive when displayed on a pedestal or raised surface.

Water regularly during the spring and summer to keep its compost moist. But allow it almost to dry out between waterings during the winter. Mist its leaves regularly, especially when it is hot.

Feed every two weeks during the spring and summer, and once a month during the fall and winter.

Pot on in spring, into multipurpose compost. To encourage bushiness, prune it severely in spring and perhaps pinch out its growing tips. Remove any shriveled leaves as soon as you see them.

Propagate by taking stem cuttings in spring (break them off at a stem node). Then place them in compost or water, where they should easily root. For a bushy display, plant several cuttings in one pot.

This plant attracts aphids. If the tips of its leaves turn brown, its conditions are too wet or too dry. If its leaves shrivel, it probably hasn't been watered enough.

# Zygocactus

The Christmas cactus, *Zygocactus truncatus* (which is sometimes sold as *Schlumbergera truncata*), is a Brazilian plant. Its branched and jointed, arching stems grow to 11 in (30 cm) in length and comprise dark-green, leafless, flattened segments with rounded ends. Its solitary, tubular flowers appear at the end of the stems from early winter to early spring. When they open, they reveal protruding stamens and swept-back petals in shades of red, orange, pink, violet, white, and magenta.

When choosing a Christmas cactus, look for one that has tight buds, but be warned that there is a danger that they will soon fall off because this plant dislikes being disturbed when it is in bud.

## Cultivating *Zygocactus*

*Z. truncatus* should be positioned in a shady spot outside during the summer, protected from slugs, and watered only occasionally (this will toughen its stems and encourage it to produce flower buds). Bring it inside in September and position it in a cool and light location. Keep its compost on the dry side until buds begin to form, then move it to its final display position. Do not disturb it again until it has finished flowering.

Keep its compost moist by watering it with soft water or rainwater, but do not allow it to become wet or waterlogged.

Once the buds have formed, feed every two weeks until it has finished flowering.

When it has stopped flowering, pot it up into compost that contains plenty of peat and grit (it suits both pots and hanging baskets). Do this by decreasing the amount of water that you give it so that its compost remains almost dry, then placing it in a light position with a temperature between 50 and 53.6°F (10 and 12°C).

Propagate by cutting off the end section of a stem in summer and allowing the cut end to dry before planting it. To create a large specimen plant, position a few cuttings around the edges of a pot or hanging basket.

Although this plant is immune to pests, its roots will rot if its compost is too wet. Its foliage may turn a reddish color if it is exposed to too much direct sunlight.

# Index

Index

## A

African violet (*Saintpaulia*) 223
aluminum plant (*Pilea cadierei*) 208
Amazon lily (*Alocasia* x *amazonica*) 89
angel's wings (*Caladium* x *hortulanum*) 107
angel trumpet (*Datura candida*) 135
Arabian violet (*Exacum affine*) 147
arum lily (*Zantedeschia aethiopica*) 250

## B

baby's tears (*Helxine soleirolii*) 164
banana plant (*Musa coccinea*) 187
Barbeton daisy (*Gerbera jamesonii*) 156
basil (*Ocimum basilicum*) 194
bay (*Laurus nobilis*) 179
bead plant (*Nertera granadensis*) 193
begonia vine (*Cissus discolor*) 119
belladonna lily (*Amaryllis belladonna*) 91
bird of paradise (*Strelitzia reginae*) 238
bird's-nest fern (*Asplenium nidus*) 99
black-eyed Susan (*Thunbergia alata*) 242
blue-flowered torch (*Tillandsia lindenii*) 244
bonsai 64
Boston fern (*Nephrolepis exaltata* 'Bostoniensis') 191
bottlebrush plant (*Callistemon*) 110
box (*Buxus*) 106
bride's plant (*Myrtus communis*) 188
bromeliads 68
bronze inch plant (*Zebrina pendula* 'Purpusii') 251
*Brugmansia* (*Datura* x *candida*) 135
bulbs 60-61
bunny ears (*Opuntia microdasys*) 196
burn plant (*Aloe vera* or *A. barbadensis*) 90
busy Lizzie (*Impatiens*) 171

## C

cabbage tree (*Cordyline australis*) 126
cacti 65
calla lily (*Zantedeschia aethiopica*) 250
Canary date palm (*Phoenix canariensis*) 207
Cape cowslip (*Lachenalia aloides*) 176
Cape ivy (*Senecio macroglossus*) 233
Cape leadwort (*Plumbago auriculata*) 212
Cape primrose (*Streptocarpus*) 239
carniverous plants 73
cast-iron plant (*Aspidistra elatior*) 98
century plant (*Agave americana*) 86
cherry pie (*Heliotropium arborescens*) 163
chili pepper (*Capsicum acuminatum*) 113
Chinese evergreen (*Aglaonema modestum*) 87
Chinese primrose (*Primula sinensis*) 215

chive (*Allium schoenoprasum*) 88
Christmas cactus (*Zygocactus truncatus*) 252
Christmas pepper (*Capsicum annuum*) 113
Christmas-tree plant (*Araucaria heterophylla*) 95
cider gum (*Eucalyptus gunnii*) 144
cigar plant (*Cuphea ignea*) 129
cineraria (*Senecio cruentus*) 233
clog plant (*Hypocyrta glabra*) 169
club moss (*Selaginella*) 231
cobweb houseleek (*Sempervivum arachnoideum*) 232
cockscomb (*Celosia cristata*) 115
coconut palm (*Cocos nucifera*) 122
common fig (*Ficus carica*) 150
compost 26-27
corn plant (*Dracaena fragrans* 'Massangeana') 141
creeping fig (*Ficus pumila*) 150
creeping Jenny (*Pilea depressa*) 208
croton (*Codiaeum variegatum pictum*) 123
crown of thorns (*Euphorbia milii* or *E. splendens*) 146

## D

daffodil (*Narcissus*) 189
date palm (*Phoenix dactylifera*) 207
desert privet (*Peperomia magnoliifolia*) 204
devil's ivy (*Scindapsus aureus*) 229
dinner-plate aralia (*Polyscias balfouriana*) 214
donkey's tail (*Sedum morganianum*) 230
dragon tree (*Dracaena draco*) 141
dumb cane (*Dieffenbachia picta*) 137
dwarf fan palm (*Chamaerops humilis*) 116

## E

Egyptian star cluster (*Pentas lanceolata*) 203
elephant-foot's plant (*Beaucarnea recurvata*) 102
elephant's ears (*Caladium* x *hortulanum*) 107
emerald fern (*Asparagus densiflorus* 'Sprengeri') 97
*Euphorbia pulcherrima* 213
European fan palm (*Chamaerops humilis*) 116

## F

fairy duster (*Calliandra tweedii*) 109
fairy primrose (*Primula malacoides*) 215
false aralia (*Dizygotheca elegantissima*) 140
false castor-oil plant (*Fatsia japonica*) 149
false holly (*Osmanthus hetero-

phyllus*) 197
felt plant (*Kalanchoe beharensis*) 175
feng shui 74-75
ferns 70
fig (*Ficus*) 150
finger aralia (*Dizygotheca elegantissima*) 140
firecracker plant (*Crossandra infundibuliformis*) 128
flame nettle (*Coleus blumei*) 124
flame of the woods (*Ixora coccinea*) 172
flaming Katy (*Kalanchoe blossfeldiana*) 175
flamingo flower (*Anthurium scherzerianum*) 92
flaming sword (*Vriesea splendens*) 248
foxtail fern (*Asparagus densiflorus* 'Meyeri') 97
freckle face (*Hypoestes*) 170
fruits 48-50

## G

genista broom (*Cytisus canariensis*) 134
geranium (*Pelargonium*) 201
glossary 10-11
golden barrel (*Echinocactus grusonii*) 143
golden Pothos (*Scindapsus aureus*) 229
goldfish plant (*Columnea*) 125
goosefoot plant (*Syngonium podophyllum*) 241
gout plant (*Jatropha podiatrica*) 174
grapefruit (*Citrus paradisi*) 120
grape ivy (*Cissus rhombifolia*) 119
grape ivy (*Rhoicissus rhomboidea*) 220
grass palm (*Cordyline australis*) 126
ground ivy (*Glechoma hederacea* 'Variegata') 157

## H

heliotrope (*Heliotropium*) 163
herringbone plant (*Maranta tricolor*) 183
*Hippeastrum* 91
hot-water plant (*Achimenes*) 82
houseleek (*Sempervivum*) 232
houseplants
    cleaning 39
    conditioning 14
    dangerous 77-78
    eco-friendly 76
    feeding 34
    grooming 40
    positioning 19-23
    potting on 30-32
    propagatng 41-51
    repotting 32
    resting 39
    selecting 13-14
    watering 35-38
humidity 18-19
hyacinth (*Hyacinthus*) 168
hydroponics 33

# IndexIndex

## I

Indian azalea (*Azalea indica*) 101
Indian shot (*Canna indica*) 112
Indian strawberry tree (*Duchesnea indica*) 142
iron-cross begonia (*Begonia masoniana*) 103
ivy (*Hedera*) 162
ivy tree (x *Fatshedera lizei*) 148

## J

jade plant (*Crassula argentea*) 127
Japanese maple (*Acer palmatum* 'Dissectum Atropurpureum') 81
Japanese sedge (*Carex morrowii* 'Variegata') 114
jasmine (*Jasminum*) 173
Joseph's coat (*Codiaeum variegatum pictum*) 123

## K

kaffir lily (*Clivia miniata*) 121
kangaroo vine (*Cissus antarctica*) 119
kris plant (*Alocasia*) 89
kumquat (*Fortunella margarita*) 153

## L

lemon (*Citrus limon*) 120
leopard lily (*Dieffenbachia picta*) 137
lettuce (*Lactuca sativa*) 177
light 16-17
little lady palm (*Rhapis excelsa*) 219
living stone (*Lithops salicola*) 181
lobster claws (*Vriesea carinata*) 248
lollipop plant (*Pachystachys lutea*) 199

## M

Madagascar dragon tree (*Dracaena marginata* 'Tri-color') 141
Madagascar jasmine (*Stephanotis floribunda*) 237
maidenhair fern (*Adiantum*) 83
maple (*Acer*) 81
marmalade bush (*Streptosolen jamesonii*) 240
mind your own business (*Helxine soleirolii*) 164
mint (*Mentha*) 184
money tree (*Crassula argentea*) 127
monkey plant (*Ruellia mackoyana*) 222
moonstones (*Pachyphytum oviferum*) 198
mother-in-law's tongue (*Sansevieria trifasciata* 'Laurentii') 226
mother of thousands (*Saxifraga*) 227
mother of thousands (*Tolmiea*) 245
myrtle (*Myrtus communis*) 188

## N

nettle spurge (*Jatropha podiatrica*) 174
Norfolk Island pine (*Araucaria heterophylla*) 95

## O

oleander (*Nerium oleander*) 192
olive (*Olea europaea*) 195
orange (*Citrus sinensis*) 120
orchids 71-72

## P

painted tongue (*Salpiglossis sinuata*) 224
palms 69
panda plant (*Kalanchoe tomentosa*) 175
paper plant (*Bougainvillea*) 105
papyrus plant (*Cyperus papyrus*) 133
parlor palm (*Neathe bella*) 190
parsley (*Petroselinum crispum*) 205
partridge-breasted aloe (*Aloe variegata*) 90
passionflower (*Passiflora*) 200
peace lily (*Spathiphyllum wallisii*) 236
peacock plant (*Calathea makoyana*) 108
pearl plant (*Haworthia margaritifera*) 160
Persian violet (*Exacum affine*) 147
pests 54-58
pick-a-back plant (*Tolmiea menziesii*) 245
piggyback plant (*Tolmiea menziesii*) 245
pig-tail plant (*Anthurium*) 92
pineapple lily (*Eucomis*) 145
pink jasmine (*Jasminium polyanthum*) 173
plant
   names 7
   parts 8-9
plantain lily (*Hosta*) 166
plume flower (*Celosia argentea plumosa*) 115
poison primrose (*Primula obconica*) 215
polka-dot plant (*Hypoestes*) 170
polyanthus (*Primula* x *tommasini*) 215
pomegranate (*Punica granatum*) 218
pony-tail plant (*Beaucarnea recurvata*) 102
pots 27-29
powder-puff plant (*Calliandra tweedii*) 109
prairie gentian (*Lisianthus russelianus*) 180
prayer plant (*Maranta leuconeura*) 182
prickly pear (*Opuntia robusta*) 196
primrose (*Primula vulgaris*) 215
problems 52-58

## R

rainbow fern (*Selaginella uncinata*) 231
rainbow tree (*Dracaena marginata* 'Tri-color') 140
rat's-tail cactus (*Aporocactus flagelliformis*) 94
regal elk-horn fern (*Platycerium grande*) 210
resurrection plant (*Selaginella lepidophylla*) 231
roof houseleek (*Sempervivum tectorum*) 232
rose of China (*Hibiscus rosa-sinensis*) 165
rosemary (*Rosmarinus officinalis*) 221
rubber plant (*Ficus elastica* 'Decora') 150

## S

sage (*Salvia officinalis*) 225
sago palm (*Cycas revoluta*) 130
saucer plant (*Aeonium tabulaeforme*) 85
scarlet star (*Guzmania lingulata*) 158
sensitive plant (*Mimosa pudica*) 185
shrimp plant (*Beloperone guttata*) 104
shrubs, indoor 62-63
silvery inch plant (*Zebrina*) 251
small-leaved box (*Buxus microphylla*) 106
snake plant (*Sansevieria trifasciata*) 226
snakeskin plant (*Fittonia verschaffeltii argyroneura* 'Nana') 152
soft tree fern (*Dicksonia antarctica*) 136
Spanish moss (*Tillandsia usneoides*) 244
spider plant (*Chlorophytum comosum* 'Vittatum') 117
spleenwort (*Asplenium*) 99
spotted laurel (*Aucuba japonica* 'Variegata') 100
stag's-horn fern (*Platycerium birfurcatum*) 210
stonecrop (*Sedum morganianum*) 230
stonecrop crassula (*Aeonium*) 85
strawberry tree (*Arbutus unedo*) 96
string of beads (*Senecio rowleyanus*) 233
succulents 66-67
sugar-almond plant (*Pachyphytum oviferum*) 198
Swedish ivy (*Plectranthus*) 211
sweet orange (*Citrus sinensis*) 120
Swiss cheese plant (*Monstera deliciosa*) 186

## T

tangerine (*Citrus reticulata* or *C. deliciosa*) 120
temperature 15-16
thyme (*Thymus vulgaris*) 243
tomato (*Lycopersicon esculentum* or *L. lycopersicum*) 182
tools 24-29
Transvaal daisy (*Gerbera jamesonii*) 156
trees, indoor 62-64
Turkish temple (*Euphorbia obesa*) 146

# Index

Index

## U

umbrella plant (*Cyperus alternifolius*)
133
umbrella tree (*Schefflera actinophylla*)
228
urn plant (*Aechmea fasciata*) 84

## V

vegetables 48, 50, 51
velvet plant (*Gynura aurantiaca*) 159
Venus flytrap (*Dionaea muscipula*) 138

## W

wandering Jew (*Tradescantia
fluminensis*) 246
wax flower (*Stephanotis floribunda*)
237
wax plant (*Hoya carnosa*) 167
weeping fig (*Ficus benjamina*) 150
winter cherry (*Solanum capsicastrum*)
235

## Y

yellow arum (*Zantedeschia elliottiana*)
250
yellow sage (*Lantana camara*) 178
youth on age (*Tolmiea menziesii*) 245

## Z

zebra plant (*Aphelandra squarrosa*) 93

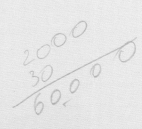

# Bibliography

Beckett, K.A., *The R.H.S. Encyclopaedia of Houseplants*, Simon & Schuster, Godalming, 1995.

Coussins, C., *Bonsai for Beginners*, D & S Books, Bideford, 2002.

Davidson, W,. *The Houseplant Survival Manual*, Guild Publishing, London, 1986.

Greenwood, P., *Pippa's Organic Kitchen Garden*, Dorling Kindersley, London, 1999.

Greenwood, P., and Halstead, A., *The R.H.S. Pests and Diseases*, Dorling Kindersley, London, 1997.

Hessayon, Dr. D.G., *Houseplant Expert*, Transworld Publishers Ltd., London, 1998.

Jantra, I., and Kruger, U., *The Houseplant Encyclopaedia*, Key Porter Books, Toronto, 1997.

Keen, B., *Cacti and Succulents*, Crowood Gardening Guides, Marlborough, 1999.

McHoy, P. (Ed.), *Houseplants: A Complete Guide to Indoor Gardening*, Book Club Associates, London, 1982.

McVicar, J., *New Book of Herbs*, Dorling Kindersley Ltd., London, 2002.

Wolverton, B.C., *Eco-friendly House Plants*, Seven Dials, Cassell & Co., London, 2000.

# Credits and Acknowledgements

A big thank-you from the author to Clare Haworth-Maden for her patience, encouragement, and invaluable skills in editing this book.